NatWest Business Handbooks

This series has been written by a team of authors who all have many years' experience and are still actively involved in the day-to-day problems of the small business.

If you are running a small business or are thinking of setting up your own business, you have no time for the general, theoretical and often inessential detail of many business and management books. You need practical, readily accessible, easy-to-follow advice which relates to your own working environment and the problems you encounter. The NatWest Business Handbooks fulfil these needs.

- They concentrate on specific areas which are particularly problematic to the small business.

- They adopt a step-by-step approach to the implementation of sound business skills.

- They offer practical advice on how to tackle problems.

The authors

Geoffrey Whitehead has been a teacher and lecturer in accounting for over forty years, and was formerly Head of the Professional Studies Division at Thurrock Technical College. Today he acts as small business accounts adviser to Croner Publications, the publishers of *Reference Book for the Self-employed and Smaller Business*. He also acts as consultant to the Simplex Advice Bureau, solving book-keeping problems for many small businesses. As a self-employed author who has sold nearly three million books, he has practical experience of running a small business.

Other titles in this series

NatWest Business Handbooks

Book-keeping and Accounting

Second Edition

Geoffrey Whitehead BSc (Econ)

Pitman

Pitman Publishing
128 Long Acre, London WC2E 9AN
A Division of Longman Group UK Limited

First published in 1989
Second edition first published in Great Britain 1991

© Longman Group UK Ltd 1989, 1991

A CIP record for this book can be obtained from the British Library

ISBN 0273 03516 9

Typeset, printed and bound in Great Britain

Contents

Preface

This book has been prepared as a practical accounting guide to all those entering business for the first time. It is based on my experiences in over forty years' lecturing and consultancy work at a grass roots level. It starts at 'Dawn on Day One', and explains how to open very simple account books, using one of the systems readily available at any stationer's shop.

It then goes on to look at all the other systems available, giving a detailed account of several of them. This section includes a full explanation of double-entry, and also a section on computerized accounting. A full list of all the manual and computerized systems on the market is given in Chapter 13. How to do bank reconciliation statements is covered in this section also, and VAT records are explained fully.

The book then proceeds to explain the final accounts of manufacturers, sole traders, partnerships and limited companies. It concludes with chapters about control of the business in its various profit-making activities, analysis of the results using the commoner accounting ratios, and ends with some practical advice on dealing with the Inland Revenue and submitting accounts to them directly where a trader wishes to do so.

In this new edition I have also included a chapter on accounts for clubs and charities, since many business people take an interest in such activities.

In writing this book I have been greatly helped by all the firms whose systems are described, and by numerous other people. Their assistance is acknowledged overleaf. Whilst their help and encouragement has been invaluable I must take responsibility for all the statements made, which have been made in good faith. In using names for exercises, etc., no intentional reference was made to any particular firm or company, and I must apologise if I have inadvertently clashed with any true name.

Geoffrey Whitehead

Acknowledgements

The assistance of the following persons and organisations is gratefully acknowledged. Some kindly permitted the use of artwork to illustrate their systems, and permission to reproduce this copyright material is much appreciated.

The Accounting Centre
Diane Baker, of Kalamazoo plc
Casdec Ltd (Finco system)
Central Computer Services Ltd
Croner Publications Ltd
Controller General, Her Majesty's Stationery Office
Kalamazoo plc
Micro-Retailer Systems Ltd
Micro-Simplex Ltd
Tom Moffat, of Casdec Ltd
National Westminster Bank plc
Robert Piper, of Croner Publications Ltd
Brian Senior, of George Vyner Ltd
Nick Smith, of the Charity Commission
Paul Tugby, of Central Computer Services Ltd
Ross Tye, of Safeguard Systems Ltd
Safeguard Systems Ltd
George Vyner Ltd (Simplex system)

1 Solving the book-keeping problem

1

Why do we need to keep book-keeping records at all? □ What sort of records do we need? □ Solving the book-keeping problem for different types of business □ The importance of documents in business □ About this book □ Checklist

Why do we need to keep book-keeping records at all?

There is no law which requires sole traders and partnerships to keep book-keeping records, but if we set up as a limited company there is a positive requirement in s.221 of the Companies Act 1985. It begins 'Every company shall cause accounting records to be kept in accordance with this section' and it goes on to require that the accounts shall be sufficient to show and explain the company's transactions, financial position, etc. So if we set up as a company we must keep accounts. Even if we are to trade only as a sole trader or in partnership, it is possible under the Insolvency Act 1986 to be charged with an offence of 'failing to keep proper books of account', so that it seems that if we do not keep proper books of account we must be careful not to become bankrupt.

We need to keep proper books of account for the following reasons.

- We need to keep track of all aspects of our business activities, and the simplest way to do this for the financial aspects of the business is to keep a set of books of account.
- If our turnover (in other words the takings of the business) exceeded £25,400 in the past 12 months, or if the likely turnover in the next 30 days will bring the past 11 months' total over the £25,400 threshold figure, we must register for VAT. Many traders whose sales are not so high as £25,400 per annum register voluntarily for VAT (because this means we can reclaim the input tax we pay on everything we buy and on our overhead expenses). In that case we must keep VAT records from the moment we start business – which we will call 'Dawn on day one' – a vital moment in the life of every business. These VAT records must by law be kept for six years, so they must be put into apple-pie order each year and then archived in the bottom drawer

of a convenient filing cabinet so that we have them available if Customs and Excise require them.

● The Inland Revenue requires us to submit accounts every year which can be used as a basis for assessment of income tax (or corporation tax in the case of companies). Apart from companies, it is not necessary for these accounts to be drawn up by a professional accountant, and this book will explain how to draw up your own accounts with very little trouble. Of course many people do have their accounts drawn up by an accountant and therefore have the peace of mind which comes from having professional support in their financial affairs. One consultant told the author of this book, 'A sole trader would be as well advised to draw up his own accounts as he would be to draw his own teeth.' Actually that is going a bit too far – at least half a million sole traders and partnerships draw up their own accounts and send them to the Inland Revenue every year, without any real trouble. On the other hand, we all need the help of accountants at times – for example when the business grows, or perhaps when we wish to prepare a submission in connection with a loan request to a finance company or institutional investor – so there is much to be said for establishing a link with a reputable accountancy firm.

For these three main reasons, we need to keep book-keeping records.

What sort of records do we need?

Since the Middle Ages the system of book-keeping has traditionally been the double entry system. Every time people discuss book-keeping they refer to this system, which is fully described later in this book (see Chapter 6). Most of the words commonly used in accountancy relate to the double-entry system, for example the *Ledger* is the main book of account, and is full of pages called '*accounts*'. An account is a leaf in the ledger (i.e. two pages), though these days it may just be some pattern of magnetic records in the memory store of a computer. If we have an account with one of the High Street banks it simply means that they have allocated us a page in their ledger, and they tell us the page number so it can be referred to at any time. The number is embossed on the bottom of every cheque in magnetic ink, as shown in Fig. 1.1. The bank's computer can read this magnetic ink and it is used to speed up cheque clearing, and debit the amount of the cheque in the customer's account.

Today a full double entry system is not essential for most businesses, though those who have studied double entry book-keeping will always have a great advantage in understanding their accounts. You can learn

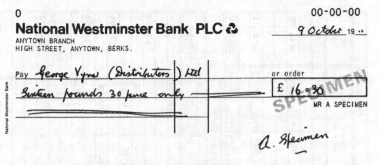

Fig. 1.1 Cheque showing the customer's account number in the bank's ledger

double entry book-keeping at an evening class, or you can use one of the many self-study textbooks on the market – a good one edited by the author of the present book is *Discover Book-keeping and Accounts*, by David Spurling, published by Pitman Publishing, 128 Long Acre, London WC2E 9AN. However it takes a year to learn the subject really well.

For the person starting up in business this full knowledge of double entry is not necessary, as explained in the next section. What records then do we need? To some extent that depends upon the type of business we are running, but to begin with we could make a list as follows.

- VAT records.
- 'Dawn on day one' records.
- Cash records (to keep track of receipts and payments) and enable us eventually to work out the profit or loss we have made in the year.
- Wages records (if we employ anyone).
- A full double entry system if we prefer to keep full records, without taking any short-cuts.
- Specialized records (which are chiefly short-cuts on a full double entry system). These are described later.
- We might keep computerized records, which involves some small capital cost at the start, though we can buy everything we need for about £1,000.
- Then we need to be able to prepare our final accounts at the end of the year, for submission to the Inland Revenue. These are called the *Trading Account* (in which we find the *gross profit*), the *Profit and Loss Account* (in which we find the *net profit*) and the *Balance Sheet* (which gives us a snapshot picture of the state of our business after closing the doors on the last day of the financial year). Preparing these is really very simple, and you will find lots of practice exercises to help you in the book.

Example No. 1 – Bank in Credit — Week No. 14 — Commencing: 6TH APRIL 19

RECEIPTS / PAID TO BANK

Day	Date	Gross Daily Takings (cash) Col 1	Gross Daily Takings (cheques) Col 2	Other Receipts Col 3	Particulars	CASH Col 4	CHEQUES Col 5	TOTAL Col 6
Sunday	6/4	186 27						
Monday	7/4	232 44	25 80	35 60	TAX REFUND	420 00	66 89	486 88
Tuesday	8/4	256 26	12 64	5 48	DEBTOR P. SMITH			
Wednesday	9/4	112 27						
Thursday	10/4	299 85	19 74					
Friday	11/4	364 24	26 34			520 00	58 72	578 72
Saturday	12/4	382 72	62 50					
Totals		1924 05	147 02	41 08		940 00	125 60	1065 60

PAYMENTS FOR BUSINESS STOCK

Date or Chq. No.	To Whom Paid	Amount Paid By Cash Col 7	Amount Paid By Cheque Col 8
7/4	J. COWLAN & SONS	48 50	
7/4	J. BRADLEY & Co. LTD.		36 50
8/4	A.J. GOOD LTD.		136 85
8/4	J. BROWN & Co LTD.	33 80	
11/4	F. LINDSAY & Co.	26 70	
11/4	A. NEWCOMBE		86 25

PAYMENTS OTHER THAN FOR STOCK

Nature of Payment	Amount Paid By Cash Col 9	Amount Paid By Cheque Col 10
Rent	35 00	
Rates		
Light and Heat		63 50
Carriage		
Postages £1·70 24p. £2·38	9 45	
Paper	4 32	
Motor Expenses PETROL	16 12	
-do- REPAIRS		27 46
Travelling	7 32	
Cleaning	5 00	
Printing & Stationery		86 50
Repairs & Renewals		
Insurance (Business)		23 20
Advertising		15 79
Telephone		
Wages (Wife)		

- Finally, and it is really a part of the Balance Sheet work, we need to understand the effect of the year's trading on the owner of the business, whether we are trading as a sole trader, as partners in a partnership or as a limited company, with shareholders.

That may sound quite a lot, but actually it isn't too bad. In any case, the first lesson we must learn in business is that whatever duties the state

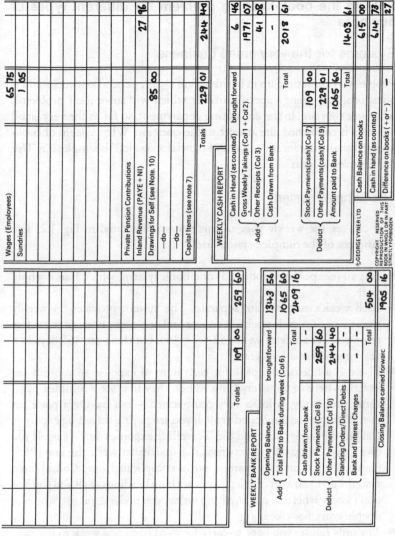

Fig. 1.2 The Simplex weekly page

imposes on us – like collecting VAT for the government or keeping proper wages records if we employ anyone – we have to carry out, even if they are a bit of a problem. It is no good throwing up your hands in horror as if it was all too much for you. Parliament has imposed certain duties upon you, and you must carry them out or get someone to do them for you. None of this is very difficult, as this book hopes to show you.

Solving the book-keeping problem for different types of business

Systems for the very small business

People who are setting up in business don't want general answers to their questions, they want a specific answer which will solve their problems, whatever they are. In the accounting department, so far as the very small business is concerned, the answer to the question 'What system of book-keeping shall I use for my ordinary financial accounts?' is simple: it is 'Use the Simplex system.'

The Simplex system

You can see the weekly page of this system illustrated in Fig. 1.2. The advantages of the Simplex system are:

- It is an inexpensive (about £5) one-book system, which lasts a whole year.
- Each week's accounts are separate. The system provides 53 weekly pages – one for each week in the year and one extra, because every few years you get an extra week (52 × 7 = 364, but there are 365 days in a year and 366 in a leap year).
- There is a line on the page for each item of expense so you can see exactly where to put everything. When they first see a Simplex page, some people say 'It looks very complicated' – but having a place for everything isn't complicated at all. If you are paying travelling expenses you put the money spent on the 'Travelling expenses' line – easy. If you don't pay any travelling expenses that particular week the line is left blank. So it *is* an easy system, not a complicated one. Complicated systems give you a set of ruled paper with no headings at all and you just don't know where to put anything unless you understand the whole of double entry book-keeping.
- The only figures you have to carry forward from one week to the next are your bank balance (according to your weekly page) and your cash in hand at the end of the week. You count that up and carry it forward to next week.
- You don't have a lot of accounts to keep – there are no accounts – only summaries where you gradually build up the profits and losses of the business.
- At the end of the year all these summary figures are ready to carry into the Trading Account and Profit and Loss Account to find the profits of the business.

- Finally, you draw up a Balance Sheet and are ready to send your accounts to the Inland Revenue.
- You can buy the Simplex D Account Book from any reputable stationer, or by post from George Vyner Ltd, PO Box 1, Holmfirth, Huddersfield HD7 2RP. Phone them on 0484 685221 to ask the current price and send a cheque with your order. When you have purchased your Simplex book you will be entitled to enrol in the Simplex club, free of charge, which entitles you to book-keeping advice on any problem connected with the systems, and any problem you pose will be answered in great detail, at absolutely no cost to yourself.
- They do sell a book called *Simplified Book-Keeping for Small Businesses*, which is by the author of the present book but of course deals only with their systems. It explains every detail of the system – although much of it is explained later in this book anyway. What is more, every query which might seem to be of interest to other Simplex users is added to the book at each reprint and thus it is very up to date.

The Simplex VAT system

I did say the Simplex system was a one-book system, but if you are registered for VAT you do need a Simplex VAT book as well. A good set of VAT records is simple enough, but there are a number of VAT systems and nearly all VAT users have three sets of records to keep:

- *Input tax*: based upon the invoices we receive from our suppliers, and kept by what is known as the 'normal method' – the method used by people who have invoices to cover every purchase/or sale.
- *Output tax*: based either upon the invoices we issue to our customers or on one of the 12 special retailers' schemes. A 'retailer' in VAT terms is not just a shopkeeper, but anyone who supplies good or services for payment without making out an invoice for every supply. If we issue invoices these output records are kept by the normal method.
- If we don't issue invoices, we have to use a special retailers' scheme, and these records are based on a 'reconciliation of daily takings' figures.

All these records are kept in the Simplex VAT book – very easily – and once again you have the backing of the Simplex advisory service if you run into any difficulties.

Micro-Simplex

If the owner of a small business wishes to avoid tedious manual book-keeping it is possible to use Micro-Simplex, a computerized version of the

Simplex system in which the rulings of the Simplex D book appear on the screen of a visual display unit (VDU) and entries can be made on the screen directly by means of a keyboard. The system is user-friendly in that it has been designed with safeguards to prevent a trader making wrong entries. For example, suppose the trader is entering the 'daily takings', which today come to £428.37. When the entry has been keyed in the computer asks a friendly question, for example:

> You are asking me to record £428.37 as your daily takings.
> Is this correct?   Y/N

Y means 'Yes' and N means 'No'. A touch on the Y key will bring another question:

> Are you sure?   Y/N

Another touch on the Y key will instantaneously (a) record the figure for daily takings in the records, (b) add it to the previous total to give a total figure for the month to date, (c) carry it to the summary of takings for use in working out the profits at the end of the year and (d) make the necessary VAT entries including calculating the amount of VAT in £428.37, and so on.

A touch on the N key will delete the entry which is not correct and the screen will read something like:

> Ready to enter your correct daily takings figure.

Micro-Simplex is described fully later in this book (see Chapter 12).

Systems for the slightly larger business

Simultaneous records systems

An embryonic business will be perfectly happy with the Simplex system or with Micro-Simplex. A business which has been growing for a year or two, and is becoming too large for these basic systems should move on to one of the more advanced systems that give the benefits of full double entry but do so by means of short-cuts that reduce some of the more laborious work of double entry. Such systems are often called 'three-in-one' systems, or simultaneous records systems because three sets of records are prepared at one time, using carbon or NCR paper (paper where no carbon is required). In the latter case the paper itself is covered with tiny droplets of colourless ink, which becomes visible only when pressed with a ballpoint pen to burst the tiny globules. These systems, marketed by firms such as Kalamazoo Business Systems Ltd and Safeguard Systems Ltd, are described in detail later in this book. A good example of a three-in-one system is one for wages which prepares a payroll, an employee's individual wage record and a payslip for the week, all in one operation. The payslip gives you an account of the pay earned and the deductions made, to go in the wage packet. The employee's record card builds up to give the total pay and tax deducted etc. for the whole year, while the payroll has every employee's wage on it for the week (or the month) and thus gives a clear record of wages paid and deductions made, for the week (or month) concerned.

A full double entry system

Any business can of course use a full double entry system, but to keep it properly you do have to understand double entry book-keeping. The system is explained in detail in Chapter 6, but you cannot really say you have mastered the system without doing a great many exercises in keeping the various books. The books required include:

- Five *day books*, or *journals*: the Purchases Day Book, the Purchases Returns Book, the Sales Day Book, the Sales Returns Book and the Journal Proper (which deals with all the rather tricky things that happen, such as bad debts, depreciation, dishonoured cheques, etc.).
- The *Ledger*, which is the main book of account. It may be split up into a Debtors Ledger, a Creditors Ledger, a General Ledger and a Private Ledger.
- Finally we need a *Four-Column Cash Book* (formerly called the Three-Column Cash Book, but in the United Kingdom we need an extra column now for VAT) and a Petty Cash Book.

With these books (and we could have several more) we can keep a full accounting record for every type of firm and company.

Systems for large companies

Generally speaking it is true to say that the books of even the largest company can be kept with the double entry system and the books listed in the section above. In fact, practically every large company has a computerized accounting system. However, this is not a book about large companies and we will not try to describe these systems in detail here. Most small traders will become very familiar with computerized records from their banking activities, and their purchasing from wholesalers and large suppliers of every kind.

The importance of documents in business

It is impossible to over-stress the importance of documents in business. Whatever the nature of the activity there is almost always a document to trigger it and another to bring it to an end. Documents have important legal consequences – not just documents like the deeds to property, wills, summonses, etc. but ordinary documents like invoices, credit notes, receipts, petty cash vouchers, statements, cheques and the like. They may be presented as evidence in court; VAT inspectors and the Inland Revenue authorities expect to see documents to bear out the statements made in sets of figures presented to them, and severe penalties can be imposed for falsifying records. It follows that you should always take great care of documents, even the tiny till receipts for small items purchased and the VAT slips you demand from the garage for petrol purchased. All these documents supplied by outsiders (people not in your own business) have to be kept as financial records and if you are registered for VAT they must be retained for six years as part of your VAT records.

Petty cash vouchers

For some purchases it is impossible to obtain proof of purchase from an outside organization. For example, railways issue a ticket which is collected

Petty Cash Voucher		Folio____23____ Date____17 · 11__19··		
For what required			AMOUNT	
			£	p
Fares to Royston	Train		3	25
	Bus			52
			3	77
Signature____R. Harris____				
Passed by____G. M. W____				

Fig. 1.3 An internal petty cash voucher

at the other end of the journey. In such cases it is advisable to make out an internal Petty Cash Voucher, signed by yourself to prove that money was disbursed. Of course this might seem a bit pointless if you are writing a certificate for your own expenses, but it is certainly essential for expenses incurred by an employee. In general the principle is: 'Have a piece of paper to cover every item of expenditure.' The general name for these chits is '*Petty Cash Vouchers*' and internal vouchers for your own use can be purchased in pads of about 50 copies at any stationery shop. Such a voucher is illustrated in Fig. 1.3.

Invoices

The most important document is the invoice, which is often made out in

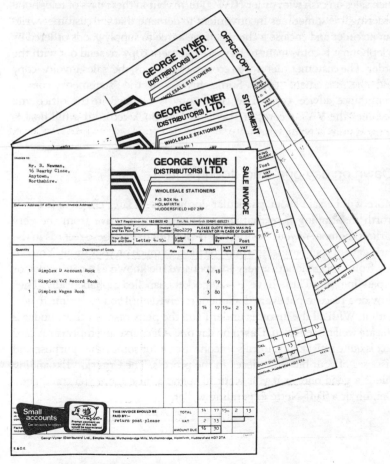

Fig. 1.4 A simple three-copy invoice set (*courtesy of George Vyner Ltd*)

sets. The smallest set consists of two copies: the top copy for the customer who is purchasing the goods (or services) you supply; the second for your own book-keeping records. It will probably finish up in your VAT file, but if you are not registered for VAT put it in a lever-arch file. Lever-arch files are the very best files for small businesses and will keep your records in apple-pie order. They are very cheap – from about £1.75 to 3.75 according to quality. They can be purchased from any stationery shop, or by mail order over the telephone from such firms as Neat Ideas, Freepost, Sandall Stones Road, Kirk Sandall, Doncaster DN3 1BR (telephone: 0302 890999).

A typical simple set of invoices is shown in Fig. 1.4. It is an appropriate set for a small trader who supplies goods on mail order and wishes to collect the cash for the order as soon as possible. Of course we often make such sales on cash with order (CWO) terms but in these days of telephone ordering it is sometimes inconvenient to demand that the customer write out an order and enclose a cheque. If we agree to supply goods ordered by telephone it is convenient to have a 'statement copy' to send out with the order. The customer therefore receives two copies, the 'sales invoice' copy and the 'statement' copy. Some firms call the 'statement' copy a 'remittance advice' copy. The third copy is retained in the office and becomes the VAT record, or the Sales Day Book record if a full double entry system is being used.

'Dawn on day one' and documents

More will be said about particular documents in later chapters but it is worth mentioning here that documents begin to arrive from the very earliest moment of your business. It is vital not to lose these records in the early days of your business, when you have so much on your mind. You can buy from any stationers a very inexpensive file known as a concertina, or expanding, file. These have 16–20 pockets, labelled alphabetically. They provide a place to put every document received until you have time to deal with it. With all the invoices under I and the petty cash vouchers under P you are well placed from 'Dawn on day one'. Of course an empty cardboard box is quite satisfactory, until someone uses it for some other purpose and disposes of your bits and pieces in the process. The Criterion Expanding File is a good one, or if you want to spend a little more you could get a Denton or a Tuff-Nette expanding wallet.

About this book

This book is intended to give you practical down-to-earth advice on how to start your book-keeping records and keep them going until you come to the end of your first financial year. You will then submit your final accounts (your Trading Account, Profit and Loss Account and Balance Sheet) to the Inland Revenue. The book does not suggest that you do not need an accountant, but it does argue that the vast majority of your routine records should be kept by you, or someone in the family who is prepared to do the work. The finishing touches can then be done by an accountant if you wish, at very little inconvenience to the accountant and very little cost to you.

Naturally there are many systems on the market and it has been impossible to mention them all, but those mentioned have been well tried over a number of years and have proved satisfactory. Whatever system you use you may find it necessary to adapt it to suit your own business, but without destroying the accounting principles on which the system is based. Don't be afraid to ask for help from the advice bureau run by the system you adopt, or to telephone the suppliers if for any reason your computer system won't work. They will soon tell you what is wrong and how to correct it. Remember that the office side of the business is still the relatively easy side, given a little attention, especially in the first year. Later it will become a routine activity.

One final point is this: the first requirement of any business person is to keep honest records. Don't worry if you make a mistake, cross the figure out, initial the alteration and put the correct figure in. *Never re-write your records*, whether for the sake of neatness or because you have made a lot of alterations. The Inland Revenue expects a few mistakes in placing figures in the books. A neat record is a false record, generally speaking, especially in the first year. All account books are coded and if the Inland Revenue finds that your January accounts are written in a book that didn't roll off the presses until July, it will not like it. Keep a proper record from 'Dawn on day one'; have all your pieces of paper neatly filed to support your written records and cheerfully pay what little tax you are charged. Only those making profits have to pay taxes, and the amount you will be charged will be fair and reasonable. Put something away every week for taxes and put away your VAT money every week, in a deposit account. Then when the time comes to pay it you can look cheerful and pay up.

1

Checklist

These are the vital points made in this chapter.

1. Make up your mind early whether you want to register voluntarily for VAT. If you do you can reclaim your input tax right from the start, but of course you must charge your customers output tax, i.e. add 15 per cent (at present) to their bills.
2. If you don't register for VAT at once you must keep an eye on your takings. If these are likely to rise above £25,400 per annum in the next 30 days' trading you must register for VAT immediately.
3. The main method of book-keeping is the double entry system handed down to us by our ancestors from the Middle Ages. You can keep a full set of books for double entry yourself if you wish to (see Chapter 6).
4. Better, for the very small business, is a simple system like Simplex. This has been computerized as Micro-Simplex, and Micro-Simplex Plus (see Chapter 12).
5. Other useful systems for slightly larger businesses are the three-in-one systems of simultaneous records, such as the Kalamazoo and Safeguard Systems.
6. Documents are vital parts of any record-keeping systems. Never throw documents away. Have a concertina file (an expanding file) to put documents in as they arrive. After recording them, file them in a permanent file – preferably a lever-arch file. Have a piece of paper for every outlay. If necessary make out an internal petty cash voucher.
7. VAT documents must be kept for six years.
8. *Never re-write your records*! The Inland Revenue does not demand neat accounts; it does demand honest records. If you make a slip by entering something in the wrong place, cross out the wrong figure, initial the correction and write in the correct figure.

2 'Dawn on day one'

The significance of 'Dawn on day one' □ The 'opening entries' of the business □ Enterprise allowances □ Opening the books on day one □ How to repay Aunt Lucy! □ Ready to go at 'Dawn on day one' □ Checklist

The significance of 'Dawn on day one'

The first moment of the first day of your new business is a very important moment. It signals the start of your new business and a new *business entity* is born. It may be a sole trader enterprise, a partnership or a limited company but it comes into existence at dawn on day one. It is separate from you in many ways, and in the case of a limited company is totally separate from you – with a separate legal personality. A company can own assets, borrow money, employ people, buy and sell goods, supply services and demand payment for them, and so on. A company is a totally separate legal person, and you are just a director of the company. Do not be misled by that title. We often see company directors referred to as if that status conferred rank, honour and position upon them. It doesn't. Anyone can become a company director by buying a company off the shelf for about £100. No particular merit or attribute is required, no skill or qualification is implied. Company directors are just as fallible as other mortals; perhaps more so.

Sole traders and partnerships are not separate legal personalities from their owners, and consequently sole traders and partners are responsible for their businesses directly and personally to the full extent of their worldly wealth. They do not have the *limited liability*, which the company director has, so that the latter is liable to lose only the actual capital put into the business – which is often as little as £100. More of this later.

The most important aspects of 'Dawn on day one' are:

1. Since that is the start of the business, it is a moment which should be recorded carefully so that the accounting activities begin in a proper manner and everyone who needs to look at our books can see what the starting position was. The chief people who might want to look at our books at some time in the future are:

- our accountants, if we decide to use the services of an accountant
- HM Customs, if we register for VAT
- the Inland Revenue, should it query the accounts we have submitted
- our lawyers, should we die and they need to sort out our will, or our financial position if we died intestate (without leaving a will)
- our partners or other persons interested in the business, such as the representatives of shareholders or debenture holders or the receiver if the company goes into liquidation.

The records that such people would want to look at start with the 'opening entry', which is the official accounting term for the entries made at 'Dawn on day one'. We shall see how to make these entries later in the chapter.

2. The other aspect of 'Dawn on day one' is that the pieces of paper (documents) that trigger every sort of business activity begin to arrive from that time and we should be ready for them and have somewhere safe to put them. A full explanation of start-up requirements is given later in this chapter.

The 'opening entries' of the business

Every new trader starts with a certain accumulation of goods and money which enables him or her to commence trading. This may consist of physical assets, such as premises, machinery, tools, motor vehicles and stock, but it may also include money, cash at the bank or in a building society, etc. A certain amount of confusion exists about the terms to be used for these assets, because the word 'capital' has several different meanings. For example, a person seeking to start up in the clothing trade may say, 'I must see the bank about some capital – I shall need about £30,000.' The use of the word capital to mean 'money capital' is very common, but actually money capital is only a part of the true capital of a business, as we shall see.

To digress for a moment, consider the Enterprise Allowance Scheme, run by the government to assist new small enterprises. It is a condition of joining the Scheme that the budding entrepreneur (one who shows enterprise) should have capital of £1,000, or if two people are going into partnership the sum required is £2,000. It is easy enough to find such capital, for almost any bank will lend you the money at the drop of a hat, provided you make a reasonable case for borrowing it. Joining the Scheme is reason enough in most cases. What is the purpose behind the requirement? Probably it is the feeling of those officials who run the scheme that it is some sort of guarantee that the new business will have a minimum amount of liquid funds (that is, funds in cash form) for the first few weeks of its life. There is no requirement to leave the money in the business beyond that time, and a great many people do not. The first question they ask is, 'Is it all right if I repay the bank (or repay Aunt Lucy who loaned me the money) because I don't need it for the business really?' We will consider this problem later when we have learned how to open the books of a business.

To open the books of a business you take a piece of paper and write down on it all the assets you have contributed to the business, and any liabilities the business is taking over. A list of assets and liabilities is called a *Balance Sheet*. That name is appropriate because the total value of the assets and the total value of the liabilities are always exactly the same, and therefore if put into the scales of a balance the balance would settle horizontally, as shown in Fig. 2.1.

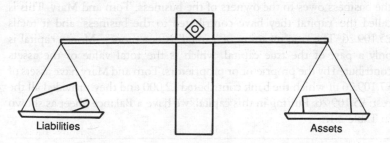

Liabilities   Assets

Fig. 2.1 Assets and liabilities always balance

Let us draw up a list of the assets and liabilities of Tom Smith, who is starting off in business under the Enterprise Allowance Scheme, as the proprietor of a snack bar operating from a layby on a busy main road. His wife Mary is a partner, and at 'Dawn on day one', 1 July 19X9 they had:

- A caravan, newly purchased for £2,850.
- Various items of crockery, kitchenware, gas cylinders etc., worth £340.56.
- A car to tow the van, which is worth £2,250 but only two-thirds of this is to be regarded as business, the other third is for domestic use. This means the business value of the car is £1,500.
- Stocks of various types of food, confectionery etc., worth £168.30.

They had borrowed £2,000 from the Helpful Bank plc as required by the Enterprise Allowance Scheme and this money, together with £225.40, which is all that is left of their own savings after purchasing the items listed above, is in a current account at Helpful Bank plc. They also have £25 cash in hand, which is regarded as a till float for use on the first day. The list of assets and liabilities is as follows:

Assets	£	Liabilities	£
Caravan	2,850.00	Bank loan	2,000.00
Crockery, etc.	340.56		
Car (⅔)	1,500.00		
Stock	168.30		
Cash at bank	2,225.40		
Cash in hand	25.00		
	£7,109.26		

It is clear that the assets and liabilities do not balance; the assets total £7,109.26 while the liabilities (owed to the bank) are only £2,000. The reason for the imbalance is that we have left out one of the liabilities: what the business owes to the owners of the business, Tom and Mary. This is called the 'capital they have contributed to the business' and it totals £5,109.26. The true meaning of 'capital' is not money. Money capital is only a part of the true capital, which is the total value of the assets contributed by the proprietor or proprietors. Tom and Mary have assets of £7,109.26 of which the bank contributed £2,000 and they provided all the rest: £5,109.26. Putting in this capital, we have a Balance Sheet as shown in Table 2.1.

Tom and Mary Smith
Balance Sheet as at dawn on 1 July 1989

Assets	£	Liabilities	£
Caravan	2,850.00	Bank loan	2,000.00
Crockery, etc.	340.56	Capital	5,109.26
Car (⅔)	1,500.00		
Stock	168.30		
Cash at bank	2,225.40		
Cash in hand	25.00		
	£7,109.26		£7,109.26

Table 2.1 Balance Sheet for Tom and Mary Smith

It is worthwhile learning this definition of capital by heart:

Capital is what the business owes to the owner of the business. It is the difference between the total value of the assets and the total external liabilities, owed to people like banks, building societies and other creditors.

This capital will be repaid to the proprietor when the business ceases to trade, at close of business on the last day. Close of business on the last day

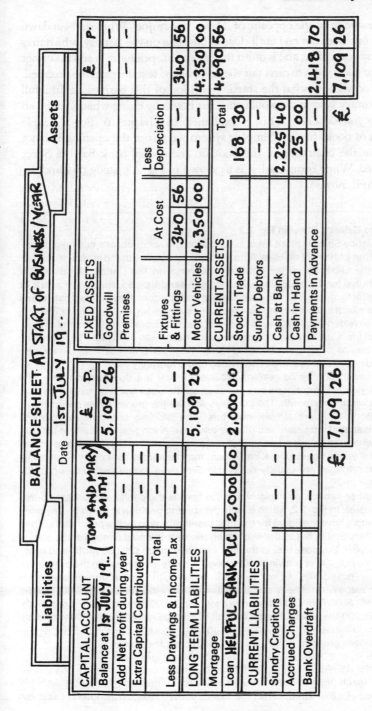

Fig. 2.2 The opening Balance Sheet of a new business *(see notes overleaf)*

may be said to be the opposite of 'Dawn on day one'. What starts at dawn on day one does not end until close of business on the last day, which may be many years after, and is often the day the proprietor dies and his or her solicitor takes steps to carry out the last will and testament of the deceased.

We now know what the starting position of this business is. In a full double entry system we would start the books by doing what is called an *Opening Journal Entry*. This is explained in Chapter 6. For a simple system of books like the Simplex system we record the opening Balance Sheet at the beginning of the book on the special bank Balance Sheet provided. When completed, it is as shown in Fig. 2.2. Study this, and the notes to it, now.

Notes to Balance Sheet in Fig. 2.2

- A Balance Sheet is just a list of balances on the accounts of a business, listed as either assets or liabilities. It may be written down with the assets on the left and the liabilities on the right, or vice versa. In the United Kingdom it is traditional for the assets to be on the right-hand side, as shown in Figure 2.2.
- The assets are divided into *Fixed Assets* and *Current Assets*. Fixed assets are those which are used in the business over many years, and are sold only when they have depreciated to such an extent that they have come to the end of their useful life. Current assets are those which have been purchased to sell again. This means that the stock in trade is sold, and turns into cash; or it may turn into debtors and becomes cash when they eventually pay.
- The liabilities may be current liabilities, which are due for payment very shortly. For example, if we buy goods on credit to sell again we usually pay for them within one month. The suppliers we owe the money to are called 'trade creditors', or more simply, creditors. The dividing line between current liabilities and long-term liabilities is one year. A long-term liability is usually one where we have made a contractual arrangement to repay over a period of several years. For example, bank loans may be spread over one to five years, and mortgages are usually repayable over even longer periods – up to 25 years.
- The other liability, as explained in the text, is the capital owed back to the proprietor. In Fig. 2.2, which is only the starting position at dawn on day one, we simply have the figure for the total assets supplied by the proprietors, Tom and Mary Smith, but as the illustration shows this would change at the end of every year. Suppose that in the first year they made £20,000 profit, and each drew out £6,000 as drawings. 'Drawings' is the term used when the proprietor of a business draws out money to live on during the year. A proprietor cannot draw 'wages', what he or she does draw is 'drawings in expectation of profit earned'. So if Tom and Mary drew a total of £12,000 and the profits proved to be £20,000 there would be £8,000 left in the business. This £8,000 would be added to the capital to give them £13,109.26 by the end of the year. That is how a business grows in value – by ploughing back the profits.
- There is one final point which we will not go into here. It is explained in Chapter 15. As this is a partnership business we should really show how much each partner has contributed as capital, instead of showing a single figure of £5,109.26. The partners could have contributed equally

(i.e. £2,554.63 each) or unequally – say £1,000 by Mary and £4,109.26 by Tom. For the moment, to save a long explanation of partnership accounts we will leave it as a joint figure.

Opening the books on day one

Having recorded the 'Dawn on day one' position does not actually get the books open. We now know what the assets and liabilities were at dawn on day one, but we still have to enter them all in the books, whatever system we decide to use. With the Simplex system we enter all these items on the first weekly page, which is of course Week 1 of our business. As already shown in Fig. 1.2, the weekly page has separate sections for 'receipts', 'paid to bank', 'payments for business stock' and 'payments other than for stock'. For convenience the entries from our Opening Balance Sheet have been shown in their separate sections in Figs 2.3, 2.4, 2.5 and 2.6. What we are pretending is that all these assets and liabilities were taken on at the first moment of Day 1, even if in real life some of them were bought or arranged in the weeks before the business actually opened. If you look down the list of activities necessary to get the Week 1 page started and then look at the figures you will follow the ideas.

- The 'receipts' section: We pretend that the £2,000 kindly loaned to us by Helpful Bank plc, and the £5,109.26 put into the business by Tom and Mary Smith are both contributed in cash on Day 1. Of course they weren't; the arrangements had really been made in the run-up period before Day 1 (see Fig. 2.3).
- The 'payments for business stock' section: We pretend that stock to

RECEIPTS		Week No. 1.		Commencing: 1st JULY 19..		
Day	Date	Gross Daily Takings (cash) Col 1	Gross Daily Takings (cheques) Col 2	Other Receipts Col 3		Particulars
Sunday	: 1 JULY			5,109	26	CAPITAL (T.&M. SMITH)
Monday	:2 "			2,000	00	LOAN FROM HELPFUL
Tuesday	:3 "					BANK PLC.
Wednesday	:4 "					
Thursday	:5 "					
Friday	:6 "					
Saturday	:7 "					
	Totals					

Fig. 2.3 Receiving the capital, etc., on to the books

PAYMENTS FOR BUSINESS STOCK			
Date or Chq. No.	To Whom Paid	Amount Paid	
		By Cash Col 7	By Cheque Col 8
1 JULY	A. SUPPLIER.	168 30	
	Totals		

Fig. 2.4 Pretending to purchase the stock on Day 1

the value of £168.30 is purchased at this time with some of the money received (see Fig. 2.4).

- The 'payment other than for stock' section: Three of the items we started business with are capital items, in other words fixed assets. We need a small digression here to explain the term capital items, or capital expenditure.

Capital expenditure and revenue expenditure

It is very important to understand these two terms, capital expenditure and revenue expenditure.

Capital expenditure is expenditure on fixed assets, which last a long time, and are used in the business during their lifetime. They are not bought to sell again – we sell them only at the end of their working life when we may trade them in for a new item, or sell them for scrap. They are bought to use in the business and make it possible to carry out our activities. Thus Tom and Mary have a car to tow the caravan, the caravan itself is fitted out as a mobile canteen and has various items of crockery, frying pans, etc. These are all capital items.

Revenue expenditure is expenditure on things that do not last a long time. For example, we buy business stock and sell it the next day, or in the next few days. It is part of our turnover. We buy petrol, postage stamps,

PAYMENTS OTHER THAN FOR STOCK				
Nature of Payment	Amount Paid			
	By Cash Col 9		By Cheque Col 10	
Rent				
Rates				
Light and Heat				
Carriage				
Postages				
Paper				
Motor Expenses				
—do—				
Travelling				
Cleaning				
Printing & Stationery				
Repairs & Renewals				
Insurance (Business)				
Advertising				
Telephone				
Sundries				
Wages (Wife)				
Wages (Employees)				
CAPITAL ITEM (CROCKERY ETC)	340	56		
CAPITAL ITEM (⅔ OF A CAR)	1,500	00		
Private Pension Contributions				
Inland Revenue (PAYE + NI)				
Drawings for Self (see Note. 10)				
—do—				
—do—				
Capital Items (see note 7)(CARAVAN)	2,850	00		
Totals				

Fig. 2.5 Bringing the assets on to the books as capital items

stationery, etc. These are revenue expenses, incurred in the process of earning 'revenue', i.e. takings. If you like you can remember these revenue expenses as items you will account for at the end of the year when you have dealings with the Inland Revenue, who will expect to see your Profit and Loss Account, showing the revenue you earned (your takings) and the revenue expenditure you incurred (your expenses) and the difference between them is your profit (on which the Inland Revenue will levy a fair rate of tax).

Returning to those capital items, the car, caravan and crockery, they are recorded on the capital items line of the weekly page. We have only one line for this, but if there is more than one item we use one of the spare lines provided, as shown in Fig. 2.5.

- *The 'Paid to Bank' section*: We now have to pretend that we are paying into the bank the £2,225.40 (which in fact is in the bank already). We enter this in the 'Paid to Bank' section as shown in Fig. 2.6.

PAID TO BANK					
CASH Col 4		CHEQUES Col 5		TOTAL Col 6	
2,225	40			2,225	40

Fig. 2.6 Paying the funds (apart from the till float) into the bank

Do you understand the 'Cash' situation now?

On the Balance Sheet it says that the proprietors provided £5,109.26 and the bank provided a loan of £2,000, making £7,109.26. We have entered this as if it came in, in cash, at 'Dawn on day one'. We have then pretended that we paid out for the following:

	£
Three capital items	340.56
	1,500.00
	2,850.00
Business stock	168.30
Cash banked	2,225.40
Total	£7,084.26

Since they contributed £7,109.26 and we have 'spent' £7,084.26, the balance left unspent is £25.

$$
\begin{array}{r}
£ \\
7,109.26 \\
-\ 7,084.26 \\
\hline
£25.00
\end{array}
$$

This £25 is left in our till, as a till float. We don't need to enter it anywhere, our books are open and we are ready for the first week of our business, up and running.

How to repay Aunt Lucy!

Of course a person who has just started up in business is usually short of capital, and doesn't want to repay any loan borrowed until the business has really started to pay off. However, this business of providing capital to satisfy the Enterprise Allowance requirement does mean that many small traders who start in business are forced to borrow a capital sum that they don't really need. How do they repay it if they don't really want the money, and would rather not be in debt? The answer is very simple. You write Aunt Lucy a cheque for £2,000, and enter it in the 'payments other than for stock' section, on one of the spare lines:

Repaid Aunt Lucy   2,000.00

The £2,000 is entered in the 'By cheque' column because you have paid by cheque. Aunt Lucy has her money back again, and you have only £225.40 in the bank. There is nothing difficult about paying any debt – just write out the cheque and post it to your creditor, and enter the payment on the appropriate line in 'Payments for Business Stock' or 'Payments other than for Stock', whichever is the correct section for the payment you are making.

Ready to go at 'Dawn on day one'

This chapter has explained how important a moment 'Dawn on day one' is. It remains to say that you should be ready to be 'businesslike' on the day your business begins. Whatever it is, you can't just concentrate on the technicalities; you have to get the business side organized as well. Of course the budding pizza restaurateur is worried about producing good pizzas, and is busy ordering flour, salt, and fillings and all the rest of the paraphernalia of a pizza parlour. What he or she must not do is forget to register for VAT; £25,400 per annum is only £488 a week, and a pizza parlour will take a lot more than that, so VAT registration will be compulsory. Other traders may only be going to register voluntarily, but don't delay if you are planning to register so you can claim back your input tax straight away. To be businesslike and ready to go you should:

- Decide on your accounting system. The author recommends you consider the Simplex system first, because it is cheap, easy, comprehensive and has a sound advisory service to help you if you get into any book-keeping difficulty. Buy a Simplex D book, and a Simplex VAT book well before 'Day One'. If you want a computerized system try Micro-Simplex, or Micro-Simplex Plus. If you understand double entry book-keeping and need a full double entry system decide what system to use after reading this book – and actually buy the system and be ready to do your opening entries in it.
- Decide whether you are going to register for VAT, and if you are, register well in advance before Day One arrives. Buy a Simplex VAT book, and go into the whole subject of VAT (see Chapters 11–12) so you know which scheme you are going to use. If you are not going to use a special retailers' scheme you have to issue an invoice to every customer, so visit your local print shop and have a good invoice designed and printed before Day One. Make sure your full details are on all documents – including postcode and telephone numbers. You will lose orders if people can't find your postcode and telephone number; it is very frustrating to want to place an order and not be able to locate the supplier, even when you are looking at his or her printed document.
- Buy a basic set of office requirements – an expanding file for documents, a filing cabinet helps (however old), a two-hole punch, a stapling machine, a pair of scissors, a decent telephone system that meets your needs, a couple of lever-arch files, a calendar, a memo pad for telephone messages, some paper clips, etc. All these things are very cheap, they last for years and will soon be 'all shiny from long years of handling' – as much a part of you as an arm or a leg. Obtain bills for all of them –

remember we want a piece of paper for everything we buy (and sell – though the sales might be on a till roll).

With this sort of set-up you are poised to start in business. Like the British soldier, who is said to have a field marshal's baton in his knapsack if he just knows where to find it, you are ready to become a tycoon. Whether you become one or not, enterprise activity is never dull, and there are nearly always new avenues to explore as you become more knowledgeable and more experienced. Life begins at 'Dawn on day one'.

Exercise on opening entries

To practise drawing up opening entries you might like to try the following exercise. You will find it a lot easier to draw up your own opening entry if you have tried this first.

A. Startup commences business on 1 February 19.X, bringing in the following assets:
- tools and equipment £1,240
- an electronic till £380
- supplies for resale already purchased £1,585.50
- a motor vehicle (to be shared 50 per cent business, 50 per cent domestic) and valued at £3,850
- cash in hand £48.50
- cash at bank £1,732.85

He has an outstanding bank loan of £2,500 from Helpful Bank plc. Draw up his opening Balance Sheet.

Answer

Capital £4,411.85, totals of Balance Sheet £6,911.85.

Checklist

These are the vital points made in this chapter.

1. 'Dawn on day one' is the moment when your new business comes into existence.
2. Be ready for it by:
   - Registering in advance for VAT if you intend to register voluntarily, or feel sure your takings will exceed £488 per week, on average, so that registration will be compulsory for you.
   - Getting your accounts system ready, either a Simplex book for small businesses or a full double entry system, or a computerized system.
   - Buying an expanding file to hold all documents as they arrive or are generated in-house.
   - Establishing a basic office set-up, so you are not driven frantic for the sake of a paperclip or a petty cash voucher.
3. Draw up your opening Balance Sheet at 'Dawn on day one', using a piece of scrap paper. When you have written down all the assets you are bringing into the business, and placed a fair value upon them, and all the liabilities the business is taking over, work out your capital.
4. Record this Balance Sheet on the opening Balance Sheet in the front of your Simplex D book, or do an opening entry if you are using a full double entry system.
5. Carry these opening figures into Week 1 of your book-keeping records so that all the assets and liabilities are properly recorded on the books.

---

3 Recording takings (sales)

The nature of takings □ Recording takings and other receipts □ Carrying the weekly takings to the 'Summary of Takings' □ Paying money and vouchers into the bank □ Use of the 'Summary of Takings' figure in determining profits □ Keeping a record of debtors □ Security and daily takings □ Checklist

The nature of takings

Every business must have 'takings' in some form or another. If a business is to survive it must have cash flows into it, and we often hear business advisers talking about the importance of 'cash flow'. The trouble is of course that cash can flow out as well as in, and if too much flows out and too little flows in we shall finish up in the bankruptcy court.

Takings may be defined as sums of money received as a result of business activity. The easiest forms of takings to understand are the takings of a shop dealing only in cash – in other words payment is demanded as the goods are supplied and the property (right of ownership) in the goods passes to the buyer as he or she gives the money payment (the price) to the seller. These terms, 'buyer', 'seller', 'property' and 'price', all come from the Sale of Goods Act 1979, where Parliament has laid down a whole host of rules about the sale of goods which make very interesting reading. Even in such a simple matter as cash sales the payment may be made in cash, by cheque, by credit card, by EFTPOS (electronic funds transfer at the point of sale) cards such as NatWest's 'Switch' card, and by tokens and vouchers from some of the minor trading houses that help poor people buy household goods, for which they pay a local tally man who calls weekly.

Shop takings of this sort occur every business day, and also lead to a considerable amount of banking. It is unwise to keep excessive amounts of cash on the premises and cheques and vouchers must be paid in before they can be turned into cash at the bank. Always pay in every day if you can, and if you do have amounts overnight, cash them up at closing time and take them home with you, including the separate till float, which you keep for change next day. It is better to have a small safe at home for these overnight moneys than to leave them in a safe in a small shop premises. Leave the till open and empty; this saves the burglars having to break it open, only to find it empty. The loss of your till can be as big a nuisance as the burglary itself.

Other traders do not handle cash every day, but are paid only when they finish a job. If your business is of that kind record each amount you receive on the day you receive it. You should supply an invoice for the job done, and if you do not give invoices for some reason at least give the person concerned a receipt. You can buy pads of receipts from any good stationers, usually with counterfoils so that the customer is given the original and you retain the counterfoil. Giving a receipt is a way of proving your good faith in financial matters, for not only has your customer proof of payment but you have proof of the amount of your takings, which is very useful in your dealings with the VAT authorities and the Inland Revenue. The person who takes payments in cash and does not record them may think he or she is getting away with it, but untraced income shows up sooner or later and is subject to serious penalties when discovered. Many a householder has complained that the burglars stole a tin containing savings from his or her wardrobe only to find that the next letter received is from the Inland Revenue asking how the press reports can be true in view of recent tax returns, and enclosing a supplementary assessment, with an immediate deadline for payment. The Inland Revenue watches for such press reports, since unbanked savings are usually a sign of undeclared income.

Recording takings and other receipts

All firms record their cash takings in some sort of *cash book*. In the Simplex system we are considering here the weekly page has a special section for recording receipts. In Fig. 3.1 we can see this 'receipts' section, showing how a shopkeeper taking cash on a regular daily basis will record it. These daily takings records are important because they form the basis of the VAT records for use in determining the VAT payable under the special schemes for retailers. The takings figures are entered gross (i.e. inclusive of VAT), either in the cash column (Col. 1) or in the cheques column if payment is made by cheque, credit card or EFTPOS card. Study the notes to Fig. 3.1.

RECEIPTS		Week No. 4		Commencing: 14 MAY 19..	
Day	Date	Gross Daily Takings (cash) Col 1		Gross Daily Takings (cheques) Col 2		Other Receipts Col 3		Particulars

Day	Date	Gross Daily Takings (cash) Col 1		Gross Daily Takings (cheques) Col 2		Other Receipts Col 3		Particulars
Sunday	:14/5	—	—	—	—	—	—	
Monday	:15/5	234	62	—	—	1,000	00	LOAN FROM HELPFUL BANK.
Tuesday	:16/5	385	71	42	90			
Wednesday	:17/5	192	60	17	26			
Thursday	:18/5	426	75	64	73			
Friday	:19/5	538	40	117	29	26	50	REFUND ON ADVERTISEMENT.
Saturday	:20/5	729	62	78	42			
Totals		2,507	70	320	60	1,026	50	

Fig. 3.1 Recording daily takings and other receipts

3

RECEIPTS

Week No. 17   Commencing: 13TH AUGUST 19..

Day	Date	Gross Daily Takings (cash) Col 1	Gross Daily Takings (cheques) Col 2	Other Receipts Col 3	Particulars
Sunday	: 13/8				
Monday	: 14/8				
Tuesday	: 15/8		246 50		MRS. T. SMITH – REDECORATIONS
Wednesday	: 16/8				
Thursday	: 17/8				
Friday	: 18/8		188 90		MR. AHURA – REGLAZING
Saturday	: 19/8				
Totals			435 40		

Fig. 3.2 Recording receipts for a trader who does not receive cash every day

Notes to Fig. 3.1

- The daily entries are simple enough. Towards the end of the day – say 30 minutes before closing time – the till is emptied, and any till float in use – say £25 – is returned to the till in small coins etc., for change. The rest – which is the day's takings – is put into suitable bags for banking purposes, notes are put together with rubber bands, and cheques and credit card vouchers are prepared for paying in. Any further takings that day are left in the till with the float and will count as tomorrow's takings.
- The paying-in book for the next day can be prepared at this time if preferred.
- The entries are now made on the appropriate line and in the appropriate column as shown in Fig. 3.1. If the trader is registered for VAT the total takings will be entered in the Simplex VAT book in the 'Daily Takings' section (see Chapter 11). The figures are entered gross, i.e. inclusive of VAT.
- At the end of the week the total takings for the week, both cash and cheques, will be taken to the 'Weekly Summary of Takings' (see Fig. 3.3 overleaf).
- Any receipts which are not ordinary takings are entered in the 'other receipts' column and a short explanation of them is written in the 'particulars' column. These are then carried to summaries at the back of the book – the £1,000 loan will go in the 'Loan Summary' and the refund on advertisement will actually be carried to the 'Summary of Miscellaneous Expenses' as a 'red ink' entry. This £26.50 is not an expense, but a refund. You write it in red in the summary of expenses and deduct it from the advertising expenses because you have received a refund of the money. That sounds a little bit tricky but if you have a Simplex book you will see it is easy enough.

Figure 3.2 shows the much more sparse entries for a trader who is paid only when a job is completed. Thus plumbers, electricians, decorators, etc., may spend several days on a job and consequently have only one or two entries a week. Authors are paid only once or twice a year and consequently have very few entries in the 'Receipts' section of the book.

Carrying the weekly takings to the 'Summary of Takings'

The whole purpose of keeping accounts is to discover the profits made by the business, both for management purposes (to decide whether it is worthwhile being self-employed at all) and for taxation purposes (to supply figures for the Inland Revenue). One of the vital figures is the 'sales' figure for the trading year. This is often called the *turnover* of the business. Under the Simplex system we find it by transferring the weekly takings figure, both cash and cheques, into a *Weekly Summary of Takings*, which builds up into four quarterly totals, and eventually into an annual total. This is illustrated in Fig. 3.3. Note that in the Simplex system these figures are all gross of VAT, in that the takings figures include the VAT – it is actually removed later when preparing the final accounts of the business. Study Fig. 3.3 now and the notes to it.

WEEKLY SUMMARY OF TAKINGS

WEEK No.	AMOUNT	WEEK No.	AMOUNT	WEEK No.	AMOUNT	WEEK No.	AMOUNT
1	1,725.62	14	1,386.48	27	3,172.95	40	1,729.47
2	1,326.73	15	2,238.72	28	2,281.84	41	2,686.38
3	1,684.48	16	2,176.32	29	2,364.73	42	3,877.26
4	2,828.30	17	2,528.64	30	2,772.27	43	3,138.42
5	2,726.50	18	1,736.20	31	2,246.92	44	2,948.54
6	2,529.65	19	988.76	32	3,938.64	45	2,391.60
7	2,814.73	20	2,148.94	33	2,471.71	46	2,472.72
8	2,736.29	21	3,188.28	34	2,692.42	47	2,256.61
9	2,468.42	22	2,384.79	35	2,166.63	48	1,563.70
10	1,989.64	23	1,864.26	36	3,875.74	49	2,677.32
11	2,176.77	24	3,175.77	37	2,334.29	50	3,476.46
12	1,284.81	25	2,234.72	38	2,272.72	51	1,381.72
13	994.36	26	1,989.76	39	1,786.56	52	2,274.55
						53	
Total 1st Qtr	27,286.30	Total 2nd Qtr	28,041.64	Total 3rd Qtr	34,377.42	Total 4th Qtr	32,874.75

Total Summary for Year	
1st Qtr	27,286.30
2nd Qtr	28,041.64
3rd Qtr	34,377.42
4th Qtr	32,874.75
Trade Debtors	126.50
TOTAL	121,706.61

Fig. 3.3 Building up the 'total sales' figure

Notes

- Each week the total takings figure, both 'cash' and 'cheque' added together, is taken to the 'Weekly Summary of Takings'.
- Every quarter the figures are totalled and carried to the 'total summary'.
- Depending on the way they are treated it may be necessary at the end of the year to add in any outstanding debtors.
- This gives us the total sales for the year, in other words the turnover of the business.
- Note that in the Simplex figures the gross figures, inclusive of VAT, are used. The VAT will be removed when the final accounts are done. This need not bother us at this stage.

Paying money and vouchers into the bank

Every day, or every few days, we have to pay our funds into the bank. We make out the usual paying-in slip as illustrated in Fig. 3.4. Note the warning on the paying-in slip that, as it is not unknown for cheques to be lost in the course of clearing, it is wise to keep a note of the names and addresses of those who are paying us by cheque. Where a cheque is valued at less than £50 it is advisable to ask for a cheque card and record the number of the card on the back of the cheque. This causes the bank to honour the cheque, for it has virtually validated the payment made. Cheques over £50 are not covered, and if we accept them we run the usual risk of taking a cheque; that it may be dishonoured. This is of course a criminal offence, which may lead to the person passing the cheque being punished, but that will not get us the money.

A rather similar paying-in slip is provided by credit card companies for paying in vouchers signed by customers and imprinted with their card details. It is not necessary to reproduce this here since you will be instructed in its completion when you become an authorised retailer for

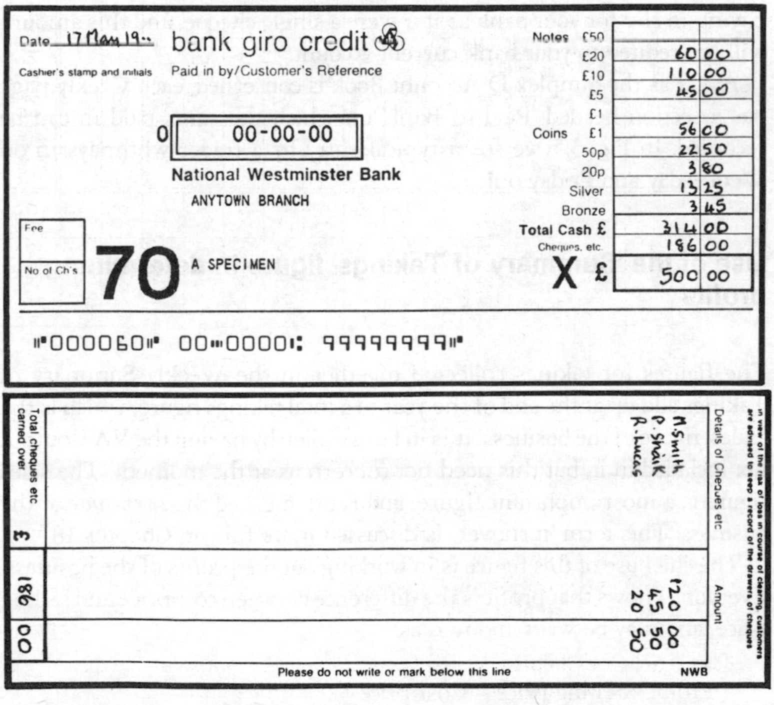
Date 17 May 19.. bank giro credit
Cashier's stamp and initials Paid in by/Customer's Reference
0 00-00-00
National Westminster Bank
ANYTOWN BRANCH
Fee
No of Ch's
70 A SPECIMEN

Notes £50		
£20	60	00
£10	110	00
£5	45	00
£1		
Coins £1	56	00
50p	22	50
20p	3	80
Silver	13	25
Bronze	3	45
Total Cash £	314	00
Cheques, etc.	186	00
X £	500	00

⑈000060⑈ 00⑉0000⑆ 99999999⑈

In view of the risk of loss in course of clearing, customers are advised to keep a record of the drawers of cheques

Details of Cheques etc	Amount	
M. Smith	120	00
P. Shaik	45	50
R. Lucas	20	50

Total cheques etc carried over 3 186 00

Please do not write or mark below this line NWB

Fig. 3.4 A paying-in slip (*courtesy of National Westminster Bank plc*)

RECEIPTS		PAID TO BANK					
Day	Date	CASH Col 4		CHEQUES Col 5		TOTAL Col 6	
Sunday	: 14/5						
Monday	: 15/5						
Tuesday	: 16/5						
Wednesday	: 17/5	314	00	186	00	500	00
Thursday	: 18/5						
Friday	: 19/5	726	00	332	80	1,058	80
Saturday	: 20/5						
Totals		1,040	00	518	80	1,558	80

Lodgements made

Total carried to Weekly Cash Report (to reduce the cash balance) and to the Weekly Bank Report (to increase the bank balance).

Fig. 3.5 The 'Paid to bank' section

any particular card. (If you wish to become an authorised retailer your local NatWest branch will be happy to put you in touch with the Access authorities.) The total amount of the vouchers submitted is recorded on a paying-in slip for your bank as if it were a single cheque, and this amount will be credited to your bank current account.

As far as the Simplex D Account Book is concerned, each weekly page has a section headed 'Paid to Bank' on which the sums paid in can be recorded. In Fig. 3.5 we see a typical entry by a trader who pays in on Wednesday and Friday only.

Use of the 'Summary of Takings' figure in determining profits

The figures for takings collected together in the Weekly Summary of Takings add up at the end of the year to a total takings figure, which is the 'Sales' figure of the business. It is in fact swollen by having the VAT output tax included in it, but this need not concern us at the moment. The sales figure is a most important figure, and is often called the *turnover* of the business. This term 'turnover' is discussed more fully in Chapter 18.

The chief use of this figure is in working out the profits of the business. Everyone knows that profit is the difference between cost price and selling price, and may be written down as:

Profit = Selling price − Cost price

In business we can extend this to a slightly different formula since we are not dealing with the profit on a single item, but with a vast number of goods or services supplied in the trading period under consideration. Profit is still very much concerned with cost prices and selling prices, but we also have many *overhead expenses* to take into account as well. For this reason we deal with the profits of a business in two parts. We first consider the *gross profit*, which means 'fat' profit or 'overall' profit found by taking the cost price from the selling price. We do this in the form of an account, called the *Trading Account*, but the formula is:

Gross profit = Sales figure (turnover) − Purchases figure

We then find the *net profit*, which means 'clean' profit, by taking away the overhead expenses from the gross profit. The formula is:

Net profit = Gross profit − Overheads

We shall find out how to do this later in the book, but here all we need to say is that the records we have kept so far (see Fig. 3.3) have found one of these vital figures for us. The sales of our business are the total takings, which come to £122,706.61. This figure will be used in the Trading Account when we find the Gross Profit at the end of the year (see Chapter 4).

Keeping a record of debtors

Debtors present many problems. For many small businesses there is no need to become involved with debtors, and one often sees notices saying 'Please do not ask for credit as a refusal may offend'. These days if people cannot pay cash for something, or pay by cheque backed by a banker's cheque card (for items costing £50 or less) they can usually use a credit card instead. In this way the retailer, provided he or she has kept within the operating rules laid down by the credit card company concerned, has no fear of a bad debt. The organization that knows how to arrange credit, is a registered credit broker and has vetted the customer for creditworthiness has all the problems; you as the retailer have none. The first rule then about debtors is:

'Don't offer credit unless you have to.'

Where you do supply goods or services without immediate payment the following problems arise:

- You must record the debt in some simple way.
- You have to exercise credit control, not only over that transaction but over all future transactions.
- You must make up your mind how to do the book-keeping entries, because of course, although you have sold the goods, no 'takings' have been received.

A word about each of these problems is necessary.

Recording the debt

With a full double entry system every debtor is allocated a separate account, with the sum owing appearing on the debit side of the account. The debit side is the left-hand side, and such an account looks like this:

T. Smith, 1275 Camside, Cambridge CB4 1PQ

19X9		£	
23 May	Goods	118.54	

Simple systems of book-keeping do not have such accounts, and instead work on the 'butcher's-book method'. Victorian butchers, to help customers in temporary difficulties, used to keep a book near the till in which they recorded any unpaid bills. When the customer paid up the date of payment was recorded in the customer's presence, and the debt struck through with a ruled line. A simple example is shown in Fig. 3.6.

19..		Date paid	£	P
May 17	Mrs. J. Brown, 21 River Walk		3	27
17	Mr. T. Appleyard, 4 Deansbury	21 May	7	32
19	R. Grimes, 19 Caffice Way		7	48
21	T. Lark, 27 Totterdown Passage		24	25
24	K. Ahura, 19 High St.		19	36
		£	61	68

Fig. 3.6 A simple record of debtors

Exercising credit control

For straightforward debtors kept under personal control by the proprietor of a business there is little difficulty. You simply decide on a policy and stick to it, except on rare occasions when you exercise discretion within a policy. Thus the policy for some debtors might be 'no further credit until an outstanding earlier item has been settled'. With another customer it might be: all the previous month's transactions to be settled by the seventh of the following month. On special pleading – for example where there is a postal strike and allowances are held up – you might use your discretion and still supply goods even though the seventh had passed.

Some small businesses (and medium-sized businesses too) are held to ransom by larger firms who won't place orders unless they can have three months' credit. This is a big problem and is dealt with in detail later, in Chapter 17. An excellent booklet about is it available from the Small Firms Service, called *Prompt Payment Please*. Telephone your local branch on Freefone Enterprise to obtain a copy. Included in it are stickers which the small firm can place on its invoices. They are brightly coloured and read 'Prompt Payment Please – Help small businesses'.

The book-keeping entries

Apart from recording your customer's debt in the 'butcher's book' you have purchased for that purpose, how will you deal with the problem of the book-keeping records? There are two ways to treat these sales, which we will call the 'Sale of Goods Act' method and the 'Sales deferred' method. In strict law the former is the correct method but it is less convenient than the 'Sales deferred' method, which is therefore often used.

The 'Sale of Goods Act' method

The Sale of Goods Act says that when a contract for the sale of goods is made the property in the goods passes at the time the parties intend it to pass, irrespective of when payment is made. Thus, if a customer takes goods from you and promises to pay later, the sale of the goods has taken place and they are now the customer's goods, and as far as you are concerned they are sales (and should be included in your daily takings even though you haven't received the money for them, but only a debtor's promise to pay). Therefore, strictly speaking, you should add these sales in with your daily takings at the end of the day.

It then becomes a problem what to do with the money when the customer comes in and pays; you can't put it into the till because that would swell the daily takings for the day, when in fact this sale has already been included in daily takings much earlier. The money must be kept separate. As a result the 'Sale of Goods Act' method, while legally correct, is a little awkward in everyday practice.

The 'Sales deferred' method

With the 'Sales deferred' method we record the debt in the 'butcher's book' but we don't regard the sale as having been made until we actually receive the money. When the customer comes in and pays the debt we cross out the debt in the book and put the money in the till, where it becomes takings of the payment date, not takings of the earlier date when the sale was actually made. In strict legal terms we regard the stock sold as not sold at all, but only out on location with the customer, until the day of payment arrives. Of course, that is really a silly idea because the customer's family may have eaten the stock, so we can hardly pretend that it is still available and could be reclaimed. There does come a time though when we do have to recognize that these debts do represent actual sales, and that is on the last day of the year. At this date, when we do the final summary of daily takings, we record the outstanding debts in the butcher's book as sales, on the summary. You can see this figure for trade debtors, £126.50 if you look back to Fig. 3.3 for a moment.

Security and daily takings

Takings are always vulnerable – from burglaries, highway robberies, embezzlement and petty theft. Some of the more obvious security measures are:

- Use proper tills with in-built security devices so that cash is properly handled, till receipts are given and sharp practices are avoided
- Collect high-value notes from tills at regular (or irregular) intervals
- Insist that staff call witnesses when giving change for large notes, or when giving change to young children
- Pay in regularly, if necessary more than once a day, and avoid taking the same route to the bank each time
- Watch out for shoplifting, credit-card frauds and passing-out (staff giving excess change to friends and accomplices)
- Remove overnight money and till floats and either use the night-safe service at your local bank or a secure safe at home to protect it
- Never discuss the level of your takings with anyone, especially in places like public houses
- Leave tills empty and open at night (*Continued on p. 42*)

RECEIPTS

Week No. _____   Commencing: _____

Day	Date	Gross Daily Takings (cash) Col 1		Gross Daily Takings (cheques) Col 2		Other Receipts Col 3		Particulars
Sunday	:							
Monday	:							
Tuesday	:							
Wednesday	:							
Thursday	:							
Friday	:							
Saturday	:							
Totals								

Fig. 3.7 A blank Simplex 'receipts' section of the weekly page
(courtesy of George Vyner Ltd)

3

Note:

You may photocopy this page for training purposes only, and do the exercises on these copies. Do not do any entries on this blank page, or you will spoil it for copying purposes.

- Do see your local crime prevention officer if you feel uncertain about the adequacy of your security measures.

Exercise on recording receipts

In Fig. 3.7 there is a blank ruling of the 'receipts' section of a Simplex page. You may photocopy a few copies of it and use them to do the exercise which follows, to give you practice in recording receipts.

Peter Morgan uses the Simplex D Account Book. It is Week 21 and the week commences on Sunday 22nd May. Sales in cash each day are as follows:
- Monday £197.20
- Tuesday £285.50
- Wednesday £248.90
- Thursday £886.50
- Friday £879.25
- Saturday £662.

On Monday he also sold goods for £78.65, paid by cheque. On Wednesday he is notified that he was won £928.50 on the football pools and decides to put £600 in as extra capital. On Tuesday he banks £300 cash and a cheque for £78.65, and on Friday £1,250 cash and the football pools money – a cheque for £600 from his personal bank account. Make all these entries and total the various columns.

Answer

Peter Morgan: cash takings £3,159.35; cheque takings £78.65; other receipts £600; total paid to bank £2,228.65.

Checklist

---

1. 'Takings' is another word for 'sales'. The takings of a business are the sole source of funds to run the business, apart from the original capital provided by the proprietor. From the sales money we must be able to afford to purchase all the goods and materials we need, and to pay all the overheads.
2. Takings should be recorded every day, and surplus funds not required in the business should be banked as soon as possible. This includes cash, cheques and credit card vouchers.
3. Ensure that you take adequate security measures with takings. Think though all the possibilities and if necessary seek advice from your local crime prevention officer.
4. The daily takings form the basis of our VAT figures if you are using one of the special schemes for retailers. Remember, in VAT, the word 'retailer' means anyone who provides taxable supplies of goods or services without issuing an invoice to the customer.
5. The daily takings figures accumulate into weekly, quarterly and annual totals for sales. It is the annual total which is used to work out the profit at the end of the financial year.

3

4 Recording purchases (payments for business stock)

The meaning of 'purchases' in business □ Purchases of business stock □ Invoices, delivery notes and advice notes □ The summary of purchases □ Use of purchases in finding the profits of the business □ Calculating the gross profit in the Trading Account □ Checklist

The meaning of 'purchases' in business

In business the word 'purchases' has a special meaning: items purchased for resale, or items purchased to be embodied in a product or in a finished piece of work. The test whether an item is a 'purchase' or not is whether an invoice will eventually be raised to charge a customer for the goods supplied, or the work done. Equally, if a future supply will be made only against a cash payment by a customer, the goods purchased for resale, or the goods embodied in the work done, are 'purchases'.

It follows that many things you may buy are not 'purchases'. For example, if you buy tools, machinery, motor vehicles, furniture and other assets of the business these are not 'purchases' because they are bought for use in the business, not for resale. Similarly, if you buy stationery, advertising brochures, pencils and ballpoint pens for use in the office these are not 'purchases'.

By contrast, to a grocery business, cheese, bacon, butter, sugar, coffee and similar products are 'purchases' which are bought to sell again. To a landscape gardener, paving stones, gravel, trees and shrubs etc., are 'purchases', for when embodied in the landscaped grounds which are the subject of his or her contract they will become the customer's property, embodied in the price for the job.

To take another example, suppose a garage buys 12 cars, two of which are to be used by the managing director and the sales director, while the other ten are for resale. Clearly the first two are assets of the business, and the last ten are 'purchases' for resale. We may refer back to an earlier section in which we distinguished between capital expenditure

(expenditure on assets) and revenue expenditure (expenditure on items which will be part of our revenue accounts in the current financial year and used in the calculation of our profits). The first two cars are capital expenditure; the other ten cars are revenue expenditure, in this case 'purchases of the business'.

Purchases of business stock

Whether goods are purchased for resale (without any alteration) or to be embodied into a finished product as a result of some manufacturing or craft process, they are purchases and form part of the stocks of the business. They can be paid for in three ways:

- in cash, on delivery
- by cheque, on delivery
- at a later date, in other words we are given a credit period (time in which to pay)

Where credit is given, in many trades the period is not very long, for example perishables like meat are usually required to be paid for within three days. In other trades we may get 7, 15 or 30 days to pay, from invoice date. If we are dealt with by our suppliers on 'open account' terms it usually means that we will be sent a 'statement' once a month showing all the purchases made in the month (and any returns for which credit notes have been given). We are then required to pay the balance on the statement within a given period, usually 30 days. To avoid having to send out thousands of accounts at the end of the month, most firms use a system of *cyclical billing* in which 4 per cent of their accounts are sent out every day. This means that we may get an account on the 16th of every month, which will be payable within 30 days of that date.

In the Simplex system which we are considering closely in these first few chapters, we record these payments in the following ways:

- *Cash payments* are recorded in the cash column, as shown in Fig. 4.1, on the day they are made.
- *Payments by cheque* are recorded similarly, but in the 'by cheque' column.
- *Credit deliveries* are not entered until they are actually paid for, when the entries are made on that date. Clearly it is important to keep the invoice safely until the due date. A useful tip here is to have an expanding file labelled 1–31. You can buy one from Neat Ideas by telephone on 01–449 9949. The labels are A–Z but you can change these

PAYMENTS FOR BUSINESS STOCK					
Date or Chq. No.	To Whom Paid	Amount Paid			
		By Cash Col 7		By Cheque Col 8	
1 FEB 19..	BANBURY & CO.	37	56		
3 FEB 19..	F. GILES	3	50		
4 FEB 19..	R. HAYSEED	27	55		
326541	NEAT IDEAS			8	73
326543	R. T. MORGAN			214	27
6 FEB 19..	BANBURY & CO.	49	84		
	Totals	118	45	223	00

Fig. 4.1 Recording purchases (payments for business stock)

Notes

- The date is the date of payment or, if paid by cheque, the cheque number may be inserted instead (it helps with bank reconciliations later).
- Cash payments and cheque payments are differentiated in columns 7 and 8.
- The total of payments for the week will be carried to the 'Summary of Payments for Business Stock' at the back of the Simplex book.

---

to numbers. When an invoice or a monthly statement arrives you work out the date by which it must be paid and put it in the file accordingly. If it offers a discount if paid within a certain time put it in the date that will earn you the discount. On that date you write the cheque, enter it into your records, and post it off.

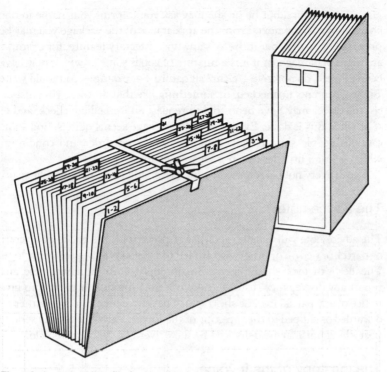

4

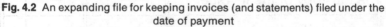

Fig. 4.2 An expanding file for keeping invoices (and statements) filed under the date of payment

Now look at Fig. 4.1 to see how the 'purchases' entries are made, and Fig. 4.2 to see an expanding file for storing invoices until the date of payment.

Invoices, delivery notes and advice notes

An invoice from a supplier for goods for resale is usually spoken of as a purchase invoice. It will usually be part of a multicopy set, as shown in Fig. 1.4, though many invoice sets have more than the three copies shown in that illustration. The copies you are likely to see are the following.

The delivery note

The delivery note will usually be presented by the delivery driver, who will ask you to sign it. What the driver wants is a 'clean' signature, preferably just your signature, but he or she may ask you to print your name in one box and sign in the next. From the appearance of the package you may be prepared to do this, but if there is any unsatisfactory feature, for example any signs of damage, or if it is a mixture of goods some of which may have been pilfered, do not give a 'clean' signature. For example, you could write 'Signed, contents unchecked' or something like that. In these circumstances the driver may have been told to request an immediate check, and to wait while this is done. Even when the package seems quite sound some cautious people sign 'Received in apparent good order and condition', which is just a little less than a 'clean' signature.

The delivery note is retained by the driver and you will not see it again.

The advice note

The advice note will usually be either enclosed with the goods in its crate or parcel, or tied on or otherwise affixed to the goods in a special envelope. The idea is that you should check the contents against the advice note, and report any discrepancy (usually there is a time limit of three days to give notice of any partial loss, or shortage). The advice note can then either be discarded or clipped to the top copy of the invoice, which is usually sent by post, though it may be delivered by the driver of a delivery vehicle.

The top copy of the invoice

This copy may be labelled 'customer's copy' and is the purchase invoice for your purposes. It will often go into the VAT records in the first place and then be used to record payment for the purchases, on the day of payment, as recorded in Fig. 4.1. If you are being supplied as a trusted customer on 'open account' terms you will not pay on the invoice but on the monthly statement as explained above. Keep your top copy of the invoice, with the advice copy clipped to it if you received one, as part of your VAT records. If this means you cannot keep it in a concertina file until payment, put a piece of scrap paper giving the details in your concertina file so that you do not fail to pay it on the due date.

The summary of purchases

At the end of the week the total of the payments for business stock is carried to the 'Summary of Payments for Business Stock' at the back of the Simplex D Account Book, and these figures total into quarterly totals and then an annual total in the special box provided. Once again, since it is possible we will have a few invoices from suppliers which we have not yet

WEEKLY SUMMARY OF PAYMENTS FOR BUSINESS STOCK

WEEK No.	AMOUNT	WEEK No.	AMOUNT	WEEK No.	AMOUNT	WEEK No.	AMOUNT		Total Summary for Year
1	223.43	14	325.72	27	525.36	40	538.11	1st Qtr.	5,229.04
2	416.56	15	426.36	28	472.25	41	861.49	2nd Qtr.	4,922.44
3	218.72	16	375.49	29	684.46	42	772.90	3rd Qtr.	10,062.12
4	375.61	17	209.56	30	396.72	43	249.82	4th Qtr.	10,335.62
5	296.17	18	623.72	31	838.38	44	951.63	Purchases Creditors	237.25
6	341.45	19	443.21	32	925.29	45	973.71	TOTAL	30,786.47
7	423.14	20	329.49	33	701.71	46	884.43		
8	815.29	21	217.36	34	1272.49	47	717.29		
9	316.31	22	361.72	35	1138.72	48	1103.34		
10	275.42	23	552.63	36	1047.68	49	1342.71		
11	385.58	24	449.48	37	929.86	50	1051.60		
12	426.66	25	336.59	38	456.71	51	377.32		
13	714.70	26	271.11	39	672.49	52	511.27		
Total 1st Qtr.	5,229.04	Total 2nd Qtr.	4,922.44	Total 3rd Qtr.	10,062.12	53			
						Total 4th Qtr.	10,335.62		

Fig. 4.3 The summary of payments for business stock (purchases)

paid, and consequently have not yet entered in the 'Payments for Business Stock' section, a space is provided in the annual summary to enable us to enter these purchases under the heading 'Purchases Creditors'. This total of purchases comes in Fig. 4.3 to £30,786.47. Notice that this is a great deal less than the figure for total sales for the year (see Fig. 3.3), so it is clear that we are leading up to a profitable result at the end of the financial year.

Use of purchases in finding the profits of the business

In Chapter 2 we referred to the use of the sales figure in determining the profits of the business, under the general formula:

Gross Profit = Sales figure (turnover) – Purchases figure

Now that we have seen how the total purchases figure for the year is found we can see how to work out the gross profit, because we have both figures required in the formula given above, the sales figure and the purchases figure. According to our formula the gross profit would be found, using the figures in Figs. 3.3 and 4.3, as follows:

$$\begin{aligned} \text{Gross profit} &= \text{Sales} - \text{Purchases} \\ &= £122,706.61 - £30,786.47 \\ &= £91,920.14 \end{aligned}$$

However, this isn't really the correct answer for the gross profit of our business because the formula we have used is just a little too simple. The reason is that it does not take account of unsold stock. We very rarely manage to sell out all the stock by the last day of the year and that unsold stock is included in the 'purchases' made in the year. As we haven't sold it we really need to deduct it from the 'purchases' figure for the year. Of course we may also have had some opening stock, at the start of the year, which will almost certainly have been sold during the year, and thus needs to be added in with our 'purchases' figure. We must just look at 'stock' closely for a moment.

Stock and stocktaking

What is stock? Well, obviously it is the result of purchasing goods for resale, what the Simplex system calls 'Payments for Business Stock'. However, although everything we buy goes into stock (and if we had a burglary we should certainly be asked by the police to make a list of all the stock stolen), we don't usually talk about 'stock' in that general sense. The word 'stock' usually refers to the 'Closing Stock' figure, which is the amount of stock left on the shelves at the last moment of the last day of the financial year. This 'Closing Stock' is carried over to next year, and of course becomes the 'Opening Stock' of the new year, at exactly the same figure. To value the Closing Stock we have to carry out a stocktake, and as this is rather a lot of hard work and takes a few hours we may have a *stocktaking sale* just before the end of the financial year to get rid of as much stock as possible. Having done that, we must then count the stock still on the shelves, and value it. There is a special rule for stock valuation, laid down by the professional bodies of accountants. The rule is: *Stock is valued at cost price, or net realizable value, whichever is the lower.*

This is a very important rule. Most of our stock will be valued at cost price. Suppose a menswear shop has a suit priced at £50 to the customers but it cost the shop £23.50 from the wholesaler. It will be valued at the cost price of £23.50 when we do the stocktaking. However, suppose that the suit has been used as a display model and is rather shop-soiled because customers have been feeling the quality of the material. We might decide we'll be lucky to sell it for £30, and to do that we'll have to send it to another branch in an area where people are looking for bargains. It will cost £3 to send it to the other branch, so the 'net realizable value' is only £27. However, this is still more than the cost price, so the stocktaking value is still £23.50. 'Cost price or net realizable value, whichever is the lower.' Suppose the damage is such that, honestly, we could get rid of the suit only by offering it at £15 at the other branch. The result would be that the 'net realizable value' is only £12, because of the £3 expenses involved. On the stocktaking lists this suit would be valued at only £12, because the net realizable value is less than the cost price.

The rule is an example of another rule in accountancy: the 'prudence' rule. The prudence rule says this: *Any business person behaves prudently. Never take a profit until you've actually made the profit, and always take a loss as soon as it is clear you have suffered a loss.* In the case just mentioned we don't value stock at selling price £50, or even at reduced selling price £27, because if we did that we would be pretending to ourselves that we'd made a profit, when we haven't actually sold the article. On the other hand, if the net realizable value is less than the cost price we value the item at this lower figure, because we believe we've made a loss on this garment (the most we can hope to recover is £12, so we've lost £11.50 on the garment). Always take a loss the moment you realize you've suffered one.

So, to carry out the stocktake:

- count the items on the shelves
- appraise the items to decide (a) the cost price and (b) the net realizable value (what we can hope to sell it for)
- value it at cost price or net realizable value, whichever is the lower
- if necessary multiply the value decided upon by the number of items – i.e. 26 tins of baked beans at a cost price of 24p = £6.24
- add up all the figures for all the items to reach a grand total for the 'Closing Stock' figure.

With this Closing Stock figure you are ready to calculate the gross profit of the business.

Calculating the gross profit in the Trading Account

The profits of a business are worked out in two stages, the gross profit and the net profit. The first is worked out in the Trading Account, which, as its name implies, tells us the profit we have made on trading, but before deducting the overhead expenses to find the net profit (or clean profit). As we shall see in Fig. 4.4, the process is very simple. On the 'sales' side we simply have the total figure for sales for the year. In the Simplex book there is a line for 'value of goods taken for own consumption', but we can ignore this for the present. On the 'purchases' side we have slightly more complicated figures. We need to know the cost of the sales. What did the things we sold for £122,706.61 actually cost us? The answer is that at the start of the year, at 'Dawn on day one', we had an opening stock of £168.30. We then purchased a great deal of stock to add to this opening stock, making £30,954.77 of stock which went on to our shelves during the year. At the end of the year, when we did the stocktake, we had unsold stock to the value of £3,894.68. If we take this closing stock from the total stock available we find we have sold – stock to a total of £27,060.09. We sold this stock for £122,706.61, so we made an excellent gross profit of £95,646.52. Note that some firms like to show last year's figures for comparison purposes, and companies are required by law to do so. As this is a new business we cannot show these figures anyway, but the Simplex book has a place for them to be shown in future years if we wish to do so. Study the layout of the Trading Account in Fig. 4.4 carefully.

Exercise in recording payments for business stock

In Fig. 4.5 you have an illustration of the Simplex 'Payments for Business Stock' section. Photocopy it for your personal use and then do the following exercise to make sure you understand how purchases are recorded.

R. Mansfield records on his Simplex page under the heading 'Payments for Business Stock' the following items during the week:

July 7 Paid Media Supplies Ltd by cheque £25.74 (cheque no. 725311) and R. Jones in cash £5.40

July 8 Paid Computer Software plc by cheque £885.50 and Prepared Data Ltd £46.50 by cheque (cheque nos 725312 and 725313 respectively)

July 9 Paid R. Masters by cheque £27.25 (cheque no. 725316) and the Mason Paper Co. Ltd in cash £25.85

July 13 Paid R. Jones in cash £17.25

Enter these items and total the 'cash' and 'cheque' columns.

TRADING ACCOUNT for year ending 31st DECEMBER 19..

LAST YEAR				THIS YEAR				LAST YEAR	
		Opening Stock at 1·1·19..		168	30		Sales or Work completed	122,706	61
		Purchases during year		30,786	47		Value of goods taken for own consumption	—	—
		Total		30,954	77		Total turnover	122,706	61
		Less Closing Stock at 31·12·19..		3,894	68				
		Cost of Sales Total		27,060	09				
		Gross Profit (Carried to Profit & Loss Acount)		95,646	52				
		TOTAL £		122,706	61		TOTAL £	122,706	61

Fig. 4.4 Finding the gross profit on trading

4

PAYMENTS FOR BUSINESS STOCK			
Date or Chq. No.	To Whom Paid	Amount Paid	
		By Cash Col 7	By Cheque Col 8
	Totals		

Fig. 4.5 A blank 'Payments for Business Stock' section (*courtesy of George Vyner Ltd*)

Note: May be photocopied for educational purposes only

Exercise on calculating the gross profit

Using the same layout as is shown in Fig. 4.4, draw up the Trading Account for the following business.

R. Mortenson for the year ended 31 December 19X9:

- Sales £135,856.20
- Purchases £27,386.75
- Stock at 1 January £3,727.60
- Stock at 31 December £9512.60

Answer to recording payments

Books of R. Mansfield: cash payments £48.50; payments by cheque £984.99.

Answer to gross profit exercise

Books of R. Mortenson: gross profit £114,254.45.

4

Checklist

These are the vital points made in this chapter.

1. 'Purchases' has a special meaning in business. Not everything we buy is 'purchases'. Purchases are things we buy to sell again (business stock) or things we buy to make up into a finished product, in some sort of manufacturing process, assembly work or service (such as landscape gardening).
2. Purchases of consumables (stationery, postage stamps, etc.) are not purchases, neither are purchases of assets for use in the business.
3. When we purchase business stock it may be for cash, or for a cheque (which is as good as cash) or we may purchase on credit, and promise to pay later. We pay our creditors when they send a statement, and the terms of payment will be written on it (for example 'Cash 30 days').
4. The individual payments are collected together in summaries or possibly in a Purchases Account, to give us the monthly, quarterly and eventually annual total.
5. The total purchases figure is used in the Trading Account to work out the gross profit of the business, using the formula:

   Gross profit = Sales − Cost of sales

6. Cost of sales is found by adjusting the 'Purchases' Figure for opening and closing stocks, using the formula:

   Cost of sales = (Opening stock + Purchases) − Closing stock

5 Recording payments other than for stock

Payments other than for stock □ How do I treat wages, salaries and National Insurance contributions? □ What are capital items? □ Repayment of loans and mortgages □ What are drawings? □ Recording all types of expenditure other than for stock □ carrying weekly figures to summaries to collect the annual figures □ Payments by direct debit and standing order; bank charges □ Finding the net profit of the business: the Profit and Loss Account □ Checklist

Payments other than for stock

We saw in Chapter 4 that one of the chief types of expenditure incurred in a business is expenditure on purchases; that is, expenditure on goods for resale or on raw materials, components, etc., to be worked into a finished product for which a customer will eventually be invoiced. We now have to look at all the other types of expenditure incurred in a business. Payments other than for stock consist of several types:

- Payments for *consumable items*, such as paper, stationery, cleaning materials, etc.
- Payments for *overhead expenses*, such as rent and rates, light and heat, travelling expenses, repairs and renewals, etc.
- Payments for *wages and salaries*, and National Insurance contributions (NIC) associated with employing staff.
- Payments for *capital items*, such as the purchase of premises, motor vehicles, furniture and fittings, plant and machinery, computers, typewriters, etc. Even goodwill, a rather strange asset that we have to purchase when we buy some kinds of business, is a capital item. It consists of the good opinion of customers in the area around the business, and is called an *intangible asset* because there is nothing we can really touch when we buy goodwill.
- Repayments of *loans* and *mortgages*.
- Payments of '*drawings*' to the proprietor, or partners of the business.

All these types of payment need a few words of explanation.

What are consumables?

Consumables are items that are used up in the course of business activity and, while the business gets some benefit from them, it is a very temporary benefit. For example, if we buy postage stamps, stick them on letters and post the letters we have 'consumed' the postage stamps in the course of business. Similarly, the letterhead we wrote on and the envelopes we used are consumable items. These types of expenses are revenue expenditure, a term explained earlier. They are deductible business expenses when working out the profits, since they were incurred for business purposes to advance the activities of the business. These weekly expenses must be carried to some sort of summary and added up over the year, so that at the end of the year the total expenditure on postage, stationery, etc., can be deducted from the takings to determine the profitability of the business. In the Simplex system this summary is called the 'Summary of Payments for Expenses'. Remember that the dividing line between revenue expenditure and capital expenditure is one year, and we can always decide whether an item is revenue expenditure by asking ourselves the question: 'Do I expect to have this item I have just purchased still benefiting the business one year from now?' For a postage stamp the answer would be 'No', but for a pair of scales to weigh the letters the answer would be 'Yes'.

What are overhead expenses?

Consumable items are often considered part of *overheads*, but for the moment we shall keep this term to refer to the very large body of expenses concerned with keeping a roof over our heads and a place to work in, such as rent, rates, light and heat, telephone expenses, repairs and renewals, and so on. These are similar to consumable expenses, and will be collected together in the summary of expenses, before being deducted from the profits at the end of the year as legitimate business expenses. (Note: community charges are never a business expense.)

How do I treat wages, salaries and National Insurance contributions?

Wages, salaries and any other expenses connected with the employment of staff are an expense of the business. The reason for mentioning them separately is to point out that certain legal obligations are imposed upon employers which make them unpaid collectors of taxes for the government. For example, we must operate a PAYE (pay as you earn) system to deduct tax from the employees' wage packets or salary cheques, and pay it over monthly to the Inland Revenue. We must also deduct National Insurance contributions (NIC) from the employees' wages or salaries, as well as paying a large contribution as employer, for every person we employ. Full details of these payments are given in Chapter 10. These various deductions result in a considerable amount of money being in our possession which does not belong to us, but to the government. As a result the government imposes two further burdens upon us: it requires us to pay sickness benefit (statutory sick pay) to staff entitled to receive it because of absence from work and also maternity benefit (statutory maternity pay) to female employees taking maternity leave. We are paying this money out of the funds we have collected, so it is not our money, but it does save the government a great deal of work if these payment are made through the wage packet. Of course we then need to send in only the net amount (taxes collected minus disbursements) to the Inland Revenue each month.

As far as book-keeping is concerned the important point about all these payments, whether they are in the wage packet or sent to the tax office is that they are all part of the expense of employing staff, and therefore a deductible revenue expense so far as we are concerned. The total payments (wages paid, National Insurance contributions for both employer and employee and the tax deducted from the wages) are shown in the Profit and Loss Account at the end of the year as a deduction from the gross profit – as part of the calculations to discover the net profit.

What are capital items?

Capital items have already been described as items that last longer than a year, and therefore permanently benefit the business by giving lasting service to it. Land and buildings are generally recognized as lasting for such a long time that they may be regarded as permanent assets. Plant and machinery may last 20 or 30 years, motor vehicles about five to eight years, furniture about 15 years, and so on. The important point about these is that they are capital, not revenue, expenditure and cannot be written off the profits at the end of the year. Howevever, where they do decline in value by 'fair wear and tear' we are allowed to charge a certain amount of their value against the profits each year. This is called *depreciation*, and there are many ways of working out the correct value. However, as a small business proprietor you need not worry about this, because whatever system you use the Inland Revenue will disregard it, for the following reason. Suppose Mr Smith, a decorator, has had a good year and made £20,000 profit. He purchased a new car for £8,000 this year and to save tax decides to depreciate it by 100 per cent – which will reduce the value of the car to nothing on his books, and reduce his profits to £12,000. Clearly this would not be correct, because the car is really worth about £6,000 and only £2,000 is depreciation. Mr Smith would therefore be cheating the Inland Revenue of some tax and giving a false picture on his Balance Sheet at the end of the year (it appearing that he had no car, whereas in fact he has an almost new one).

To get over this problem Parliament has enacted the rate of depreciation you may take. The £8,000 Mr Smith has deducted from his profits will be added back, and the Inland Revenue inspector gives him what he is entitled to. The figure does sometimes change on Budget Day, but at the present time it is 25 per cent, on the *reducing balance* method. To explain this, think of Mr Smith's car:

	£
Value when new	8,000
Depreciation 25%	2,000
Balance left	£6,000

This £6,000 is recorded by the Inland Revenue in Mr Smith's 'pool'. This is a pool of assets carried over from one year to the next. So the next year we have:

	£
Amount in pool	6,000
Depreciation 25%	1,500
Balance left	£4,500

The next year the figures will be as shown below, because what is deducted as depreciation is 25% of the reducing balance. So we have:

	£
Amount in pool	4,500
Depreciation 25%	1,125
Balance left	£3,375

Of course it will not be just Mr Smith's car, but all his other assets (but not land and buildings) which are in the pool, and the balance will be a composite figure for all of them. Notice also that the limit of depreciation on a car is £2,000, so if you buy a Rolls-Royce for £40,000 you will receive only £2,000 depreciation. If you want a fancy car by all means have one, but you can't expect the tax man to pay a large contribution towards it.

Repayment of loans and mortgages

When we borrow money we have to repay it, usually in monthly instalments. These are often paid by standing order or direct debit, but these terms are explained later. When we pay an amount due on a loan the payment must be recorded, and the amount paid must be deducted from the loan, since we now do not owe as much as before. Of course, from time to time the bank or building society will notify us of interest added to the loan – because our repayments are partly interest and partly repayments of the sum borrowed, but this need not worry us for the moment, it is explained later. We shall see that recording repayments is a very simple matter.

What are drawings?

The last type of payment we need to take note of is 'drawings'. The sole proprietor of a business is not allowed to receive any wages or salary, neither is a partner of a partnership business. What they are entitled to is the profits of the business, but as these are computed only at the end of the financial year, the proprietor(s) are in difficulty. They have to meet their household expenses and pay for food and clothing like everyone else. Therefore we get round the difficulty by letting them take 'drawings'. The full term for drawings is 'drawings in expectation of profits made'. We hope that our activities are making a profit, and, on the assumption that we are, we draw out some of our money and use it for domestic purposes. How much we draw depends upon our family needs, and whether we have funds. Suppose we draw £60 a week but are in fact making £200 a week profit. We shall lead a fairly frugal life, but our business will be building up useful bank balances and at the end of the year we shall have plenty of money to pay our taxes. We can then draw out the rest of our profits if we wish, or leave them in the business to keep it in good heart.

By contrast, suppose we draw £300 per week when we are actually making only £200 profit (although we don't actually know this). It won't be long before we notice that we are running short of cash, and find ourselves asking the bank for an overdraft or a loan. The first question a prudent bank will ask is: 'How much are you taking out each week as drawings?' When we reveal the figure the bank manager will say, 'Well, look here, you're not making that amount of profit.' Even if we had plenty of funds at the start of our business, at the end of the first year we would have the following figures:

PAYMENTS OTHER THAN FOR STOCK				
Nature of Payment	Amount Paid			
	By Cash Col 9		By Cheque Col 10	
Rent				
Rates			236	50
Light and Heat				
Carriage	3	72		
Postages £1·16, £1·90, 54p.	3	60		
Paper				
Motor Expenses			9	12
—do—				
Travelling				
Cleaning 89p. £1·35, £29·76	32	00		
Printing & Stationery				
Repairs & Renewals				
Insurance (Business)				
Advertising				
Telephone				
Wages (Wife)				
Wages (Employees)	68	00		
Inland Revenue (PAYE + NI)				
Sundries				
POST SCALES (CAPITAL ITEM)	8	75		
LOAN REPAYMENT			50	00
Private Pension Contributions				
Drawings for Self (see Note. 10)	60	00		
—do—				
—do—				
Capital Items (see note 7) COMPUTER			246	50
Totals	176	07	542	12

Fig. 5.1 Recording payments other than for stock

		£
Capital at start (say)		25,000
Add profits	10,400	
Less drawings	– 15,600	
		– 5,200
		£19,800

Because of excessive drawings the funds we originally contributed have declined. We are said to be 'living on our capital', and if this continues for a few more years we'll soon be in the bankruptcy court. As the Americans say, 'We're living too high on the hog' and must cut back our standard of living more in line with the profits we are earning.

Recording all types of expenditure other than for stock

Recording all these different types of payments varies with the system of book-keeping you are using. In these early chapters we have been using the Simplex system and, as we can see in Figure 5.1, this system is really a simple cash book in which we can record payments either in cash or by cheque. The notes to Fig. 5.1 explain useful points about the records. Study them now.

Notes to Fig. 5.1

- As when making purchases of stock (see Chapter 4) we record the payments only when we actually make them. For example, we have certainly used the telephone this week, but as we pay the telephone bill once a quarter there is no entry for payment this particular week on the 'telephone' line. We did pay the rates this week, by cheque, and £236.50 appears in the 'by cheque' column.
- With some items, postage for instance, we may need to use the spare space to record several items as the week proceeds, putting the total in the column only at the end of the week. It is helpful to remind ourselves what some money was spent on – for example the 'capital items' lines remind us that we purchased a computer and a weighing machine for postal items. Where there is more than one capital item purchased in a week we put the extra item on one of the spare lines provided.
- Notice that as we employ someone we must have deducted tax and National Insurance contributions, but there is no entry on the 'Inland Revenue' line. This money is paid over monthly, and we don't happen to have paid it this week. The records would be kept in a simple wages book (see Chapter 10).
- The proprietor has drawn £60 in cash this week. This money must have been taken from the till or the cash box, but it makes no difference whether cash is taken in this way or a cheque is drawn to take money from the bank (except that the £60 would be entered in the 'by cheque' column).
- Note that the 'loan repayment' has been entered in the bottom part of the spare lines, rather than on the next line below 'sundries'. This is because the

SUMMARY OF PAYMENTS

Week No.	Rent and Rates	Light and Heat	Carriage and Postages	Paper	Motor Expenses	Motor Expenses	Travelling	Cleaning	Printing and Stationery	Repairs and Renewals
1	520 00		12 36					32 00		
2			4 56		16 95			31 00		
3	236 50		7 32		9 12			32 00		
4			6 15		13 15			39 50		
5		86 26	5 29		16 12			32 00		
6		42 60	2 34	27 63			13 24	32 00		36 25
7			13 75		14 10			32 00		
8			12 94		15 12			32 00		
9			4 25		11 27			42 50		
10			6 25		36 19			32 00	36 38	
11			7 13		14 12			32 00		
12			8 01		15 06			32 00		
13			9 94		13 72			35 00		
1st Qtr	756 50	128 85	100 29	27 63	174 92	– –	13 24	437 00	36 38	36 25
14			11 36		17 46			32 00		
15	520 00		5 17		12 37			32 00		
16			8 64				23 68	32 00		
17			6 25		8 54	168 54		34 50		
18		62 30	17 83	27 63	18 49			32 00		127 32
19		36 14	1 75		13 29			32 00		
20			24 40				16 28	32 00		
21			13 25		11 63			32 00		
22			16 01		9 17			39 50		
23			19 14	14 92	19 51			32 00		
24			14 60		14 42			32 00		
25			1 75		11 72			42 50		
26			7 99		16 58			32 00		
2nd Qtr	520 00	97 44	148 14	42 55	153 17	168 54	39 96	436 50	– –	127 32
27	520 00		14 27		15 24			35 00		
28			3 18				14 92	41 25		
29			2 46		18 57			35 00		
30			15 25		27 32			35 00		
31	236 50	44 60	6 13	28 14	12 54			36 00	47 72	
32		25 50	5 73		14 46			46 25		
33			28 82					35 00		
34			7 87		16 68		16 25	35 00		
35			19 54		23 17			40 30		
36			6 75		45 76			35 00		
37			11 46	28 32	39 24			35 00		
38			4 21		15 76			35 00		
39			12 54	15 04	21 83			35 00		
3rd Qtr	756 50	70 10	138 24	71 50	250 57		31 17	477 80	47 22	– –
40			4 42		23 74			35 00		
41	520 00		14 86		12 49			35 00		
42			7 71		14 62			35 00		
43			19 39	28 32	25 57			35 00	18 15	
44			7 19				86 71	48 50		
45			13 58		26 38			35 00		
46		79 85	12 88		10 26	131 26		35 00		28 94
47		62 80	2 29		12 43			39 50		
48			3 84		27 51			35 00		
49			8 14		15 17			35 00		
50			4 12	15 14	19 36			43 25		
51			14 61		18 20			35 00		
52			17 16		11 44			35 00		
53										
4th Qtr	520 00	142 65	130 19	43 46	217 17	131 26	86 71	481 25	18 15	28 94
Annual Total	2553 00	439 04	516 83	185 14	795 83	299 80	171 08	1832 55	101 75	192 51

Fig. 5.2 Summary of payments for expenses

FOR EXPENSES

Week No.	Insurance (Business)	Advertising	Telephone	Sundries						Wages	Inland Revenue	Total
1										68 00		632 36
2										68 00		121 51
3										68 00		352 94
4										68 00	148 50	275 30
5	50 00									78 00		303 91
6			324 00							78 00		519 81
7										85 00		444 85
8		272 50								85 00	156 20	573 76
9				24 30						165 00		247 32
10										165 00		275 82
11										165 00		218 25
12										165 00	176 30	396 37
13										165 00		223 66
1st Qtr	50 00	272 50	324 00	24 30						1423 00	481 00	4285 86
14										165 00		225 82
15										165 00		734 54
16										165 00	176 30	405 62
17				1 52						165 00		384 35
18			423 00							124 50		833 07
19				3 56						124 50		210 23
20										124 50	138 20	335 38
21		86 40								124 50		267 78
22				29 61						124 50		218 80
23										168 00		253 57
24										168 00	143 40	372 42
25										168 00		223 97
26										168 00		224 57
2nd Qtr	— —	86 40	423 00	34 70						1954 50	457 90	4690 12
27										168 00		752 51
28										168 00	159 90	387 25
29										168 00		224 03
30										168 00		245 57
31			375 00							168 00		953 13
32	95 20									168 00	86 94	441 68
33										85 55		165 62
34				29 85						85 55		174 95
35										85 55		168 56
36										85 55	112 25	285 31
37										85 55		199 57
38										85 55		140 52
39										85 55		169 96
3rd Qtr	95 20	— —	375 00	29 85						1606 85	358 69	4308 66
40										173 40	147 27	383 83
41										173 40		755 75
42				12 17						173 40		242 90
43			416 00							173 40		715 83
44										173 40	169 50	485 30
45		163 60								173 40		411 96
46										173 40		471 59
47				14 97						173 40		305 39
48										173 40	108 24	347 99
49										173 40		231 71
50										168 00		249 87
51										168 00		235 81
52										168 00	106 72	338 32
53												
4th Qtr	— —	163 60	416 00	27 14						2238 00	531 73	5176 25
Annual Total	145 20	522 50	1538 00	115 99						7222 35	1829 32	18460 89

5

top group of entries are all revenue expenses, which can be carried to summaries and eventually appear on the Profit and Loss Account as losses for the year. The items at the bottom are all to do with rather more unusual things, which go into special summaries and are dealt with rather differently from revenue expenses.

Carrying the weekly figures to summaries to collect the annual figures

The payments incurred every week have to be carried to summaries where the annual totals can be collected together, and of course every type of payment must have its appropriate summary. This requires the reader to look at the illustrations in Figs. 5.2, 5.3, 5.4 and 5.5 carefully and read the related notes so that the system is followed fully.

Notes to Fig. 5.2 on pp. 64 and 65

This is arranged in four quarters of 13 weeks, and totals to annual figures on each category of expense. The entries in Fig. 5.1 are actually line 3 of the Summary, but the figures for a whole year have been entered to show how the total expenses for the year are arrived at. These become important, as explained later in this chapter when we come to work out the profits of the business.

Since some firms may have particular expenses which they need to keep track of besides the general headings listed, there are a number of spare columns which can be headed appropriately.

Notice that all the items in the top section of Fig. 5.1 appear in the Summary of Payments for Expenses, but the items in the bottom part of Fig. 5.1 do not. They are either capital items, drawings or the repayment of a loan, and are entered in other summaries.

Notes to Fig. 5.3

As may be seen the loan and any interest notified are entered in the top half of the summary, and the repayments in the lower half. The balance outstanding at any given time is the difference between the two. Note that the interest paid would be a deductible business expense and would be transferred to the Profit and Loss Account at the end of the year when the profits are being calculated, as one of the losses of the business.

SUMMARY OF LOANS AND REPAYMENTS		
LOAN FROM: **HELPFUL BANK PLC**		

DATE	LOAN	£	
1st JAN.	AMOUNT OF LOAN ARRANGED	2,000	00
1st JAN.	INTEREST AS AGREED **FOR YEAR**	220	00
		2,220	00

5

DATE	REPAYMENTS	AMOUNT	
JAN.	CHEQUE 174268	50	00
14 JAN.	CHEQUE 174279	50	00
21 JAN.	CHEQUE 174295	50	00

NOTES

1. Enter the amount of the loan or loans (with interest) in the top section.

2. Enter the repayments, as they are made, in the bottom section.

Fig. 5.3 Summary of loans and repayments

CAPITAL EXPENSES INCURRED DURING THE YEAR

DATE	NATURE AND FULL DETAILS OF EXPENSE	INVOICE VALUE		NET VALUE OF ASSET		VAT	
1ST JAN	SECOND HAND MOTOR CAR (XYT 997 H)	460	00	400	00	60	00
18TH JAN	POST SCALES	8	75	7	61	1	14
18TH JAN	COMPUTER	246	50	214	35	32	15
TOTALS							

Fig. 5.4 Summary of capital expenses

SUMMARY OF DRAWINGS FOR SELF

Week No.	Partner 1	Partner 2	Partner 3	Week No	Partner 1	Partner 2	Partner 3
1	150 00			27	150 00		
2	150 00			28	150 00	750 00	
3	150 00			29	150 00		
4	150 00	750 00		30	150 00		
5	150 00			31	150 00		
6	150 00			32	150 00	750 00	
7	150 00			33	150 00		
8	150 00	750 00		34	150 00		
9	150 00			35	150 00		
10	150 00			36	150 00	750 00	
11	150 00			37	150 00		
12	150 00	750 00		38	150 00		
13	150 00			39	150 00		
1st Qtr	1950 00	2250 00		3rd Qtr	1950 00	2250 00	
14	150 00			40	150 00	750 00	
15	150 00			41	150 00		
16	150 00	750 00		42	150 00		
17	150 00			43	150 00		
18	150 00			44	150 00	750 00	
19	150 00			45	150 00		
20	150 00	750 00		46	150 00		
21	150 00			47	150 00		
22	150 00			48	150 00	750 00	
23	150 00			49	150 00		
24	150 00	750 00		50	150 00		
25	150 00			51	150 00		
26	150 00			52	150 00	750 00	
TAX	2174 00	2856 00		53			
2nd Qtr	4124 00	5106 00		4th Qtr	1950 00	3000 00	

Yearly Summary Partner 1	
1st Qtr	1950 00
2nd Qtr	4124 00
3rd Qtr	1950 00
4th Qtr	1950 00
Total	9974 00

Yearly Summary Partner 2	
1st Qtr	2250 00
2nd Qtr	5106 00
3rd Qtr	2250 00
4th Qtr	3000 00
Total	12606 00

Yearly Summary Partner 3	
1st Qtr	
2nd Qtr	
3rd Qtr	
4th Qtr	
Total	

Fig. 5.5 Summary of drawings for self

Notes to Fig. 5.4

Here we record any capital items purchased in the course of any week. Note that the two items in Fig. 5.1 have been recorded, and show the element of VAT in their purchase prices (which will in fact be reclaimed as VAT input tax). The figures at the end of the year would be totalled and the value of the assets purchased would be added to the assets shown on the Balance Sheet. As these are capital expenses they cannot of course be treated as expenses deductible on the Profit and Loss Account at the end of the year.

Notes to Fig. 5.5

In this illustration, just to show how partnership drawings are recorded, the summary has been completed as if there were two partners, and it can be seen that they have different patterns of drawings. One draws £150 a week while the other draws £750 a month. Notice also that if they pay their tax out of the business bank account it is treated as extra drawings. What happens with drawings is that at the end of the year we divide the profits between the partners, and they are then entitled only to whatever amount is due to them *less* amounts already drawn. Remember drawings are really 'drawings in expectation of profits made'. Of course, if a partner has already drawn more than he or she is entitled to, it would present a problem. This is explained later in the book.

Payments by direct debit and standing order; bank charges

Besides payments in cash and by cheque we do pay sums of money for all sorts of purposes by standing order and by direct debit. These types of payment are dealt with more fully later under *bank reconciliation statements*, in Chapter 8. For the present let us just say that if we authorize the bank to make a series of regular payments for us (for example mortgage payments or hire-purchase instalments), it is called a *standing order*. However, in some cases we may agree that instead of our paying our creditor, the creditor may demand payment instead. This is helpful where the sum to be demanded is variable (as for example with rates or electricity bills, which differ each year). Many breweries deliver variable quantities of goods to tied houses and after delivery ask the publican's bank for the amount required. This type of arrangement is called a *direct debit*, because the customer's account is debited with the sum payable. Since we don't know when the bank is doing these entries, we cannot make them in the week they actually occur. We have to wait until we receive a bank statement (usually requested on a monthly basis). When the bank sends the statement we go through it and find any direct debits, standing orders, bank charges, etc., and record them as if they all happened in the week the statement arrives. The result is that we carry out a simple bank reconciliation process which reconciles our cash book with the bank's ledger account in our name. See Chapter 8 for a full explanation of this process.

Finding the net profit of the business: the Profit and Loss Account

We have already learned how to prepare a Trading Account and find the gross profit on trading. We are now able to go further and work out the net profit of our business, for we have now discovered the total value of all the expenses (overheads) of the business. When these figures are brought into the Profit and Loss Account, we have the situation shown in Fig. 5.6.

Notes to Fig. 5.6

● You will note that the gross profit figure of £83,170.89 is not the same as the figure for gross profit in Fig. 4.4. This is because the Simplex figures arrived at in that Trading Account had VAT included in them. This has to be removed, but it need not concern us at the moment, it is discussed later in Chapter 11. The figure shown for gross profit is the gross profit after the VAT element has been removed.

PROFIT AND LOSS ACCOUNT for year ending 31st DECEMBER 19..

LAST YEAR		THIS YEAR		LAST YEAR			LAST YEAR		THIS YEAR	
	Rent and Rates	2,553	00			Gross Profit (brought down from Trading Account)			83,170	89
	Light and Heat	439	04			Miscellaneous Receipts			150	00
	Carriage and Postages	516	93			ENTERPRISE ALLOWANCE			2,080	00
	Paper	185	14							
	Motor Expenses	1,095	63							
	Travelling	171	08							
	Cleaning	1,832	55							
	Printing and Stationery	101	75							
	Repairs and Renewals	192	51							
	Insurance (Business)	145	20							
	Advertising	522	50							
	Telephone	1,538	00							
	Sundries	115	99							
	Wages (gross) & N.I. Contributions	9,051	67							
	Bank Charges	—	1							
	Depreciation (Fixtures & Fittings)	85	00							
	—do— (Motor Car)	450	00							
	Total	18,995	89							
	Net Profit During Year	66,405	00							
	TOTAL	85,400	89			TOTAL			85,400	89

Fig. 5.6 Calculating the net profit in the Profit and Loss Account

- The miscellaneous receipts, and the Enterprise Allowance have been included just to show that other figures contribute to profit apart from the gross profit coming in from the Trading Account.
- On the left-hand side the losses of the business are those coming from the Summary of Expenses (see Fig. 5.2), but some depreciation figures have been inserted as well. When the total expenses are deducted from the total receipts we find the net profit of the business, which will be the basis for taxation when we send our figures in to the Inland Revenue.
- You should now try the exercise given in the next section.

Exercise on calculating the net profit

In the exercise you are required to draw up a Profit and Loss Account in the style shown in Fig. 5.6, using the figures supplied.

Books of Tom Price:
- Gross profit £37,217
- Miscellaneous receipts £350
- Enterprise Allowance £2,080
- Rent and rates £2,140.50
- Light and heat £420.65
- Carriage and postage £238.60
- Paper £128.60
- Motor expenses £756.55
- Travelling £280
- Cleaning £856.50
- Printing and stationery £85.60
- Repairs and renewals £328.50
- Insurance £100
- Advertising £238.80
- Telephone expenses £396.50
- Wages and NIC £7,856.50
- Bank charges £18.95
- Sundries £228.46
- Depreciation:
  - Fixtures £280
  - Motor car £1,350

Answer

Books of Tom Price: net profit £23,942.29

Checklist

These are the vital points made in this chapter.

1. The chief types of payments apart from purchases of goods for resale are payments for consumables, for overhead expenses, for wages and salaries, for capital items, to repay loans and mortgages and payments to the proprietor.
2. Of these expenses payments for consumables, overheads, and wages and salaries are revenue expenses, deductible on the Profit and Loss Account at the end of the year as legitimate business expenses.
3. Capital items and repayments of loan and mortgages are not business expenses as that term is used by the Inland Revenue, but capital expenditures which are not deductible from the profits at the end of the year.
4. The weekly expenses of all types have to be collected together in some sort of summary to give annual totals which can then be used in preparing the final accounts. The revenue expenditures are losses of the business and go in the Profit and Loss Account.
5. The capital expenditures finish up on the Balance Sheet at the end of the year, but do not affect the profits of the business, except for depreciation charges for fair wear and tear.

6 Using a full double entry system

Nature of the full double entry system □ Layout of the double entry system □ Practical requirements to keep a full set of double entry books □ Adaptations of the double entry system □ Conclusions about the double entry system □ Checklist

Nature of the full double entry system

The double entry system is the basis of all book-keeping systems, whether they are manual (handwritten) sytems or computerized systems. To be able to *think in double entries* is a great advantage, because it can answer every problem that ever presents itself in accountancy. You can learn the double entry system at any evening school or technical college in the United Kingdom, and it takes only one year, one evening a week, to master the whole subject. Alternatively, you can use one of the simple introductions, such as *Book-Keeping Made Simple*, written by the present author. Those who already have this knowledge, or are prepared to acquire it before going into business, will find it a very great help in running any system of accounts, and if you keep a full double entry system you will certainly know exactly where you are. On the other hand, it is time-consuming and that is why this whole book is largely about short-cuts on double entry. These are best understood if the reader has some general knowledge about the double entry system. The whole layout is illustrated in Fig. 6.1. The numbers (1)–(5) guide us through the system and the reader should look at the part numbered (1) and study the illustration and then read the notes which begin with section (1) below. Having followed that section, proceed to part (2) of the illustration, and so on.

(1) Every transaction has a business document related to it

A *'transaction'* is a business arrangement of any sort whatsoever. The most common transactions, which we are already familiar with because of our studies of Chapters 1–5, are listed below. At the end of each is the document related to it, as illustrated in Fig. 6.1.

- *Purchases* of goods for resale or to be worked into a finished product for resale. (The document is the *invoice*; the top copy of the invoice from the supplier who sold us the goods.)
- *Sales* (the document is the *second copy of our invoice* – the top copy having gone to the customer).
- *Purchases returns* (the document is the *credit note*, the top copy of the supplier's credit note which is sent to us when the supplier receives back the returned goods).
- *Sales returns* (this time it is the *second copy of our credit note*, the top copy having gone to the customer who returned the goods to us).
- Purchases of consumables (there will usually be an *invoice* or *bill* for the supply of these items. It will be the top copy of the supplier's invoice. If there is no invoice for a small item the till receipt or some other *petty cash voucher* – perhaps an internal petty cash voucher made out and signed by the proprietor – will be used.)
- *Purchase of capital items* (there will always be an invoice from the supplier of the capital item, and it will be the top copy). With some items there may be a *deed* (premises) or a formal *hire-purchase document*, etc.
- *Payments in cash and by cheque.* Here the *receipt* we obtain (the top copy) or give (the duplicate copy) or the *cheque* (inwards or outwards) will be the valid document. If we use a petty cash book (see Chapter 9) these receipts will become *petty cash vouchers.*

(2) These documents are entered in books of original entry

Originally, in the Middle Ages, there were only two books: a book of original entry called the Journal, or day book, and the main book of account which was called the Ledger. Later it was found that having only two books was inconvenient, as only two book-keepers could work on the books at any one time. It was therefore found to be helpful if the journal was divided into five parts. These were:

- The Purchases Day Book
- The Sales Day Book
- The Purchases Returns Book
- the Sales Returns Book
- The Journal Proper. Note that the first four are all to do with the things we buy and sell; activities which repeat themselves many times every day. The Journal Proper was kept for rarer items, such as the purchase of capital items, bad debts and depreciation, etc.

76 Using a full double entry system

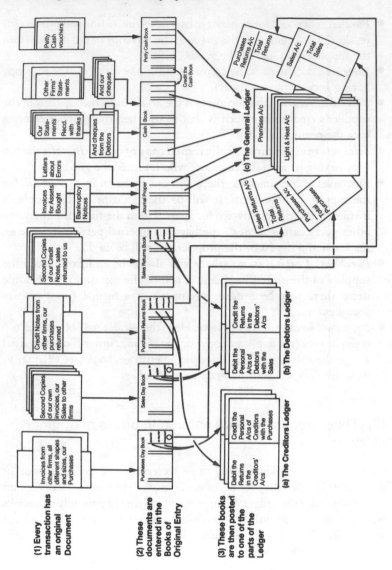

(1) Every transaction has an original Document

Petty Cash vouchers

Other Firms' Statements — And our cheques

Our Statements — Recd. with thanks — And cheques from the Debtors

Letters about Errors

Invoices for Assets Bought — Bankruptcy Notices

Second Copies of our Credit Notes, sales returned to us

Credit Notes from other firms, our purchases returned

Second Copies of our own invoices, our Sales to other firms

Invoices from other firms, all different shapes and sizes, our Purchases

(2) These documents are entered in the Books of Original Entry

Petty Cash Book — Credit the Cash Book

Cash Book

Journal Proper

Sales Returns Book

Purchases Returns Book

Sales Day Book

Purchases Day Book

(3) These books are then posted to one of the parts of the Ledger

Credit the Returns in the Debtors' A/cs — Debit the Personal A/cs of Debtors with the Sales — **(b) The Debtors Ledger**

Credit the Personal A/cs of Creditors with the Purchases — Debit the Returns in the Creditors' A/cs — **(a) The Creditors Ledger**

(c) The General Ledger

Purchases Returns A/c Total Returns — Sales A/c Total Sales — Premises A/c — Light & Heat A/c — Sales Returns A/c Total Returns — Purchases A/c Total Purchases

The other two books of original entry are the Cash Book and the Petty Cash Book, which as their names suggest, refer to incoming cash and cheques and outgoing cash and cheques. The chief idea of books of original entry is to make a permanent record of documents which can easily be lost. Keeping books of original entry in this way does give a great deal of work for very little benefit, and it is chiefly in this field that short-cut systems are widely used today. Computers do all such things with effortless ease, and this explains why computerized systems are so popular.

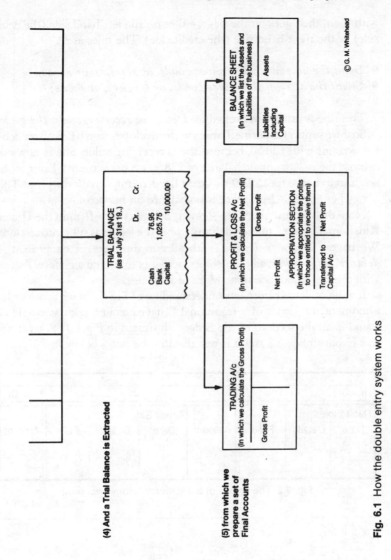

Fig. 6.1 How the double entry system works

(4) And a Trial Balance is Extracted

TRIAL BALANCE
(as at July 31st 19..)

	Dr.	Cr.
Cash	76.95	
Bank	1,025.75	
Capital		10,000.00

(5) from which we prepare a set of Final Accounts

TRADING A/c
(In which we calculate the Gross Profit)

Gross Profit

PROFIT & LOSS A/c
(In which we calculate the Net Profit)

Net Profit | Gross Profit

APPROPRIATION SECTION
(In which we appropriate the profits to those entitled to receive them)

Transferred to Capital A/c | Net Profit

BALANCE SHEET
(In which we list the Assets and Liabilities of the business)

Liabilities including Capital | Assets

© G. M. Whitehead

6

(3) The books of original entry are then posted to the Ledger

The Ledger is the main book of account in the double entry system. An account is a page in the Ledger, or rather a leaf in the Ledger, because both sides of a page are devoted to each account. If we open up an account with someone it simply means we give them a page in our Ledger, with their name and address, telephone number etc., at the top. Every transaction with them then goes on the page, either on the left-hand side (the debit side) or the right-hand side (the credit side). The rules are:

- *Debit the account that receives goods, or services, or money*
- *Credit the account that gives goods, or services, or money*

This rule is usually shortened to: *Debit the receiver, credit the giver.*
So if we supply Catherine Timms with envelopes worth £28.50 we debit her account with £28.50, because she is receiving value. She is now our debtor (she has an unpaid balance of £28.50 on her account). Later, if she sends us a cheque for £28.50 we credit her account – credit the giver. This leaves her account clear; there is no balance on her account.

Note that because there are so many accounts (one firm in the United Kingdom has over 8 million debtors alone) the ledger is split into sections. We have a *creditors' ledger* (with all our suppliers' accounts in it) a *debtors' ledger* (with all our debtors' accounts in it) and a *general ledger*, with the rest of our accounts. More of this later.

It will not detract from our understanding of Fig. 6.1 if we consider for a moment the layout of a traditional Ledger account, such as would be found in all the sections of the Ledger illustrated in Fig. 6.1. You can see this layout in Fig. 6.2 and it is described in the notes below it.

Dr.							Cr.
Debit Side				Credit Side			
Date	Details	Folio	Amount	Date	Details	Folio	Amount

Fig. 6.2 The layout of a traditional Ledger Account

Notes

- The page is divided down the middle.
- The left-hand side is called the debit side, or debtor side, and often has the abbreviation Dr. printed at the top.
- The right-hand side is called the credit side, or creditor side, and often has the abbreviation Cr. printed at the top.
- Columns are drawn on each side for the date, details, folio numbers (to be explained later) and the amount received or given.

It is when we make entries in the ledger accounts that the term 'double entry' comes into use, for every accounting transaction requires two

19--			£				
Aug. 17	A. Trader	L2	0.00				

Dr.   FURNITURE ACCOUNT   L.1 / Cr.

				19--			£
				Aug. 17	Furniture	L1	0.00

Dr.   A. TRADER   L.2 / Cr.

Fig. 6.3 A double entry

Notes

- The two accounts affected are Furniture Account and A. Trader's Account.
- Each account (page in the ledger) has a reference number written in the top right-hand corner. It is called a 'folio number' (Latin: *folium* = leaf).
- When the entries are made it is usual to record the folio number of the other account in the folio column. This tells anyone looking at an account where to find the other half of the double entry.
- Note that the Furniture Account received value and so it is debited, but A. Trader gave value so his account is credited. Remember the rule: debit the account that receives value, credit the account that gives value.
- Later, when A. Trader is paid by cheque, A. Trader's account will be debited and bank account (which is giving the money) will be credited.

entries, not one. Imagine a transaction in which we purchase a piece of furniture worth £100 from A. Trader, on credit, payable in one month's time. A. Trader gives us a piece of furniture worth £100. Can you think in double entries? Which account will receive a piece of furniture worth £100? Obviously it must be the Furniture Account. Debit Furniture Account with £100!

Which account is giving us £100 worth of value? Clearly it is A. Trader. Credit A. Trader's account with £100! A. Trader is now one of our creditors, and we owe him £100 for furniture received.

Later of course, we shall pay A. Trader £100, probably by cheque. Who will receive the £100 cheque? Clearly it is A. Trader, so we debit A. Trader's Account, and that wipes out the debt and leaves his account clear. The Bank Account has given the cheque. Credit the giver, so we credit Bank Account, which loses £100 of the money in the bank. The first of these double entries is shown in Fig. 6.3.

(4) A Trial Balance is extracted

Under the double entry system entries are being made in accounts all the time, some on the debit side and some on the credit side. The busiest accounts are probably the Cash Account and the Bank Account, which are separated out into a special book, the *Cash Book*, kept by a book-keeper who is fairly high in the accounting team, and called the *cashier*. Other busy accounts are the Purchases Account and the Sales Account; like dealings in cash and by cheque, purchases and sales take place all day, every day, in many businesses.

As a result of all these efforts we find it helpful to check up on all our entries at least once a month, and this is done by taking out a *Trial Balance*. As the name implies we try the books to see if they balance, because if they do we must have made all our double entries correctly. To draw up a Trial Balance we balance off each account in the Ledger, including the Cash Account and Bank Account in the Cash Book. The final balance on any particular account will be on either the debit side or the credit side. If we make a list of these balances and total them, we should find that the two sides reach to the same figure.

In Fig. 6.1 we have only a very brief indication of what the Trial Balance looks like, so it is helpful now if we look at one more closely. Before we do so, look at the three accounts shown in Fig. 6.4, to see how the balancing-off procedure is done. For simplicity the accounts have been shown without the full rulings.

Mrs M. Jones A/c, 2173 Camside, Cambridge CB4 1PQ   L32

19X9	£		
27 January	137.56		

Commission Received A/c   L199

		19X9	£
		4 January Motor car sale	25.00
		11 January Motor car sale	38.94
		23 January Finance contract	72.65

Land & Buildings A/c   L252

19X9		£	19X9		£
1 January	Balance b/d	147,256.55	19 January	Sale of Pett St.	38,250.00
14 January	Garages	8,285.60	31 January	Balance c/d	122,157.15
29 January	Shop front	4,865.00			
		£160,407.15			£160,407.15
19X9		£			
1 February	Balance b/d	122,157.15			

Fig. 6.4 Balancing-off accounts before taking out a Trial Balance

Notes

• The first account has only one entry on the debit side. Clearly this is a debit balance and we can see at once what the figure is. There is no need to tidy up this account at all – we just record it on our list of balances as a debit balance of £137.56.
• With Commission Received Account there are several entries all on the same side, the credit side. You might think, with a name like Commission Received Account these would be debit entries, because of the rule that we debit the account that receives goods, or services or money. In fact, this *money* has been received but it will be debited in the Cash Account (or in the Bank Account if we received the money as a cheque). This account is the other half of the double entry – the one that says: 'Who gave this money to the business?' The answer is that it has been given by 'Commission Received Account' – though that may be a number of individuals who pay us for the service we rendered them. For example, garages often allow people wishing to sell a car to exhibit it on the forecourt and take 10 per cent of the sale price as commission. This is a profit of the business and goes on the credit side of the account.

  Do we need to tidy up this account? Yes – but we need not balance it off. All we do is add it up in pencil and enter the figure on our Trial Balance – a credit balance of £136.59.
• The third account is the Land and Buildings Account and it has items on both sides of the account. What do we do here? The answer is that we balance off the account. One side is clearly large than the other. There is £160,407.15 on the debit side, and only £38,250.00 on the credit side. Taking the smaller side from the larger we have a difference of £122,157.15. This is the balance on the account; the value of the buildings owned when we balance the books on the last day of the month. Note that we add this balance to the credit side, making both sides equal at £160,407.15, but immediately bring the balance down on to the left-hand side, where it shows clearly in a single figure the balance on the account.

Personal Accounts, Nominal Accounts and Real Accounts

There is one further point to make about these accounts. They show us the three types of account we have in every business.

Mrs M. Jones's account is obviously a *personal account*, an account with one of the persons we deal with in business. Personal accounts are always either debtors (people who owe us money) or creditors (people to whom we owe money). There is one rather special personal account, and that is the *Capital Account*, the account of the proprietor. Since we owe back to the proprietor everything he or she has put into the business, it is almost always a creditor account, with a credit balance.

Land and Buildings Account is a *real account*; that is, an account which tells us about some real asset the business owns. Thus land and buildings, motor vehicles, plant and machinery, furniture and fittings and cash are all real things you can actually touch and handle. This business has land and buildings worth £122,157.15. Assets are always debit balances, and appear on the debit side of the Trial Balance.

Commission Received Account is not a real account. It is a record of money received, but the real money is in the cash box, or in the bank. It is said to be a *nominal account*, because the money is there 'in name only'. All nominal accounts are either profits or losses, and we keep a record of them only until the end of the year so we can work out the profits of the business.

Figure 6.5 shows a Trial Balance. This one has been taken out at the end of the year, although Trial Balances are always done monthly. Written alongside each item are notes showing whether the item is an asset, a liability, a profit or a loss. Some items are called 'Trading Account Items' because they appear in the Trading Account; don't forget that to prepare a Trading Account we also need the Closing Stock figure, which is given separately at the end. One special item is the 'drawings' of the proprietor – which is explained more fully later. This Trial Balance is worked into a full set of final accounts in the next section.

T. Sanderson
Trial Balance as at 31 December 19X9

Ledger Accounts	Notes	Dr. £	Cr. £	Notes
Premises Account	Asset	86,000.00		
Capital Account			130.675.70	Liability
Debtors:				
R. Green Account	Asset	394.00		
P. Colne Account	Asset	426.60		
Creditors:				
M. Shah Account			872.50	Liability
Carried forward		*86,820.60*	*131,548.20*	

		Dr.	Cr.	
Brought forward		*86,820.60*	*131,548.20*	
P. Driver Account			729.30	Liability
Plant and Machinery Account	Asset	38,240.50		
Office Furniture Account	Asset	7,246.38		
Cash Account	Asset	294.72		
Bank Account	Asset	13,825.60		
Bad Debts Account	Loss	238.60		
Advertising Account	Loss	3,294.60		
Commission Paid Account	Loss	25.60		
Discount Allowed Account	Loss	128.54		
Discount Received Account			236.35	Profit
Business Rates Account	Loss	894.56		
Carriage Out Account	Loss	328.70		
Salaries Account	Loss	27,925.50		
Motor Expenses Account	Loss	1,727.36		
Rent Received Account			1,850.00	Profit
Stock at 1 January 19X9	Trading account item	9,275.50		
Purchases Account	Trading account item	29,312.65		
Sales Account			98,325.50	Trading account item
Purchases Returns Account			2,275.56	Trading account item
Sales Returns Account	Trading account item	2,425.50		
Drawings	Special item	12,960.00		
		£234,964.91	£234,964.91	

At 31 December stocktaking revealed that the 'closing stock' figure was £13,925.60.

Note

In abbreviated form these notes can be condensed into the following groups:

Trial Balance	Dr.	Cr.
	• Assets	Liabilities
	• Losses	Profits
	• Three trading items	Two trading items
	• Drawings	

Fig. 6.5 A typical Trial Balance

T. Sanderson
Trading Account for year ending 31 December 19X9

	£		£
Opening stock	9,275.50	Sales	98,325.50
Purchases 29,312.65		Less returns	2,425.50
Less returns 2,275.56		Net turnover	95,900.00
	27,037.09		
Total stock available	36,312.59		
Less closing stock	13,925.60		
Cost of sales	22,386.99		
Gross profit	73,513.01		
	£95,900.00		£95,900.00

Profit and Loss Account for year ending 31 December 19X9

	£		£
Bad debts	238.60	Gross profit	73,513,01
Advertising	3,294.60	Discount received	236.35
Commission paid	25.60	Rent received	1,850.00
Discount allowed	128.54		75,599.36
Community charges	894.56		
Carriage outwards	328.70		
Salaries	27,925.50		
Motor expenses	1,727.36		
Total Losses	34,563.46		
Net Profit	41,035.90		
	£75,599.36		£75,599.36

Balance Sheet as at 31 December 19X9

		£			£
Capital (at start)		130,675.70	*Fixed assets*		
Add net profit	41,035.90		Premises		86,000.00
Less drawings	12,960.00		Plant and machinery		38,240.50
		28,075.90	Office furniture		7,246.38
		158,751.60			131,486.88
Long-term liabilities		–	*Current assets*		
			Closing stock	13,925.60	
Current liabilities			Debtors	820.60	
Creditors		1,601.80	Bank	13,825.60	
			Cash	294.72	
					28,866.52
		£160,353.40			£160,353.40

Fig. 6.6 A set of sole trader's Final Accounts

(5) From which we prepare a set of 'Final Accounts'

The final stage in double entry book-keeping is to prepare a set of final accounts to discover (a) the net profit of the business and (b) the financial situation of the business at the start of the new financial year. This is done by producing a Balance Sheet. Since we have already learned how to produce a Trading Account and a Profit and Loss Account it is relatively simple to use the Trial Balance given in Fig. 6.5 to produce a set of Final Accounts which can be submitted to the Inland Revenue.

Note to Final Accounts

- The only difference on the Trading Account from the one shown in Fig. 4.4 is that there are some Purchases Returns and Sales Returns which have to be deducted from the Purchases and Sales figures to give a true 'net' figure for Purchases and Sales.
- The Balance Sheet is shown in traditional United Kingdom style with the assets on the right-hand side. This is illogical, and is the result of a mistake in an Act of Parliament in 1858. It need not bother us here. Balance Sheets are done the correct way round in Europe, and the United Kingdom should start to do this soon. Being simply a sheet of paper – the Balance Sheet – having the figures in the traditional style does not affect the double entry, though it is a bit confusing to students.

Practical requirements to keep a full set of double entry books

We now come down to the crucial point about keeping a full set of double entry books: what books do you need, and where do you get them? The answer is that you need:

- A Journal Proper
- Four day books: a Purchases Day Book, a Sales Day Book, a Purchases Returns Day Book and a Sales Returns Day Book
- A Four-column Cash Book (which used to be a Three-column Cash Book but now that VAT is a constant feature of our lives you need an extra column for the VAT)
- A Petty Cash Book (for small cash outgoings)
- A loose-leaf Ledger, divided into sections for debtors and creditors, and a 'General Ledger' section

This is an awful lot of books compared with, say, a Simplex D Account Book or one of the other systems shown later in this book. If you want to keep a full set of books, and already know how to do double entry book-keeping by all means do, but better to use the Simplex system or one of the simple adaptations of double entry book-keeping described in the chapters which follow.

Adaptations of the double entry system

In general, adaptations of the double entry system deal with sections of the system, rather than the entire system. There are, for example, clever systems for keeping the day books (such as the Sales Day Book and the Purchases Day Book) by simultaneous records, or what are called three-in-one systems. The name comes from the use of carbon paper, or perhaps NCR paper, to prepare three records at once. The term NCR stands for 'no carbon required' – the paper itself is covered with transparent ink, which when pressed by a ballpoint pen turns to a visible ink by reacting with the air.

Another three-in-one system deals with wages, and enables a payroll sheet, individual wages records for each employee and weekly or monthly pay slips for insertion in wage packets to be prepared in one operation. This system is described later in the chapter on wages.

Another system, the FINCO system, which is described in detail in the next chapter, is an adaptation of the double entry system which keeps certain parts of the records very clearly, for example Purchases and Sales records, Cash and Bank records. It is not as complete as the Simplex system, in that it does not prepare Final Accounts, and is therefore perhaps most useful to the larger firm which is definitely intending to use the services of an accountant for the finer points of its book-keeping activities.

Finally, any computerized system will offer great economies of operation once the initial familiarization with computerized activities has been undertaken. Because the computer program can decide what to do with any particular item of information it can perform all the double entry activities in the twinkling of an eye, at speeds of millions of processes per second. Thus, if we imagine the double entries for the purchase of an item of business stock, once the operator feeds in the code for the supplier concerned and the amount of the invoice with the VAT included, the computer will do both the VAT records and the financial records in a hundredth of a second, updating the supplier's account, the VAT input tax, the stock records and anything else covered by the program. The chapters on computerization later in this book explain the systems on offer and give you all the names and addresses to contact.

Conclusions about the double entry system

What can we say in conclusion about the double entry system? The chief points seem to be:

- It is the only perfect book-keeping system, which will answer every difficulty that arises.
- There is everything to be said for getting to know the full double entry system and being able to think in double entries.
- At the same time it is too cumbersome to be used by a peson who is a 'one-man (or one-woman) band'. It really needs a specialist book-keeper and is thus most suitable for the slightly larger business that has reached the stage where it can afford one. Smaller firms should use one of the simple systems, either Simplex or one of the more advanced systems described in the next few chapters.
- Even the firm which does have a specialist book-keeper should consider the use of simultaneous record systems for purchases, sales, wages, etc.
- In the last analysis the true answer to accounting problems is a computerized system. The computer *does* work on a perfect double entry system built into the programs provided by the systems analyst. The computer operator is not aware of what the computer is doing, and must ensure only that the data keyed in is correct.

6

Exercise on drawing up a set of final accounts

Here is P. Morris's Trial Balance as at 31 December 19X9. Draw up his Trading Account, Profit and Loss Account and Balance Sheet as at that date.

	Dr. £	Cr. £
Capital		83,500.00
Cash	285.50	
Cash at bank	17,350.00	
Stock at 1 January 19X9	21,334.50	
Sales returns and sales	4,998.50	219,275.60
Purchases and purchases returns	85,497.25	600.75
Debtors and creditors	21,950.00	2,226.10
Discount allowed and received	501.60	3,238.20
Repairs	14,500.00	
Stationery	2,102.50	
Light and heat	4,376.50	
Business rates	13,503.50	
Motor vehicle expenses	2,102.60	
Salaries	27,539.90	
Drawings	15,000.00	
Office expenses	6,500.00	
Freehold premises	55,000.00	
Motor vehicles	8,500.00	
Fixtures and fittings	10,560.05	
Interest received		2,761.75
	£311,602.40	£311,602.40

The stock at the end of the year was valued at £18,500.

Answer

Books of P. Morris: gross profit £126,546.10; net profit £61,419.45
Balance Sheet totals:
- fixed assets £74,060.05
- current assets £58,085.50
- capital at close £129,919.45
- current liabilities £2,226.10
- final totals £132,145.55

Checklist

These are the vital points made in this chapter.

1. Double entry book-keeping is the basis of all sound accounting and it is a great help to be able to 'think in double entries'.
2. The chief books of account are the Journal and the Ledger, but these days the journal is split up into a number of day books, and the ledger is also split into several parts, notably a Debtors' Ledger, a Creditors' Ledger and a General Ledger. The Cash Book and the Petty Cash Book are also specialized parts of the Ledger.
3. If you want to learn double entry book-keeping you can do so at an evening class, or you can study a simple introduction to the subject, such as *Book-Keeping Made Simple*.
4. Most new entrants to self-employment don't need to learn double entry, or keep a full set of books, but use a simple system like the ones described in this book.
5. As you grow large enough to employ a specialist book-keeper you may find it helpful to move on to a full double entry system but even then you will probably find that using some of the short-cuts on double entry, such as three-in-one simultaneous records systems, is advantageous.
6. Finally, the use of a computerized system, such as those described later in this book, is the ultimate solution to the book-keeping problem and enables all sorts of statistical control figures about your business to be calculated instantaneously.

6

7 FINCO: nearly a double entry system

Nature of the FINCO system □ Elements of the FINCO system □ The FINCO bank account record □ The FINCO sales record □ Appraisal of the FINCO system □ Checklist

Nature of the FINCO system

The FINCO system is a simple system of book-keeping for small businesses that is fairly close to a full double entry system in that different sections of the book-keeping records are kept on differently coloured pages in a compendium of sheets. The full system has a loose-leaf binder, while the 'one-year' version has a reasonable number of sheets for each section of your book-keeping records, bound together as a one-year book. The system is based on monthly records, rather than weekly as in some other systems, and the use of analysis columns enables the vital figures for sales, purchases, cash, bank, wages, and VAT to be collected together to give the figures required for preparing the financial accounts at the end of the year, and for ongoing financial management control.

The system is most appropriate for businesses where the proprietor has some knowledge of book-keeping and is able to follow the book-keeping entries without needing to be guided through the system too closely. The rulings are good, but those with some idea of book-keeping will take to them better than those without.

Another point is that since the system has only a limited number of analysis columns it cannot distinguish all the various headings under which expenses may occur, and this makes it fairly difficult to draw up one's own Trading Account, Profit and Loss Account and Balance Sheet. It is therefore most suitable for businesses whose proprietors intend to use the services of an accountant to prepare Final Accounts.

Elements of the FINCO system

The elements of the main FINCO system are:

• 24 monthly pages of Bank Account Records, showing receipts and payments. These are on white paper. The 32 lines on each page may be enough for most businesses.

- 24 monthly pages of Cash Records, on blue paper. These are very similar to the bank account records, and allow for the VAT element to be recorded (where applicable).
- 24 monthly pages of Sales Records. This is virtually a Sales Day Book, with analysis columns to bring out the sales activity in any particular area and to record the VAT output tax, payable eventually to Customs and Excise. There is no Sales Returns Book; any credit notes received have to be entered in red ink on the sales record and deducted at the end of the month from the total sales figure; the goods being returned to stock.
- 24 monthly pages of Purchases Records. This is virtually a Purchases Day Book, with analysis columns to divide the purchases into various departments, and to extract the recoverable VAT Input Tax. Again, purchases returns must be entered in red ballpoint pen.
- 24 monthly pages for payroll records. These are not strictly arranged on a monthly basis, the records can roll forward from month to month, the figures occupying as much space as they require. Some payroll features, such as Statutory Sick Pay (SSP) and Statutory Maternity Pay (SMP) are not specifically catered for, and the book-keeper must devise a method for using the columns to meet these particular needs.
- 24 quarterly VAT record sheets provide records of input tax and output tax drawn from the purchases, sales, cash and bank records; they are, however, a little difficult to follow for a trader using one of the 12 special retailers' schemes. The blank page provided each quarter for the 'Special Scheme Calculation' enables a trader to make his or her scheme calculation, but the daily takings figures have to be assembled from the cash records for the previous three months. Once again, as with the full double entry system, a real knowledge of the scheme adopted and an understanding of book-keeping are helpful to see your way through the system.

The FINCO bank account record

An example of the FINCO bank account record is shown in Fig. 7.1. The following points are worth noting.

- The description column appears only on one side of the page, and as it may refer to either a receipt or a payment the eye has to run right across the page to the far side where the running balance may be seen. This

ACCOUNT RECORD   Period From 1 · 1 · 19.. to 31 · 1 · 19..   Serial No. A

Total	Cash	Purchases	Payroll	Capital Items	Misc.	Details	Acc'ts use only	BALANCE
								2,000 00
46 50		46 50						1,953 50
								2,680 00
114 56				114 56		Filing Cabinet		2,565 44
								2,883 94
								3,406 54
780 54					7 80	SU (Comm. Cngt)		2,675 99
546 20			546 20					3,124 36
								2,578 16
								3,093 58
								5,730 33
137 20		137 20						5,593 13
231 60					231 6	C. Advertising		4,439 08
								4,159 48
								4,307 23
1,836 62		183 70	546 20	114 56	1012 16			5,410 03
								5,410 03

| Checked | | Analysed |

Fig. 7.1 The FINCO bank account record

FINCO   © Casdec Limited 1981   Business Name R. Peters and Co.   **BANK**

DATE	DESCRIPTION	Cheque No.	Total	Sales	Misc.	Details
Jan 1	R. Peters	100451	2000 00		2,000 00	Capital
5	M. Lark	100451				
6	Cash banked		726 50	726 50		
6	P. Lodrick	100452				
8	M. Morgan		318 50	318 50		
10	Cash banked		522 60	522 60		
14	City Council	100453				
16	Cash banked		448 38	448 38		
18	Wages	100454				
20	Cash banked		515 42	515 42		
23	"		636 75	636 75		
25	M. Lark	100455				
27	Cash banked		797 95	797 95		
29	I.O. Cawforth	100456				
30	M. Morgan		147 75	147 75		
31	Cash banked		1102 80	1102 80		
			7726 63	5724 65	2000 00	

TOTAL (c/fwd) (Month..............)

Accountants use only

balance will of course increase when a receipt is recorded and decrease when a payment is recorded.

- Where cheques are paid away the cheque number is recorded. This helps later with bank reconciliations (see Chapter 8).
- The two sides of an account have a limited amount of analysis work, but the provision of a 'details' column permits individual items, which might need special attention when doing the final accounts, to be pinpointed when required.
- The running balance gives an immediate check on the financial position relative to the bank.
- Cross-totting keeps an effective check on the entries made in the analysis columns, and one total subtracted from the other should give the running balance in the end column.

The FINCO sales record

An example of the FINCO sales record is shown in Fig. 7.2. The following points are worth noting.

- The activity under various headings for the particular business is found in the analysis columns.
- If applicable, VAT is recorded against every entry, at the standard rate. Some retailers (using the Special Schemes) might need to modify this procedure if selling goods at more than one rate, for example.
- Some items are not ordinary sales – such as the sales of scrap on 2 January. These are separated out into a 'miscellaneous' column.
- When customers are invoiced for goods and pay later the date of payment is recorded in the 'Received' column. The blank spaces in this column indicate a debtor, and these should be scanned to keep a check on late payers, and to stop further orders until earlier invoices have been paid. Summation of unpaid items in these blank spaces does conveniently give 'aged debtor' control.
- Note how quickly VAT builds up: £1,268.16 in the month. A trader paying VAT quarterly even at this rate would have to find nearly £4,000 for Customs and Excise on the due date. It is important to put away VAT regularly in a special deposit account to ensure funds are available to meet this obligation, if your business is the type where output tax collected always exceeds deductible input tax.

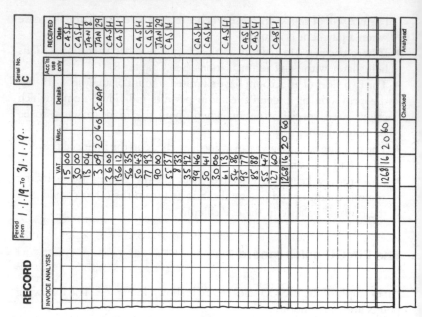

Fig. 7.2 The FINCO sales record

Appraisal of the FINCO system

The main FINCO system is a loose-leaf system capable of infinite expansion and therefore of use to businesses however large they become. More recently a 'one-year-system' with a limited number of pages has been added, for the smaller business. The reader considering using FINCO should therefore be careful to buy the system that is most suitable to the size of his or her business. For example, the Bank Account Record shown in Fig. 7.1 has 32 lines, which must cover for both receipts and payments. A person paying in takings every day would perhaps find it better to buy the larger loose-leaf system so that extra pages could be inserted if necessary. For smaller businesses 32 lines per month may well be adequate. More recently a *FINCO Open Learning Training Manual* is available, with the one-year FINCO, in a boxed pack. It is designed to take the newcomer through all stages in the use of the FINCO system.

The only criticism of the system is that it does require some knowledge of book-keeping if the trader is to continue to prepare his or her own final accounts. For those traders who, in any case, propose to leave this activity to an accountant there is no problem, of course. Full details, sample sheets and a price list are available from the suppliers: Casdec Ltd, Broadwood View, Chester le Street, Co. Durham DH3 3NJ (telephone: 091-410 5556).

7

Checklist

These are the chief points made in this chapter.

1. The FINCO system is a suitable book-keeping system for small and growing firms.
2. It is particularly suitable for a new enterprise where the proprietor understands double entry book-keeping, or a growing enterprise which has reached the point where it can employ a specialist book-keeper.
3. As the system does not automatically lead into a system of Final Accounts it is more appropriate for someone who intends to hand his or her records to an accountant at the end of the year, to prepare the Trading Account, Profit and Loss Account and Balance Sheet.
4. Since the system has both a one-year system and a long-lasting permanent system, using loose-leaf pages, it is sensible to check whether the one-year system is adequate for your needs before embarking on it. If you need the training manual the best time to buy it is at the very start of your business.
5. One of the main strengths claimed for FINCO is its facility to provide essential financial management control data. This is assisted by the supply of monthly analysis sheets for recording current data for comparison with figures from the previous year. To assist this control facility a number of optional extras are available. These include:
   - Bank Reconciliation
   - Aged Debtor Control
   - Aged Creditor Control
   - Cash flow and Profitability Control
   - Payslips
   - Purchase Ledger System
   - Sales Ledger System
   - Finco Text Book.

8 Bank statements and bank reconciliation statements

Nature of a bank statement □ Why we need to reconcile the two sets of records □ The procedure on receiving a bank statement □ records □ Drawing up a bank reconciliation statement □ What to do if you cannot reconcile the two sets of records □ Checklist

Nature of a bank statement

Every trader who runs a current account with a bank should ask for a bank statement once a month. Since the banks have millions of accounts they spread the workload of sending out statements by the cyclical billing method. Andrew Specimen's statement shown in Fig. 8.1 is dated 12 June 19XX, and he will receive a statement on the 12th of each month. The computer prints hundreds of thousands of statements every day, which are posted to customers – a considerable volume of work in itself. The statement shows every transaction between the bank and the customer since the last statement (12 May 19XX). All the debit entries on the account are called 'withdrawals', and mean that the account holder has received back some of the money previously deposited, though it may not have been drawn in cash but paid to various people at his request. All the credit entries are called 'deposits', and mean that the account holder has paid money into the account, so that the bank is a creditor for the amount deposited. In Fig. 8.1 there is only one such entry, £51.60, which is a dividend transfered to the credit of Andrew Specimen's account by a bank giro transfer.

Study the statement in Fig. 8.1 closely now, and the notes to it

Notes to Fig. 8.1

- Study the 'key', which shows the computer codes used to indicate what type of receipt or payment is involved. Thus DD is 'Direct Debit' and DV is 'dividend'.
- Note that there is only one deposit in the month, a dividend from Guardian Royal Exchange. Andrew did not pay in any cash or cheques in the month.

☊ National Westminster Bank PLC   CONFIDENTIAL

```
200 PENTONVILLE ROAD              CURRENT                      7
LONDON                    ANDREW SPECIMEN ESQ
N1 9HL
```

19XX	1234-6583		12 JUN 19XX		99999999
Date	Details	Withdrawals		Deposits	Balance
26MAY	Balance from Sheet no. 6				93.40
27MAY	037079	3.40			90.00
2JUN	EAGLE STAR INS DD	4.55			85.45
3JUN	GUARDIAN RYL EX DV			51.60	137.05
	✳ 037080	10.00			127.05
4JUN	SWANDENE COUNCIL SO	30.00			97.05
.	AA DD	21.00			76.05
5JUN	DEPOSIT A/C TR	35.00			41.05
8JUN,	KINGS CROSS AC	25.00			16.05
−	037081	9.00			7.05
10JUN	037082	10.00			2.95 %b

12JUN   Balance to Sheet no. 8   2.95 %

Key	SO Standing Order DV Dividend CC Cash &/or Cheques Auto ⎫ AC Automated Cash OD Overdrawn
	EC Eurocheque TR Transfer PY Payroll withdrawals ⎭ DD Direct Debit Interest–see over

NATWEST - THE ACTION BANK

```
To the Manager National Westminster Bank PLC    STAFF TRAINING
My/Our account number is   99999999    Please note my new address/occupation will be from_____ 198
                                                                      _____Post Code_____
New occupation_____Signature_____

                                               60-77-12          For Office Use
       MR A SPECIMEN                                                 —
       46 GRANVILLE GARDENS
       SWANDENE
       YORKSHIRE
       SD4 9AG
```

Fig. 8.1 A. Specimen's bank statement for 12 June 19X9

Rather surprisingly perhaps in view of his small balance in hand (he finished up with an overdraft) he transferred £35 into a Deposit Account.
- Where a cheque was made out and passed through the clearing system the cheque number is printed, but no other details except the amount paid to the payee named on the cheque.
- There are two direct debits (in which authorized parties asked the bank to debit Andrew's account directly and pay them the sums due to them).
- Andrew drew £25 from the automated teller machine (ATM) at King's Cross.
- Note that withdrawals reduce the running balance and deposits increase it.
- There is a standing order, paid monthly probably, to Swandene Council.
- Note that the account is overdrawn on 12 June 19XX by £2.95. The bank would conceivably have been able to return that last cheque for £10 to the bank that

presented it, there being insufficient funds in the account to honour it, but as Andrew appears to have some money in a deposit account it did honour it (the bank has a right of set-off against the money in the Deposit Account should Andrew in fact be in financial difficulties).

Having studied the statement consider the Bank Account of Andrew Specimen in his own account books. He is self-employed as a freelance artist and graphic designer. The account is as shown in Fig. 8.2.

Cash Book (Bank Account only)

19XX		£	19XX		£
13 May Balance	b/d	93.40	14 May T. Smith (037079)		3.40
12 June R. Lomax		185.75	17 May R. Lyon (037080)		10.00
			25 May M. Lark (037081)		9.00
			26 May P. Jones (037082)		10.00
			7 June P. Patel (037083)		17.50
			8 June Cash (King's Cross)		25.00
			10 June R. Shah (037084)		12.50
			12 June Balance	c/d	191.75
		£279.15			£279.15
19XX		£			
13 June Balance	b/d	191.75			

Fig. 8.2 The Cash Book (bank column only) in Andrew Specimen's books

8

Notes

- The reader will notice that according to his Cash Book Andrew Specimen has £191.75 in the bank, whereas the bank says he is overdrawn by £2.95.
- Clearly this difference needs some explanation, and to explain it we must scrutinize both records carefully, as explained in the next section, 'Why we need to reconcile the two sets of records'.

Why we need to reconcile the two sets of records

When two organizations keep records about the same thing it is always possible that one will be better informed than the other and consequently the records will differ. For example, if a bank is authorized to pay standing orders at certain times in the month, and is also permitted by direct debit mandates to allow insurance companies, district councils and clubs and associations (such as the Automobile Association) to ask for money from time to time, it will be better informed about these matters than the account holder. The first the account holder knows about a direct debit is when he or she receives the bank statement. So Andrew Specimen does not know about the direct debits for Eagle Star Insurance, and the AA. He does know that there is a standing order for the Swandene Council but he doesn't know whether the bank remembered to pay it, until he receives the statement and sees it is paid. Similarly, he doesn't know about the dividend of £51.60 received on 3 June, and he seems to have forgotten to enter the transfer of £35.00 to his Deposit Account, although he must have been to the bank to make the transfer.

Similarly, the bank is not aware of some of the things Andrew has done in the month. The cheques sent to P. Patel and R. Shah are still in the course of transmission somewhere in the clearing system, and the bank has not recorded the deposit of £185.75 made by Andrew on 12 June – it hasn't had time to key in the entries to its branch computer network or transmit them to the bank's computer centre. This will happen overnight.

We can therefore say that we need to reconcile the two sets of records because:

- the bank does not know everything the customer has done
- the customer does not know what the bank has done until the statement arrives
- there are time lags in the cheque presentation and clearing system which mean differences between the two sets of records
- either side could have made a mistake. We sometimes read in the press of a computer error leading to millions of pounds being credited to an ordinary householder's account – there have been civil and criminal cases about such events.

What is the procedure for reconciling the two sets of records?

The procedure on receiving a bank statement

When we receive a bank statement we must for our own peace of mind immediately undertake a bank reconciliation procedure to ensure that we, and the bank, have the same idea about our account. The procedure is as follows.

- Go through the two sets of records and tick the items that appear on both – on the bank statement and in our own books.
- Examine the items that are unticked on the bank statement. These will all be things that the bank has done of which the customer was

unaware. They must now be entered in the customer's bank records, either in the Bank Account or, if a special system is being used, in whatever cash book records are provided.

• This will leave some items which the account holder has entered in the cash book records of which the bank is not yet aware. These are the items that must be taken into account by drawing up a *Bank Reconciliation Statement*. They are time-lag items, which will be covered as soon as the bank gets to hear about them.

We will now do this for Andrew Specimen's records as shown in Figs. 8.1 and 8.2.

Stage 1: Ticking the items that appear on both sets of records

The bank statement for this is shown in Fig. 8.3. There are five items on the bank statement that are not ticked: two direct debits, a dividend, a standing order and an error on Andrew's part because he seems to have forgotten to enter on his own records the transfer he made into his Deposit Account.

♻ National Westminster Bank PLC   **CONFIDENTIAL**

200 PENTONVILLE ROAD	CURRENT	7
LONDON	ANDREW SPECIMEN ESQ	
N1 9HL		

19XX	1234-6583			12 JUN 19XX		99999999
Date	Details		Withdrawals	Deposits		Balance
26MAY	Balance from Sheet no.	6				93.40✓
27MAY		037079	3.40✓			90.00
2JUN	EAGLE STAR INS	DD	4.55			85.45
3JUN	GUARDIAN RYL EX	DV		51.60		137.05
	*	037080	10.00✓			127.05
4JUN	SWANDENE COUNCIL	SO	30.00			97.05
.	AA	DD	21.00			76.05
5JUN	DEPOSIT A/C	TR	35.00			41.05
8JUN,	KINGS CROSS	AC	25.00✓			16.05
	–	037081	9.00✓			7.05
10JUN		037082	10.00✓			2.95 %

Fig. 8.3 Ticking the items already known to both parties (bank statement)

Notes

• These items would also be ticked in Andrew's books.
• Note that Andrew does not know about the items for £4.55, £51.60, £30 and £21. He has also forgotten to enter the transfer for £35 in his own records.
• The first thing to do is to update Andrew's Cash Book to take account of these entries.

Andrew's Cash Book is shown in Fig. 8.4, ticked to show the items that appear in both sets of records.

Cash Book (Bank Account only)

19XX		£	19XX	£
13 May Balance	b/d✓	93.40	14 May T. Smith (037079)	3.40✓
12 June R. Lomax		185.75	17 May R. Lyon (037080)	10.00✓
			25 May M. Lark (037081)	9.00✓
			26 May P. Jones (037082)	10.00✓
			7 June P. Patel (037083)	17.50
			8 June Cash (King's Cross)	25.00✓
			10 June R. Shah (037084)	12.50
			12 June Balance c/d	191.75
		£279.15		£279.15
19XX		£		
13 June Balance	b/d	191.75		

Fig. 8.4 Ticking the items already known to both parties (Cash Book)

Notes

- We can see from this record that the bank does not know about the cheques sent to P. Patel and R. Shah. These have not reached the bank through the clearing house mechanism or BACS (the Bankers' Automated Clearing Service).
- The bank also does not know about the deposit of £185.75 made on 12 June. This has been paid into Andrew's branch, but has not yet been keyed into the bank's computer system.
- We must now update Andrew's records with the missing items revealed on the Bank Statement. This is done in Fig. 8.5.

Stage 2: Updating the entries in the records of the business to take account of those things the bank has done, which Andrew has not done

To do this we start with the balance on Andrew's books of £191.75 and make the necessary entries. These are shown in Fig. 8.5. First note the following points:

- Items that appear as deposits (credits) on the bank statement appear on the left-hand side of Andrew's books as debits. This is because the two records are kept from different points of view. The bank regards the £51.60 deposited as a liability – it credits Andrew's account because Andrew is a creditor and the bank owes him the £51.60.

- Items that appear as withdrawals (debits) on the bank statement appear as credits on Andrew's Bank Account. So far as the bank is concerned Andrew is receiving back the use of his money, but so far as Andrew is concerned he is giving the money in his Bank Account to the AA, the Eagle Star Insurance Co., etc. Now study Fig. 8.5 carefully.
- Although the bank made these entries on various dates Andrew cannot go back and make all these entries on those dates. It would make an awful mess of his accounting records if he tried to add these things at different places. Andrew makes the entries on the day he became aware of them, which is 13 June, the date the statement reached him.

Cash Book (Bank Account only)

19XX			£	19XX			£
13 June	Balance	b/d	191.75	13 June	Eagle Star Insurance		4.55
13 June	Dividend received		51.60	13 June	Swandene Council		30.00
				13 June	AA (motor expenses)		21.00
				13 June	Deposit A/c		35.00
				13 June	Balance	c/d	152.80
			£243.35				£243.35
19XX			£				
13 June	Balance	b/d	152.80				

Fig. 8.5 Specimen's revised Cash Book

Notes

- The revised balance is £152.80. This does not agree with the balance of £2.95 (overdrawn) on the bank statement, but it is a little closer than before.
- The final agreement can be achieved only when the time-lag items sort themselves out. To test whether this is so we prepare a Bank Reconciliation Statement, in which we reconcile the two balances. The word 'reconcile' means 'get them to agree'.

Stage 3: Drawing up the Bank Reconciliation Statement

Having entered all the things the bank has done into Andrew Specimen's books we now have the two records as close to agreement as we can make them, but they still don't agree. This is due to the time-lag items, where certain cheques and other information are still in the course of transmission to the bank. We can check these by preparing a Bank Reconciliation Statement. This starts with the new balance on Andrew Specimen's cash book and tries to explain why it is different from the bank's balance as given on the Bank Statement. Look at the Bank Reconciliation Statement below, and read the notes below it.

Bank Reconciliation Statement as at 13 June 19XX

		£
Balance as per revised bank account (in Andrew Specimen's cash book)		152.80
Add:		
Cheques drawn but not yet presented (because the bank thinks we still have this money)		
P. Patel	17.50	
R. Shah	12.50	
		30.00
		182.80
Deduct:		
Cheque paid in but not yet cleared (because the bank does not yet know we have this money)		185.75
Balance as per bank statement		£2.95 o/d

Notes

- We see that the two figures can be reconciled.
- We start with the Cash Book balance and consider each of the time-lag items. Since we want to arrive at the figure on the Bank Statement we ask ourselves: 'What does the bank think about this particular item?'
- In the case of the two cheques for Patel and Shah the bank thinks we still have the money, so we add them back.
- In the case of the cheque Andrew paid in on 12 June the bank does not know this money has been paid in – it hasn't been put through the computer yet. We must then deduct it to find what the bank thinks our balance is.
- The result is that the bank thinks we are overdrawn by £2.95. This is the balance on the bank statement. Since we arrive at the same figure we conclude that our books and the bank's books are correct, and when the time-lag items sort themselves out both books will read the same.

What actually happens to Bank Reconciliation Statements?

The answer is that they are filed away in a file marked 'Bank Reconciliation Statements' and kept as proof that we have checked our Bank Account, and on the bank's work, and found both to be satisfactory. Write or type a fair copy and file it away.

What to do if you cannot reconcile the two sets of records

The most likely reason is that you have not made the calculations properly, or have made a slip on your own records. Check them carefully. Find out what the difference is, and see if you can remember an item for that amount.

It is much less likely that the bank has made an error, but if you do discover one draw it to the bank's attention at once. In the United Kingdom dishonest bank staff are, fortunately, very rare – but there are a few cases every year. By drawing attention to a disparity on your statement you may reveal to the bank that it has a problem.

Never use money put into your account in error. It has been held in the courts that a person who does so deliberately is a thief – since a simple bank reconciliation procedure should have told him or her that the money had been credited to the account in error. We want our bankers to deal honestly with us, and we must be equally honest in our dealings with them.

Exercise in drawing up a bank reconciliation statement

1. M. Lever's bank statement reads as follows for the month of March 19X9:

Date	Details	Dr. £	Cr. £	Balance £
1/3/19X9	Balance C/fwd			427.40
3/3/19X9	Cheque (019260)	31.30		396.10
5/3/19X9	Sundries		460.00	856.10
12/3/19X9	Cheque (019263)	489.50		366.60
14/3/19X9	Sundries		600.00	966.60
14/3/19X9	Cheque (019262)	28.86		937.74
15/3/19X9	Sundries		750.00	1,687.74
19/3/19X9	Sundries		650.00	2,337.74
26/3/19X9	Cheque (019264)	846.24		1,491.50
31/3/19X9	Charges	22.50		1,469.00
31/3/19X9	Bank of England (transfer)		83.80	1,552.80

On 31 March his cash book (bank columns only) read:

M. Lever's Cash Book (Bank Columns only)

19XX			£	19XX		£
1 March	Balance	b/d	427.40	3 March R. Lamb (019260)		31.30
5 March	Cash	c	460.00	7 March M. Peters (019261)		24.90
14 March	Cash	c	600.00	8 March B. Green (019262)		28.86
15 March	Cash	c	750.00	10 March K. Ahmed (019263)		489.50
19 March	Cash	c	650.00	21 March R. Onobanjo (019264)		846.24
30 March	Cash	c	550.00	31 March Wages		340.62
				31 March Balance c/d		£1,675.98
			£3,437.40			£3,437.40

19XX			£
1 April	Balance	b/d	1,675.98

8

You are asked to update his cash book by entering any items not already entered and then to draw up a bank reconciliation statement to reconcile the revised cash book figure with the bank statement balance of £1,552.80.

Answer

Revised Cash Book balance £1,737.28. The two accounts can then be reconciled.

Checklist

---

1. It is most unlikely that your own Cash Book (bank) records will agree with your bank statement because:
   - The bank does things like paying standing orders and direct debits, and collecting bank giro credit transfers without telling you
   - You write out cheques and don't tell the bank
   - There are time lags in the clearing process
   - Both sides can make mistakes
2. When you receive a bank statement compare it with your own records and tick all items that appear on both records.
3. Now update your cash book by putting into the bank entries any items listed on the statement that do *not* appear in your own records, as if they happened on the day you received the statement.
4. When your records are up to date there may still be entries on your books which are not in the bank's records. You can't go to the bank and update its records, you will have to wait for the time lags to clear the bank's records in due course. What you can do is draw up a Bank Reconciliation Statement. If it tallies, write out a neat copy and file it away.
5. If it doesn't tally search all your records for an error, and if necessary approach the bank about the difficulty. (It is an offence to use money put into your account in error.)

---

9   Simultaneous records (two-in-one and three-in-one) systems

What is a simultaneous records system? □ How a simultaneous records system fits into double entry book-keeping □ The Safeguard sales ledger system □ Checklist

What is a simultaneous records system?

Any simultaneous records system depends on the preparation of several records at once, by writing on a top record which is immediately reproduced either by carbon copying or NCR copying (NCR = no carbon required) on to other records below. As the pressure exerted by an ordinary ballpoint pen (other pens are not so good for this type of system) is only enough to make two decent copies it means that a system involving three documents is best. Hence the name 'three-in-one systems' which is often used to describe these systems. In some systems only two records need to be processed simultaneously. Another name is 'one-write' systems.

There are a number of famous names in this field: two of the leaders are Safeguard Business Systems and Kalamazoo. In this chapter we are featuring Safeguard Business Systems, but a similar system from Kalamazoo is featured in Chapter 10, dealing with wages.

To return to the aspects of book-keeping that lend themselves to this treatment, the following sections describe some of them. (Note that in all the Safeguard Systems the word 'journal' has its normal meaning in book-keeping of 'day book' or 'daily record'. The journal is in sheet form and will be archived in stiff cardboard binders.

Sales

With a sales system we need to record all the invoices made out to customers including the VAT output tax. The customers of course become debtors for the amount owed. We also need to record any credit notes issued for returns, and any payments received. The Safeguard sales system is illustrated in this chapter, and need not be discussed any further here. The various components are:

- Debtor's Statement
  on top of
  Debtor's Ledger Card
  on top of
  Sales Journal and Output VAT Record

  or:

- Debtor's Statement
  on top of
  Debtor's Ledger Card
  on top of
  Sales Returns Book

- Debtor's Statement
  on top of
  Debtor's Ledger Card
  on top of
  Cash Received Journal

- As a sub-system we can have a paying-in slip which will give a list of cheques and cash amounts paid in.

- An Aged Accounts Journal can be prepared as the new statements are headed up ready for the next monthly period. This can be used for credit control.

Purchases

With a purchases system we need to record the invoices received from suppliers, the VAT on them (input tax), any credit notes received against returns or allowances subsequently made, and our payments to the supplier when made. Since the payment needs to be covered by a document (the remittance advice note) this is prepared at the same time.

- Remittance advice note
  on top of
  Creditor's Ledger Card
  on top of
  Purchases Journal and Input VAT Record

- Remittance advice note
  on top of
  Creditor's Ledger Card
  on top of
  Purchases Returns Book

- Cheque
  on top of
  Remittance Advice note
  on top of
  Creditor's Ledger Card
  on top of
  Payments Cash Book

Wages

With a wages system we need to record the pay of each individual as part of a total payroll, but also as an individual tax record which can be discussed with the employee without the other people's salaries being seen. We also need a payslip to go in the wage packet or to be given to the individual if all payments are made to the bank by bank giro credit transfers.

A further sub-system is required at the end of the year to notify the employee, the DHSS and the Inland Revenue of the total amounts earned, deductions, etc., in the year. The official forms are P14, P35 and P60.

- Payslip
  on top of
  Individual tax record
  on top of
  Payroll record

- P 14 (end of year return)
  on top of
  P60 (certificate of pay, tax and NIC)
  on top of
  P35 (end of year payroll summary)

Petty cash

With the petty cash system we can keep control of all petty cash items because an entry can be made by means of special carbon-backed petty cash vouchers, supplied in sets to give a pack of 'shingled' vouchers. The term 'shingled' implies that each voucher overlaps the one below it, the vital details being written on the top edge of the voucher, which is carbon-backed, and this reproduces itself on the Petty Cash Journal below it. Thus the document (a petty cash voucher) must be made out for every expense entered and apart from the actual details written on the edge there is ample space to describe the expenditure incurred and to clip on any bill, or receipt. The person being reimbursed for the expenditure then signs the slip and draws the money.

- Petty Cash Voucher
  on top of
  Petty Cash Journal

How a Simultaneous Records System fits into double entry book-keeping

Be clear in your mind that when you decide to cover a particular area of your book-keeping by a simultaneous records system, what you are doing is removing that area from ordinary double entry book-keeping and adopting a short-cut which will both save you work and prevent possible errors by making several entries at the same time. It involves a certain amount of preparation as you move over to the new system. You need to purchase the posting boards, posting trays, forms and binders required to start up, but once installed it will function for as long as you are in business. It is therefore well worthwhile to start the system, learn how to use it and liaise closely with the distributor in the teething-problem period.

In a book of this size we can feature only one of the systems, but there are a number that may be helpful to you. The address of Safeguard Business Systems is Centurion House, Gateway, Crewe, Cheshire CW1 1XJ (telephone 0270 500921).

The Safeguard Sales Ledger System

The system consists of six documents, three of which are used in the main system and the others in subsidiary parts. The three main documents are:

- the monthly statement, *placed on top of*
- the debtor's ledger card (a loose-leaf card that is virtually a page in the debtor's ledger, and thus forms the debtor's account), *placed on top of*
- the Sales Journal page, which is also the VAT output tax register.

Starting up the system

Before you can start up the system you must head up a ledger card for each customer whose account is active, and from whom you expect to receive orders month by month. The details required are:

Name ....   Contact ....

Address ....   Telephone No. ....

....   Balance forward £ ....

You now need to head up a monthly statement, simply with the name and address of the customer. These two documents, the statement and the ledger card, are kept together in the indexed posting tray, in alphabetical order. Having done this with all the active ledger accounts you have a posting tray with numerous ledger cards, each with its statement ready to record any events that may occur in the coming month.

You now need to take the posting board, with its spring clamp. Open the clamp and insert a Sales Journal sheet in it. Lower the spring clamp and your day book record is now ready for the first entry you wish to make.

Posting sales invoices

- Total the batch of invoices to be posted. Using an add-listing calculator draw up a list of the invoices' gross values, VAT and 'net of VAT' values and total them.
- Select the statement and ledger card to be posted and align the first blank line on the statement with the first blank line on the ledger – use the 'previous balance' column to make the alignment easier. Hold them together and place them under the spring-loaded clamp – align the first blank line of the statement directly opposite the number on the clamp which denotes the first blank line on the journal. The first blank lines on all three records are now aligned together.
- First, enter the 'previous balance' and 'account name'. Then enter on the statement (using firm pressure) 'date' (day and month is sufficient), 'invoice number', and in the two debit columns enter the 'amount of goods/services' and the 'VAT' to be charged. The account has now been debited with the value of the invoice and the statement has been updated to show the invoice which has been entered.
- Add the total invoice amount (goods/services and VAT) to the previous balance to obtain the new balance – enter this total in the balance column on the statement.
- On the right-hand side of the journal are some analysis columns that can collect details of the activity for any particular product or area. Analyse the charge for goods/services into these columns as required.
- Return the statement and ledger to the posting tray. Repeat this procedure for each invoice.
- If an item is exempt from VAT or zero-rated the word 'exempt' or 'zero' should be written in the VAT column to prove the VAT has not just been overlooked.

Posting credit notes

These may be posted at any time of the month but if you wish they can be held until month-end and posted in one straight run.

In the reference column enter 'CN' and the number – the amount of the credit should be apportioned between goods/services and VAT in the ratio in which it was originally charged and these amounts entered in the appropriate 'credit' columns on the ledger card. If analysis columns are being used on the right of the journal, the amount of the credit should be entered in brackets in the appropriate column. Entering in brackets implies that the activity in that class of goods must be reduced by the amount of the figure in brackets.

Note The total of the VAT credit column must be deducted from the VAT debit column. This will ensure you remit only the VAT which you are liable to pay.

Proving the journal

It is best to check the work done at the end of each set of postings, and at the foot of each journal page (which means after 30 entries have been made). The columns should be totalled and the totals should equal the totals obtained on the adding-listing obtained before the posting run began. This proves the entries have been correctly made. There is a check section at the bottom of the page to record the totals arrived at, and to confirm that all entries have been done correctly.

This is perhaps sufficient to show how helpful these Safeguard systems are. Similar entries will be made to record cash or cheques received, and when the end of the month arrives the statements are ready to be sent out, informing the customer of all the changes in the account during the month: purchases made, returns and payments received and the balance outstanding. This avoids telephone calls to query how the figures were arrived at – and excuses for the debtor to delay payment. The full facts are disclosed, and the customer is invited to pay the balance due.

The system is illustrated in Fig. 9.1 and the full range of Safeguard systems is shown in Fig. 9.2.

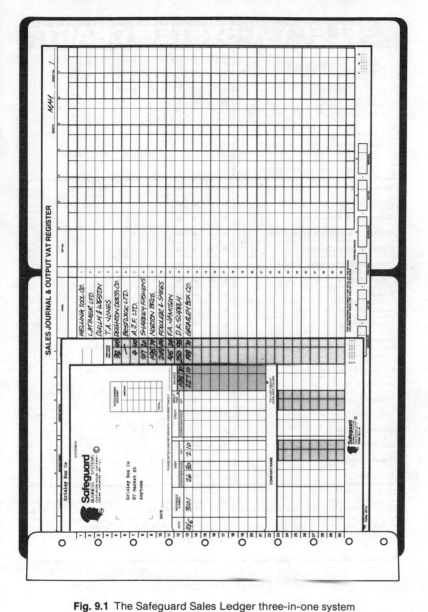

Fig. 9.1 The Safeguard Sales Ledger three-in-one system

SELECT·A·SYSTEM CHART

Safeguard BUSINESS SYSTEMS
CENTURION HOUSE, GATEWAY
CREWE, CHESHIRE, CW11XJ
Telephone : 0270 - 500921

DID YOU KNOW

. . . that most businesses can use two or even three Safeguard Systems. Locate the business classification below . . . then read across for the Safeguard systems applicable.

	Cheque-writing	Sales Ledger	Purchase Ledger	Wages/Salaries	Travel Agency Accounting	Insurance Brokers Accounting	Job Costing	Tab Ledger	Account Balance Verification	Solicitors Accounting	Time-Cost System	Cash Receipting	Goods Received	Petty Cash
Accountants	•	•	•	•					•		•			•
Associations	•	•	•	•								•		•
Auctioneers & Estate Agents	•		•	•								•		•
Builders, Contractors & Allied Trades	•	•	•	•			•						•	•
Computer Service Bureaux	•	•	•	•										•
Employment & Secretarial Agencies	•	•	•	•										•
Farmers & Nurserymen	•	•	•	•										•
Franchises	•	•	•	•										•
Garages & Motor Car Dealers	•	•	•	•									•	•
Hotels & Motels	•	•	•	•				•						•
Insurance Brokers	•	•	•	•		•						•		•
Manufacturers	•	•	•	•			•						•	•
Property Management	•	•	•	•						•		•		•
Religious & Educational	•	•	•	•								•		•
Restaurants & Entertainment	•	•	•	•				•						•
Retailers	•		•	•								•	•	•
Service Industries	•	•	•	•			•					•	•	•
Solicitors	•	•	•	•						•	•	•		•
Travel Agents	•	•	•	•	•							•		•
Wholesalers	•	•	•	•								•	•	•

In today's economy, the efficiency in office accounting routines is more important than ever. Safeguard's One-Write systems — the WORK-SAVERS — are designed to replace antiquated methods with modern, accurate, labour-saving routines. Safeguard's systems provide maximum accounting control and ensure up-to-the-minute financial information for the business managers of today . . and provides a perfect audit trail for your accountant.

Fig. 9.2 A useful range of simultaneous records systems

Checklist

These are the vital points made in this chapter.

1. A simultaneous records system is one where two or three sets of records are prepared with a single writing.
2. To do this carbon paper or NCR paper is required, and a ballpoint pen is the most efficient writing medium since it enables firm pressure to be exerted while entries are being made.
3. These systems are sometimes called 'three-in-one' or 'one-write' systems.
4. If you decide to adopt such a system, what you are really doing is removing one area of accounting (say the Debtors' Ledger or the Creditors' Ledger) from your ordinary double-entry system and using a simplified, more easily controlled system. These systems are therefore most suitable for firms that have grown enough to employ a specialist book-keeper or book-keepers. They are not so appropriate for 'embryo' firms just starting up.
5. Famous names in this area are Safeguard Business Systems and Kalamazoo Business Systems. Both offer a range of systems (for example the Kalamazoo Wages System is illustrated in Chapter 10).

9

10 Simultaneous records: wages systems

Employing staff □ The simplest wages system □ Simultaneous records systems □ The Kalamazoo wages system □ Statutory sick pay and statutory maternity pay □ Paying wages by bank giro □ Checklist

Employing staff

If every new business employed one more person it would make a considerable dent in the unemployment figures, and those who believe in encouraging enterprise believe that eventually all small businesses grow enough to take on one or two people, even if in the first few years they are often only part-timers. This is an accountancy book – not a book describing how to start up a new business – but it is helpful to give the subject of employing staff a general airing, if only for this reason. The subject is treated in great detail in a companion volume in this series entitled *Hiring and Firing* by Karen Lanz.

Once you decide to employ someone you come immediately under the general umbrella of a whole field of law called 'employment law'. You are at once 'an employer' and as such have a number of general duties to perform, such as providing a safe system of work, keeping adequate wages records, and deducting tax and National Insurance contributions and paying them over to the Inland Revenue on a monthly basis. You also have to assume certain 'social security' duties, for example to pay your employees' statutory sick pay (SSP) and statutory maternity pay (SMP) if they qualify for these benefits. You don't pay it out of your own pocket, hopefully, because the idea is that as you have certain government moneys in your possession (the tax and National Insurance contributions you have deducted from your employees' wage packets) you can use this money to pay SSP and SMP, and send in only the balance.

The Inland Revenue publishes a leaflet called *Thinking of Taking Someone On?* (IR53), and it tells you a great many things you need to know about the PAYE (pay as you earn) system of income tax, the tables you need from the Inland Revenue (Tables A and B), etc. A telephone call to your local Inland Revenue number will procure the leaflet and other explanatory material, for example about SSP and SMP. The leaflet lists five things you must do:

- Tell the tax office when an employee starts to work for you.
- Work out the tax and NIC due each pay day.
- Pay this over to the Accounts Office each month (the Accounts Office is part of the Inland Revenue and collects or receives your payments).
- Tell the tax office when an employee leaves.
- Tell the tax office at the end of each tax year how much each employee has earned and how much tax and NIC you have deducted. (The tax year runs from 6 April one year to 5 April the next. Your PAYE instructions include an income tax calendar showing how the tax year is divided into tax weeks and months).

Although this all sounds fairly daunting it soon becomes routine, and even the SSP and SMP duties are fairly easy to follow, especially if you are using one of the simple schemes outlined in this chapter.

The simplest wages system

Although the Simplex wages book is not featured in this chapter it is mentioned here because it is a very simple system for a firm that employs only a very small number; it has space for 26 employees. Those who have decided to use the Simplex D Account Book, or elect to use the Simplex VAT book – see Chapter 11 – may feel that the Simplex wages book is adequate for their records. It is obtainable from George Vyner Ltd, PO Box 1, Holmfirth, Huddersfield HD7 2RP.

Simultaneous records system

As explained in Chapter 9, a simultaneous records system is one where a number of records are prepared simultaneously, one on top of the other. There are two wages systems that can be prepared by simultaneous methods:

- Payslip
  on top of
  Individual pay record
  on top of
  Payroll record

- P14 (end of year return)
  on top of
  P60 (certificate of pay, tax and NIC)
  on top of
  P35 (end of year payroll summary)

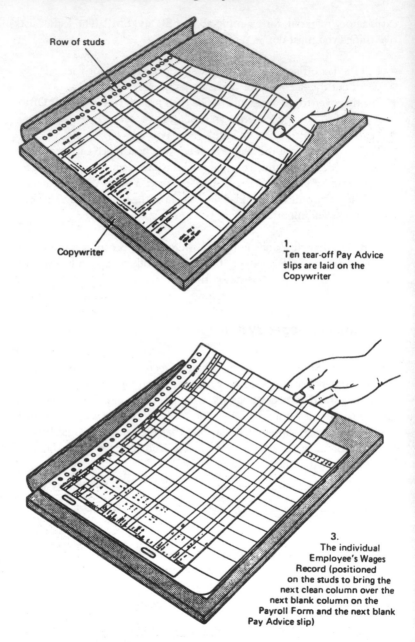

Row of studs

Copywriter

1.
Ten tear-off Pay Advice
slips are laid on the
Copywriter

3.
The individual
Employee's Wages
Record (positioned
on the studs to bring the
next clean column over the
next blank column on the
Payroll Form and the next blank
Pay Advice slip)

Fig. 10.1 The Kalamazoo wages system (*reproduced by courtesy of Kalamazoo plc*)

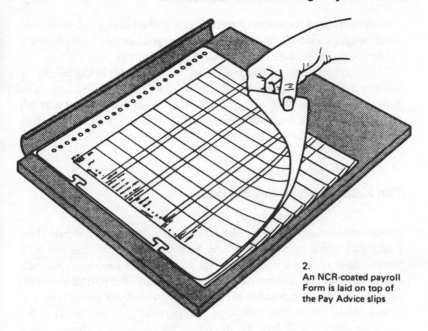

2.
An NCR-coated payroll
Form is laid on top of
the Pay Advice slips

10

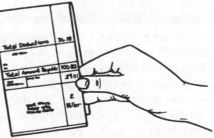

4.
The torn-off Pay Advice slips
folded once to go into the
pay packets. If paid in cash
the money is inserted in the
same envelope

Only the first of these sets of records is described in this chapter. If you decide to adopt a simultaneous records system your supplier will show you the forms and procedure for the end-of-year summary.

The two chief names in this field today, as pointed out in Chapter 9, are Safeguard Business Systems and Kalamazoo Business Systems. The illustrations in Figs. 10.1 and 10.2 are provided by Kalamazoo, and full details are available from Kalamazoo plc, Northfield, Birmingham B31 2RW (telephone 021-411 2345).

The Kalamazoo wages system

About three million people in the United Kingdom alone are paid their wages each week or month via the Kalamazoo system. The essential feature of the system is that it provides an *individual pay record* for each employee distinct from everyone else's records and not part of a general payroll. This makes it possible to take out the individual's record from the locked file in which they are kept, for personal discussions with the employee about pay, deductions, discrepancies, etc., without the employee seeing anyone else's pay details. The pay record shows either 10 or 15 weeks' records, and a year's records are kept in the file so that any difficulty can be cleared up for the financial year under discussion. Transfer binders are available for archiving past records.

Besides the individual pay record the system provides a payroll sheet showing the total payroll in any given week/month, and a payslip for the wages envelope. If an employee is paid in cash the money will be provided in the same envelope, but if payment is direct into a bank account by bank giro credit the employee receives the payslip only as a record of the payment transferred.

The system is best described by looking at the illustrations in Fig. 10.1, which shows the Kalamazoo copywriter – a solid plastic writing surface with a set of studs on which documents can be laid, with the perforations on the documents engaging the studs firmly and retained by a spring-loaded cover. First a layer of 10 (or 15) blank pay advice notes is positioned on the copywriter. A payroll sheet is then placed over them and since they are coated with NCR material anything written on one will appear on the other. As each employee's wages are dealt with the individual pay record for that employee is positioned over the top of the other two documents and positioned so that the current weekly column covers the next available column on the payroll sheet and therefore the next available payroll slip on the set of pay advice notes. Fig. 10.1 shows the way in which these documents are used. A pay advice note is shown in Fig. 10.2.

Pay Advice		
Week Month No. Date	14	10/7
Earnings		
Details		
A	92	24
B	5	00
C		
D		
E		
SSP	37	76
SMP		
Gross Pay	135	00
Superannuation		
Gross Pay less Superannuation	135	00
Gross Pay to Date for Tax Purposes	2085	00
Tax Free Pay	985	18
Taxable Pay to Date	1099	82
Tax Due to Date	296	73
Tax Refund		
Deductions Tax	18	56
• N.I. Contribution (Employee)	12	19
1 T.U.	–	75
2 Dr. Barnardo's	1	00
3		
4		
5		
Total Deductions	32	50
Net Pay		
F		
Total Amount Payable	102	50
N.I. Contribution (Employer)	12	19
N.I. Total (Employer and Employee)	24	38
G		
• Contracted Out cntb. incl. above		
Earn. on which E'ees. cntb. pybl.	135	00
Earn. on which E'ees. cntb. at CO. rate pybl.		
Your Pay is made up as shown above		

MILLER.
K.E.

Kalamazoo
business systems
T-18403
©

Notes

- The week or month number is shown and the date it commences.
- There are seven lines for types of earnings, such as basic wage, overtime, commission, etc. One of these is for SSP and another for SMP. The total of these gives the gross pay.
- Superannuation is then deducted, because it is not taxable. In this case the employee is not part of any superannuation scheme.
- The gross pay for tax purposes is then used to find the tax payable, using the tax tables provided by the Inland Revenue (Tables A and B).
- The deductions are then listed, which gives the net pay.
- There is then one line for any addition to net pay – such as refunds of tax overpaid or expenses incurred. This gives the total amount payable.
- The employer also needs to know the total cost of National Insurance – in this case the employer had to pay £12.19 making £24.38 in all.

10

Fig. 10.2 A Kalamazoo pay advice slip (*reproduced by courtesy of Kalamazoo plc*)

Statutory sick pay and statutory maternity pay

SSP and SMP are methods of paying through the ordinary wage packet what are, in effect, two types of social security payment. This is administratively convenient for the government, and rather inconvenient for the employer, since it places an obligation on employers to keep records of both schemes (to ensure that the sums reclaimed from Inland Revenue by deduction from PAYE tax and NIC contributions are correct).

The arrangements for SSP are that employees who are sick reach a 'PIW situation' on the fourth day of absence. A PIW is a 'period of incapacity for work'. Employees provide self-certificates of absence and an absence record must be kept by the employer, which may be subject to periodic checks by DHSS officers. The detailed arrangements are too involved for a book of this nature but, briefly, the absence record will reveal the days of sickness and consequently the PIWs, and from this the number of days' SSP payable. The rate will be worked out as a daily rate based on the average earnings, and the amount due will then be added to the wage packet. The maximum liability for SSP is 40 days a year – those absent for more than 40 days will be paid their sick pay direct by the DHSS. A useful record system for SSP is provided by Formecon Services Ltd, Douglas House, Gateway, Crewe CW1 1YN (telephone 0270 500800), which includes a full explanation.

The arrangements for SMP are also fairly complex. An employee who is pregnant is entitled to receive SMP for a total of 18 weeks, either before and after the EWC (expected week of confinement). Even if she ceases work earlier she cannot receive it until the 11th week before the EWC, and if she works after that date she cannot receive it until she does stop work. Details of the rates payable, the method of reclaiming money paid, etc. are available in the scheme literature. A useful record system, with all the necessary forms for control of SMP procedures is again provided by Formecon Services Ltd.

Paying wages by bank giro

Making up wage packets can be a tedious and time-consuming activity, subject to risks as money is collected in bulk from the bank and distributed from pay office windows. More and more people today receive nothing in their wages envelopes but an advice note similar to that illustrated in Fig. 10.2. The money is simply credited to their bank accounts and no actual cash is handled. This is the *bank giro credit system* and it is strongly recommended as the best way to pay wages for those who have a number of employees. The payroll is done in the usual way using the Kalamazoo system, but instead of going to the bank to draw the payroll in cash and notes, from which the wage packets may be prepared, the cashier takes to the bank a slip for each of the employees. Each slip states the amount due to that employee, which the bank will now transfer through the clearing system to the employee's account. The cashier authorizes the bank to debit the firm's account with the total payroll. The firm has thus paid the wages in a very safe and economical way. No security guards are needed; no tedious counting of notes or handling of coins. The funds are available in

---

You are asked to complete wages advice slips for the four employees shown below whose pay details are as follows:

	R. Brown	P. Green	T. Jones	F. Brand
Week	1	7	9	16
Date	12/4/19X9	24/5/19X9	7/6/19X9	26/7/19X9
Earnings A	136.30	106.25	174.62	138.62
Earnings B	4.50	14.20	15.55	24.74
Gross pay	?	?	?	?
Superannuation	8.60	5.80	9.20	8.80
Gross pay for tax purposes	?	?	?	?
Gross pay to date for tax purposes	? (NB it is week 1)	750.25	1712.20	2360.50
Free pay	48.64	191.03	676.62	642.88
Taxable pay to date	?	?	?	?
Tax due to date	20.75	139.75	258.75	429.25
Tax paid up to last week	–	124.60	272.65	401.75
Tax	?	?	? (*careful*)	?
NI contribution	7.80	9.50	10.20	11.15
Charity	0.50	0.50	–	1.00
Total deductions	?	?	?	?
Net pay	?	?	?	?
Refunds (if any)	?	?	?	?
Total amount payable	?	?	?	?
NI contribution from employer	7.80	9.50	10.20	11.15
NI total	?	?	?	?

Answers

	R. Brown	P. Green	T. Jones	F. Brand
Total amount payable	103.15	89.50	184.67	114.91
NIC total	15.60	19.00	20.40	22.30

10

the employee's account to be used at once through the ordinary banking system, and the employee has the benefit of greater security. If you want to use this system approach your local bank manager.

Exercise on Kalamazoo wages

Note: To complete a full set of Kalamazoo wages records one must have the correct stationery and invent imaginary names, code numbers, etc. Schools and colleges wishing to purchase such stationery should approach the Education Department of Kalamazoo Ltd, Mill Lane, Northfield, Birmingham B31 2RW. For the purpose of the exercise on p. 123 it is suggested that pay advice notes similar to Fig. 10.2 should be ruled up.

Checklist

1. Employing staff places onerous responsibilities upon the employer. There is no gradual path into the employer–employee situation: whoever decides to take on an employee must immediately carry the full administrative burden of record-keeping.
2. The Inland Revenue will supply you with an explanatory booklet called *Thinking of Taking Someone On*, which explains all about the PAYE (pay as you earn) system.
3. Simultaneous records systems enable us to prepare at one writing:
   • a wage record for each individual we employ
   • a payroll, and
   • a wages slip for the employee's wage packet.
4. When the end of the year arrives a further three-in-one system is available for the various end-of-year records which have to be supplied, both to employees and the Inland Revenue authorities.
5. SSP (statutory sick pay) and SMP (statutory maternity pay) both impose on employers further duties and obligations which affect the wages paid to staff.

11 Value added tax

The nature of value added tax □ Registration for VAT □ Methods of accounting for VAT □ VAT by the 'normal method' □ The special schemes for retailers □ VAT fractions □ The VAT return □ VAT inspections □ Checklist

The nature of value added tax

Value added tax is a new kind of tax first introduced in 1973. It gets its name because it is charged as a percentage of the value added to a product by each and every producer who handles it. For example, a trader who sells an item for £100 must add to it tax called 'output tax'. At the time of writing the tax is 15 per cent, so that the sale price, including tax is £100 + £15 = £115. However, the trader probably did not actually add value to the article of £100, because he or she purchased the item, or perhaps the raw material for the item, at a lesser price. Suppose we say it was purchased for £50 + VAT = £57.50. Therefore the trader actually added value to the item of only £50 (it was purchased for £50 and sold for £100). To correct the tax payable the trader is allowed to deduct the £7.50 paid to the supplier (the trader's input tax) from the £15 collected from the customer (the output tax). So we have:

Output tax – Input tax = Tax due to HM Customs and Excise
£15   –   £7.50   = £7.50

The effect of this is that although the trader collects the tax and pays it to Customs and Excise, he or she is not paying the tax at all. It is the customer who pays all the tax, £15, of which £7.50 is given to the VAT authorities by the trader, and the other £7.50 is given to the supplier. The supplier then has to account for this £7.50 to the VAT authorities, unless of course some part of it was paid to another supplier further back in the chain of production.

This is a rather awkward way of collecting tax, and some people do say it is a very cumbersome business. The fact remains that traders must become used to the idea that VAT money is not theirs: it is quite separate from their money and belongs to Customs and Excise. Not surprisingly the VAT authorities are very aggrieved if VAT is not paid promptly, or if the accounting records are inadequate. We must account for VAT accurately and we must by law keep our records for six years, and make them available for the VAT inspector when required.

Registration for VAT

The arrangements for VAT registration are important. It is compulsory to register if our turnover exceeded £25,400 in the past 12 months, or if we feel that the likely turnover in the next 30 days will bring the cumulative total of the last 11 months over the £25,400 threshold figure for the twelve-month period. £25,400 per annum is only £488 a week, and many traders will exceed this level of trading and be caught by the registration procedure. The danger is that you may find you have become liable for tax which you have not in fact collected. It is therefore safer to register for VAT voluntarily before it becomes compulsory, and thus enter the VAT system. It also means that the trader can claim back input tax added to all the things purchased for the business, both stock for resale and capital items. An unregistered trader cannot reclaim input tax, but is treated like a consumer – in other words the VAT falls upon the trader. The only way the trader can recover the VAT paid is by raising the profit margins on goods sold, which puts him or her in a less competitive position than other traders.

To register you complete form VAT 1, obtainable from your local VAT office (see your local telephone directory). Once you have registered for VAT, you must:

- Record your inputs, the figures being taken from the invoices received from your suppliers.
- Record your outputs, as shown on your invoices to your customers. Of course the top copy of the invoice will have been sent to the customer, but the second copy becomes your VAT record, and must be kept for six years.

    Some traders do not make out invoices but sell for cash over the counter. All goods sold must be marked up by 15 per cent for VAT, and the figures for calculating output tax are obtained from the 'daily takings' record under one of 12 special retailers' schemes. These are explained later.
- Complete your VAT return every three months (or every month if you are a trader dealing in zero-rated items). The VAT return is a statistical control form that enables you to calculate the VAT due, and the tax authorities to apply certain checks to ensure that your figures are roughly correct. More detailed inspection of cases where error is indicated will be made by the Inspection Department.

- Keep and maintain accurate records for these purposes.
- If the tax exceeds £1, pay it at the same time as the VAT return is sent in. Payment may be by cheque, bank giro or National Giro.

The reason the zero-rated trader completes forms monthly rather than quarterly is that he or she will usually be entitled to a refund of tax. Since the trader does not collect output tax but does buy many items (for example capital equipment) which are taxed, the trader's input tax usually exceeds output tax. The trader is therefore out of pocket, and is allowed to claim the refund each month, instead of waiting for three months for a quarterly refund.

There is a leaflet available from your local VAT office (see Customs and Excise in your local telephone directory) called *Should I be registered for VAT?*. If you are thinking of registering for VAT call them and ask for a copy. Their slogan says: 'If you have a problem, don't guess at the answer; *ask for advice.*' It saves a lot of trouble to start on the right track straight away.

Methods of accounting for VAT

There are two methods of accounting for VAT, the *normal method* and the *special scheme* method. Where a trader conducts business using invoices, in other words where all customers are invoiced for the goods supplied (output invoices on which tax has been added to the sale price) the invoices are called 'tax invoices' and form the basis of the VAT records. Since all traders buy their supplies from manufacturers or wholesalers they receive invoices from suppliers (input invoices on which VAT has been added to the purchase price). Therefore both input and output records can be made from the invoices, and this is called the *normal method of VAT*.

Some traders do not make out invoices, but sell for cash over the counter, or cash on delivery. Such people can still use the normal method for their input records but are unable to record invoices for outputs because none are issued. They have to find their output tax figure from the 'daily takings' figure when they cash up at the end of the day. Because of the wide variety of business activities there are 12 different 'special schemes for retailers'. The word 'retailers' has a special meaning in VAT law: it refers not only to shopkeepers, but to anyone who carries on a business without issuing invoices to customers. Thus a piano teacher would, if registered for VAT, be a 'retailer' of musical education. The 12 special schemes are Scheme A, Scheme B, Scheme B – Adaptation I, Scheme B – Adaptation II, Scheme C, Scheme D, Scheme E, Scheme E – Adaptation I, Scheme F,

11

Scheme G, Scheme H and Scheme J. The arrangements for these schemes are discussed later in this chapter.

VAT by the 'normal method'

The normal method for accounting for VAT is by the use of tax invoices. Input tax is calculated from the purchase invoices received from suppliers and output tax is calculated from the sales invoices sent to customers. Of course we may receive credit notes from suppliers if we return goods to them, and we may also send credit notes to customers if they return goods to us. These returns would affect the liability for VAT, reducing the input tax we can claim or the output tax we must pay. They must therefore be taken into account when calculating VAT by the normal method.

The chief point about any VAT record is that it must be clear, easy to follow, systematic and easily archived for six years. Whatever book-keeping records you keep you must have a VAT system that meets these requirements. In the author's experience the simplest record is the Simplex VAT book, which has:

- A bound book, with four quarterly records; these can each be divided into three parts if you are a zero-rated trader and need 12 monthly records.
- Adequate space for input invoices (purchases) and output invoices (sales).
- Adequate space for returns, input credit notes (from suppliers) and output credit notes (sent to customers).
- Adequate pages for recording 'daily takings' if you use a 'special scheme for retailers'.
- Each quarterly section has three VAT returns, each with room for a scheme calculation (which must be kept and be available for inspection by the VAT authorities).

The advantage of a bound book for VAT records is that it is obvious to the VAT inspectors that you have a system which cannot be rewritten or otherwise tampered with (but of course a slip can be crossed out and corrected; the alteration being initialled).

Besides the VAT book it is best to have a lever-arch file for storing the documents. The lever-arch file is divided into two sections, inputs and outputs, and each invoice recorded is filed in the correct order (with the most recent invoice on top). The number allocated to it as it was entered in the VAT book is written prominently on the invoice, and if the item is small (for example VAT vouchers issued by garages) two or three of them, each with its reference number, can be clipped to an A4 page. At the end of the year we thus have a VAT book with a file of input and output invoices, relating to the VAT records for that year and manifestly in apple-pie order.

Details of the normal method are as follows.

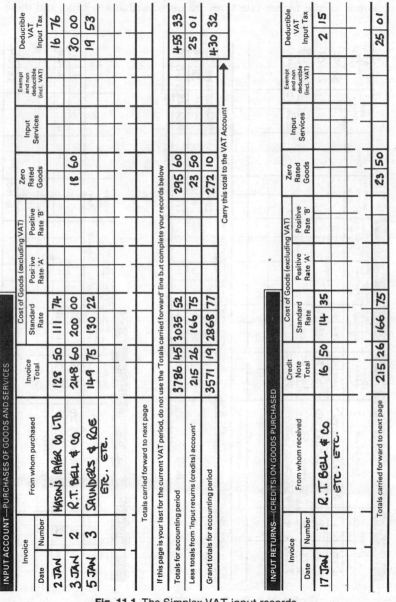

INPUT ACCOUNT—PURCHASES OF GOODS AND SERVICES

Date	Number	From whom purchased	Invoice Total	Standard Rate	Positive Rate 'A'	Positive Rate 'B'	Zero Rated Goods	Input Services	Exempt and non deductible (incl. VAT)	Deductible VAT Input Tax
2 JAN	1	MASONS PAPER CO LTD	128 50	111 74						16 76
3 JAN	2	R.T. BELL & CO	248 60	200 00			18 60			30 00
5 JAN	3	SAUNDERS & ROE ETC. ETC.	149 75	130 22						19 53
		Totals carried forward to next page								

If this page is your last for the current VAT period, do not use the 'Totals carried forward' line but complete your records below

		Totals for accounting period	3786 45	3035 52			295 60			455 33
		Less totals from 'Input returns (credits) account'	215 26	166 75			23 50			25 01
		Grand totals for accounting period	3571 19	2868 77			272 10			430 32

Carry this total to the VAT Account ↑

INPUT RETURNS—(CREDITS) ON GOODS PURCHASED

Date	Number	From whom received	Credit Note Total	Standard Rate	Positive Rate 'A'	Positive Rate 'B'	Zero Rated Goods	Input Services	Exempt and non deductible (incl. VAT)	Deductible VAT Input Tax
17 JAN	1	R.T. BELL & CO ETC. ETC.	16 50	14 35						2 15
		Totals carried forward to next page	215 26	166 75			23 50			25 01

Fig. 11.1 The Simplex VAT input records

11

The input account

As shown in Fig. 11.1, you simply record the details of each invoice received from a supplier. There are only two rates of tax at the time of writing, zero rate and standard rate, but the Simplex book has extra columns in case higher-rate taxes are introduced at any time, and these

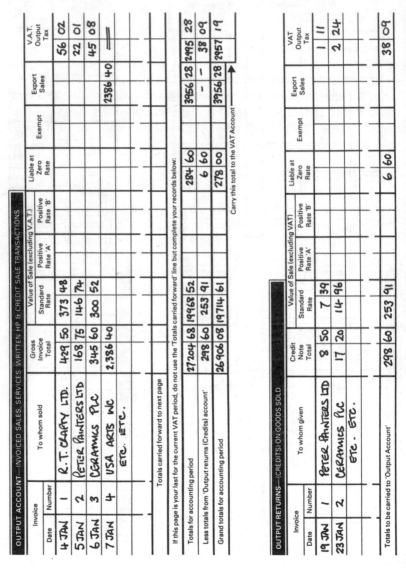

OUTPUT ACCOUNT—INVOICED SALES, SERVICES, WRITTEN HP & CREDIT SALE TRANSACTIONS

Date	Number	To whom sold	Gross Invoice Total	Standard Rate	Positive Rate 'A'	Positive Rate 'B'	Liable at Zero Rate	Exempt	Export Sales	V.A.T. Output Tax
4 JAN	1	R.T. CRAFTY LTD.	429 50	373 48						56 02
5 JAN	2	PETER PAINTERS LTD	168 75	146 74						22 01
6 JAN	3	CERAMICS PLC	345 60	300 52						45 08
7 JAN	4	USA ARTS INC	2,386 40						2386 40	===
		ETC. ETC.								

Totals carried forward to next page

If this page is your last for the current VAT period, do not use the 'Totals carried forward' line but complete your records below:

			Gross Invoice Total	Standard Rate	Positive Rate 'A'	Positive Rate 'B'	Liable at Zero Rate	Exempt	Export Sales	V.A.T. Output Tax
		Totals for accounting period	27204 68	19968 52			284 60		3956 28	2995 28
		Less totals from 'Output returns (Credits) account'	298 60	253 91			6 60		− 1	38 09
		Grand totals for accounting period	26906 08	19714 61			278 00		3956 28	2957 19

Carry this total to the VAT Account →

OUTPUT RETURNS—(CREDITS) ON GOODS SOLD

Date	Number	To whom given	Credit Note Total	Standard Rate	Positive Rate 'A'	Positive Rate 'B'	Liable at Zero Rate	Exempt	Export Sales	VAT Output Tax
19 JAN	1	PETER PAINTERS LTD	8 50	7 39						1 11
23 JAN	2	CERAMICS PLC	17 26	14 96						2 24
		ETC. ETC.								
		Totals to be carried to 'Output Account'	298 60	253 91			6 60			38 09

Fig. 11.2 The Simplex VAT output records

have been called 'Positive rate A' and 'Positive rate B'. The end column shows the input tax deductible, but note that if we return goods to our suppliers the credit notes issued record the VAT which can no longer be deducted because we did not purchase the returned items. The result is a final figure of input tax which may be deducted from the output tax collected.

The output account

The records for output tax are similar except that here we record the details from the second copies of our own invoices (the top copy having been sent to the customer as the invoice for the supply). Once again the returns (which of course will be returns inwards) are acknowledged with a credit note, and the VAT record will be made up from the second copies of our credit notes (the top copies will be with the customer). Fig. 11.2 shows some typical entries.

The VAT account

The quarterly results obtained from calculating VAT output tax and input tax by the normal method enable us to draw up a VAT account similar to that shown in Fig. 11.3. Note that for most traders the output tax will always exceed the input tax, because we always charge more for the goods we sell than we pay for them. Therefore 15 per cent of the sale prices (the

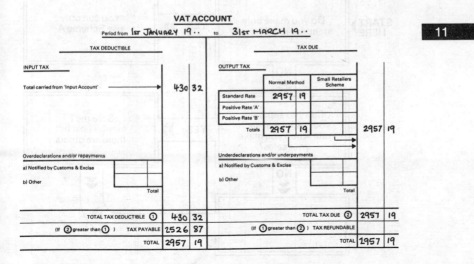

Fig. 11.3 The VAT account at the end of a VAT period

11

output tax) must be more than 15 per cent of the purchase prices (the input tax). Traders selling zero-rated items will collect no output tax, and although many of the inputs will also be zero-rated some will not – for example, plant and machinery, office supplies, etc. Therefore there will be input tax to reclaim from the VAT authorities.

Each quarter (or month for zero-rated traders) we receive a VAT return from Customs and Excise. All we have to do is to copy the figures from the VAT account on to the VAT return and send it in with the money: in Fig. 11.3 the amount is £2,526.87. This is a very considerable sum for most small traders, and it is important to put away the VAT collected. Some books will tell you that having VAT money accumulating in this way helps the small business with its working capital, but it is no help to use this money in your business if you do not have it available on the due date to pay to Customs and Excise. The wisest course is to put it in a deposit account at the bank, so that you do make a little interest out of it. Remember, it belongs to Customs and Excise, not you! You are only an unpaid tax collector.

The special schemes for retailers

There are 12 special schemes for retailers, to be used for calculating output tax by those traders who do not issue tax invoices to customers when they make a sale, and consequently cannot use the normal method of

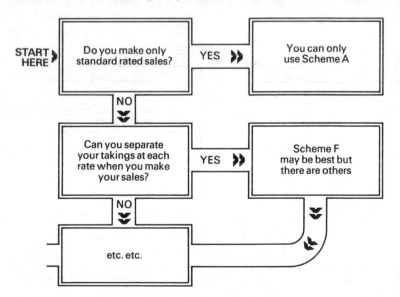

Fig. 11.4 The first few boxes of the VAT chart 'Choosing your retail scheme'

accounting for VAT. The schemes are simple enough in the actual records they require to be kept, and the method of calculation of output tax, but choosing between them is by no means an easy task. However, it has recently been made easier thanks to a really excellent chart prepared by Customs and Excise called 'Choosing your retail scheme'. You can obtain this by telephoning your local VAT office. The chart is too large to reproduce here but to illustrate its nature the first few boxes are shown in Fig. 11.4.

All the schemes require you to know your daily gross takings figure though they use various methods to arrive at the output tax figure. Once you have chosen the retail scheme which is best for you, a scheme leaflet is obtainable from the VAT office which explains exactly what records to keep and how to make your scheme calculation.

Figure 11.5 shows the method used in the Simplex VAT book to find the daily takings figure, and thus arrive via the scheme calculation to the correct output tax figure.

VAT fractions

One cause for concern when making VAT calculations is the nature of VAT fractions. In the special schemes for retailers the calculations are based on selling price figures and the fraction of the selling price which is VAT is often a source of puzzlement. For example, the present standard rate of 15 per cent has a VAT fraction of $\frac{3}{23}$ – a rather difficult fraction. We add $\frac{15}{100}$ to the intended selling price to increase it for output tax, but this becomes $\frac{3}{23}$, not $\frac{3}{20}$ of the final selling price. The explanation is quite simple.

Let us call the intended selling price 100. When we add 15 per cent to this we have 115 per cent as the final price. Now the VAT element in this final price is $\frac{15}{115}$, not $\frac{15}{100}$: 15 of the 115 parts represent output tax. And when we cancel by 5, $\frac{15}{115} = \frac{3}{23}$. So the output tax in our sales figure is $\frac{3}{23}$ of the total sales.

11

Example

A. Smith has total sales, including VAT, of £8,756.50 in July. How much of this is VAT output tax?

Output tax = $\frac{3}{23}$ × 8,756.50

= £1,142.15 (using a calculator)

Check: If we take £1,142.15 from £8,756.50 we arrive at a true selling price (without tax) of £7,614.35. If we find 15 per cent of this we shall have the VAT figure to be added on: and 15 per cent = £1,142.15, which is the answer we found by our calculation above – the VAT is £1,142.15.

Day	Date	Week No.	1. Daily Takings	2. Tax incl price of goods applied to personal use	3. Amounts charged on goods supplied against credit cards	4. Face value of trading checks, coupons, vouchers accepted	5. Total, Daily takings (add cols 1, 2, 3 and 4)	6. Cash refunds for damaged or returned goods or redeemed trad. stamps	7. Output Taxable Services (except Schemes A and F)	8. Takings against HP or credit sale agreements	9. Cash/Cheque payments to trading companies for trading stamps	10. Sub total (add cols 6, 7, 8 and 9)	11. Daily Gross Takings for calculation of output tax (subtract col 10 from col 5)
					RECONCILIATION OF DAILY TAKINGS — ONE MONTH								
Sun	1/4	14	236 72	–	–	–	236 72	–	–	–	–	–	236 72
Mon	2/4	14	344 65	4 65	–	–	349 30	–	–	36 20	–	36 20	313 10
Tues	3/4	14	299 85	–	–	–	299 85	3 25	–	–	–	3 25	296 60
Wed						ETC. ETC. FOR THE WHOLE MONTH							
Thurs													
			16284 40	156 25	–	–	16440 65	27 50	–	1350 00	–	1377 50	15063 15

Use this Figure in Schemes A, D, G, H, J,

Use this Figure in Schemes B–F

ZERO RATED OR LOWEST RATED TAKINGS

Day	Week No. 1 Date	Week No. 1 Amount	Week No. 2 Date	Week No. 2 Amount	Week No. 3 Date	Week No. 3 Amount	Week No. 4 Date	Week No. 4 Amount	Week No. 5 Date	Week No. 5 Amount
Sunday	1/4	112 35								
Monday	2/4	189 78								
Tuesday	3/4	136 52								
Wednesday		ETC. ETC. FOR THE WHOLE MONTH							Total	
Thursday										
Friday										
Saturday										
Total		1145 15	Total	1186 17	Total	1333 04	Total	1308 65	Total	363 45

Total 5336 46

Deduct 5336 46

Daily Gross Takings total: 9726 69

Where calculations are made on a quarterly basis, add together the three monthly figures.

Fig. 11.5 Finding the daily takings figures for VAT purposes

Suppose the Chancellor were to announce a higher rate of VAT for luxury items, at 25 per cent. We shall have to add 25 per cent to the intended selling price for output tax.

- *Question*: What is the VAT fraction when 25 per cent is added to the intended selling price to reach the final selling price?

- *Answer*: the VAT is $^{25}/_{125}$ of the final price.

$^{25}/_{125} = ^1/_5$ (cancelling by 25)

The VAT fraction for a tax rate of 25 per cent is therefore $^1/_5$.

Example

A. Smith's higher-rate sales total £16,274.60 in the month. What is the VAT element in this? The answer is one-fifth.

$^1/_5$ × £16,274.60
= £3,254.92

Check: Take £3,254.92 from £16,274.60 to find the intended selling price: £16,274.60 − 3,254.92 = £13,019.68. Twenty-five per cent, or $^1/_4$, of £13,019.68 = £3,254.92, which is the figure found for VAT above. Our VAT fraction of $^1/_5$ of the final selling price is therefore correct.

The VAT return

Each month, for zero-rated traders, or each quarter, for other traders, the VAT computer sends out an official form of VAT return to every registered trader. It must be completed to show the essential abbreviated details of your VAT trading. Some imaginary figures have been inserted below, but the final values 8 and 9 always include some exempt and zero-rated items, so the calculations do not work out at an exact 15%.

		£
VAT due in this period on outputs	1.	5,724.65
Under-declarations on previous returns	2.	None
Total VAT due	3.	5,724.65
VAT deductible on inputs	4.	826.50
Over-declarations in previous period	5.	None
Total VAT deductible	6.	826.50
Net VAT payable (3 − 6) or repayable (6 − 3)	7.	4,898.15
Value of outputs (excluding VAT)	8.	39,250.55
Value of inputs (excluding VAT)	9.	5,895.60

VAT inspections

Certainly in your first year, and from time to time later you will receive a visit from the VAT inspector. The newspapers often feature horror stories about people in difficulties with the VAT office, and such incidents are also featured in television documentaries. The vast majority of Customs investigations relate to sophisticated frauds which need not concern us here; so far as the normal trader is concerned the inspector wants to see that the records are kept in an honest and systematic way and are being preserved for the requisite period of six years. If a manifest error is found, such as VAT being reclaimed on expenses which were not business expenses but domestic expenses, the investigation would lead to an assessment of the tax thus wrongfully reclaimed, and possibly to some financial penalty. The legal rule is that 'ignorance of the law excuses no one'; we are all deemed to know all the details of VAT law, even though in fact none of us does. However, any penalty imposed would be fairly nominal in the case of a genuine error. It would be quite different if deliberate misdeclarations had been made, and a persistent misdeclaration penalty can be imposed.

To avoid trouble with Customs and Excise the following rules should be observed:

- Get to know the VAT system thoroughly as it affects you. Familiarize yourself with your own scheme, and the calculation it entails.
- Whichever system of VAT records you adopt keep them systematically, and preserve each year's records as a separate collection filed away in a filing cabinet or archived in a special cardboard box. You can buy quite reasonable boxes for about £2 in most stationers, or from postal sources such as Neat Ideas, Sandall Stones Road, Kirk Sandall, Doncaster, South Yorkshire DN3 1QU.
- Put away your VAT output tax regularly in a separate savings or deposit account in your own name. This will earn you interest, but it will be available for Customs and Excise when it becomes payable. Remember it is not your money, except to the extent that you can reclaim from it the input tax you have paid. The vast majority of it is tax you have collected for the VAT authorities, and they will expect it to be available. You must pay it before the due date, which is the last day of the month after your VAT period ends.

Checklist

1. Value added tax is a tax added to every supply we make of either goods or services, except that certain supplies are exempt and some are zero-rated.
2. The tax is added to the invoice price of the goods or services, and is called *output tax*. At present there are only two rates, standard rate (15 per cent) and zero rate. Other rates may be introduced at any time, to give a 'multiple-rate' system.
3. Traders must register for VAT if sales exceeded £25,400 in the past 12 months or if you believe that the next 30 days sales will bring the year's sales over the threshold figure of £25,400. These limits rise each year as part of the Budget and the latest figures can be obtained from the VAT office. Many traders register voluntarily so that they can reclaim input tax.
4. The tax payable is the output tax collected, less the input tax suffered on purchases for the business, whether these purchases are goods for resale, consumable items or capital items for use in the business.
5. If tax invoices are used as the basis for keeping VAT records the system of record-keeping is called the *normal VAT method*. All traders keep their input tax records by the normal method, but if they do not issue tax invoices for every supply they are unable to use this method for output tax and must use one of the 12 special retailers' schemes.
6. A chart called 'Choosing your retail scheme', which helps you select the most appropriate scheme for your business, is available. All the schemes depend on keeping accurate records of daily takings, and the scheme calculation is then based on these records (except for Scheme C where a different approach is used – although the daily takings figures are still required).
7. The VAT return sent to traders each month or quarter must be returned, with the VAT due, by the last day of the month following the end of any VAT record period.
8. The simplest VAT book on the market is the Simplex VAT book, obtainable from most stationers, or by post from the address given on page 7.

11

12 Computerized accounting

The nature of computers □ Advantages of computerized accounting □ Micro-Simplex accounting □ More sophisticated accounting for retailers □ Conclusions about computers for small businesses □ Checklist

The nature of computers

Computers can be programmed to do a great number of routine business activities at very fast speeds. Most of them operate at speeds in excess of ten million processes per second, so that complicated activities (such as calculating the percentage of VAT in today's daily takings) appear to be done in the twinkling of an eye. A computer system is made up of *hardware* and *software*. Hardware consists of pieces of technical equipment, such as the computer itself, a keyboard for gaining access to the computer and for keying in instructions to it, a visual display unit (VDU) which is exactly like a television screen) and a printer. Their uses are described below.

The computer

The computer is the 'thinking' end of the system, though it does not really think. It consists of a number of parts, the chief of which is the *central processor*. This is able to accept a program of instructions, and further data which it will process according to the program – hence the term 'data processing'. Since the computer works so fast it can be instructed to do numerous things one after the other. For example, if the 'daily takings' figure was keyed in at the end of the day it would not only be recorded on the Sales Account records, but the VAT output tax would be calculated and recorded as a credit in the VAT Account because the VAT officer is now a creditor for this amount. The total sales would be added to the sales figure for the year, and would eventually be used to find the gross profit in the Trading Account. A particular figure needs to be entered only once and all the activities and uses it can be put to are carried out automatically and instantaneously.

The keyboard

This allows us access to the computer and enables us to input new data. However, it is a slow method of inputting data, and to leave the computer free for other activities a great deal of keyed data is 'queued' up on some sort of storage device like magnetic tape or magnetic disks. Eventually the stored data will be fed in very rapidly at a moment when the computer is free.

The visual display unit

The VDU is an instantaneous output device that will display on its screen any particular set of information as it is presently stored in the computer. It will then display any item keyed in and, after a number of user-friendly hesitations, will pass the new data into the computer for processing. For example, suppose we have a debtor, D. Smith, who has just sent us a cheque to settle the balance owing on her account on 31 January. We first call up the Debtors' Ledger and ask to see the account of D. Smith. This will be displayed showing the balance on 31 January, £226.50, and one further invoice for goods sold to her on 4 February. We now instruct the computer to deduct £226.50, cheque received. The computer program might then display the following user-friendly question:

> You are asking me to deduct £226.50 from D. Smith's account.
> Is this correct?   Y/N

A touch on the Y key, meaning 'Yes', brings a further question:

> Are you sure?   Y/N

A further touch on the Y key and the computer will perform the following:

- Deduct the £226.50 from D. Smith's outstanding balance
- Add £226.50 to the Bank Account balance because a cheque has been received
- Issue a 'transaction number' which will appear on the screen: 'The transaction number for this entry is 213'

The computer records every transaction on an *audit trail* so that the auditors can see every entry made in the accounts. It may do several other things with the number if the program includes some sort of statistical analysis (for example an 'age of debtors' analysis).

If the operator making this entry is looking at a remittance advice note

12

and the cheque, he or she will record the transaction number 213 on the remittance advice note to show that it has been entered in the accounts, and the cheque can now be paid into the bank.

The printer

The VDU gives an instantaneous picture of the item requested, but once it is cleared from the screen there is no record of what was displayed. If we need a printed copy (called in computer language a *hard copy*) we can instruct the printer to print out what we require. It will chatter away at a rapid pace and produce the copy required. For example, if we wish to send D. Smith a statement of her account because she telephones to say that no account has been received this month, we can call up the account, print off a hard copy and put it in the post to her at once. The printer will, if a suitable program is prepared, print out a Trial Balance of the accounts, a list of unpaid creditors or a list of overdue debtors, or draw up a Trading Account and Profit and Loss Account, whenever we request it to do so.

Software

A piece of software is a program of instructions written to enable the computer to perform a particular task. For example, we could have a Payroll program, a Debtors Ledger program, a Paid to Bank program or a Cash Sales program. Writing such programs is a very expensive business, and those businesses that write their own programs have large staffs of programmers to do the work. Fortunately, for the needs of any small business, there are countless programs (packages) on the market which can be purchased 'off the shelf' from any computer shop. Very few people need to write their own software these days, certainly in the accountancy field, but if you want to use your computer for some technological purpose (such as detecting dangerous waste in the effluent from your factory) you are sure to be able to find someone who will write it for you (at a price). Your local Small Firms Service will advise you and help you to find a specialist programmer in the field of expertise you require.

The advantanges of computerized accounting

The advantages of computerized accounting are:
- Every accounting procedure can be computerized, and most businesses will find that suitable software of proven quality, with all the problems sorted out years ago, is available on the market at reasonable prices.
- Any figure needs to be entered only once, and the computer will then

undertake every process required with the item of data, automatically. Thus an invoice from a supplier will be credited to the supplier's account and debited to Purchases Account – which is the basic double entry process. If the trader is registered for VAT, the VAT on the purchase will be extracted and debited to Customs and Excise as it is deductible input tax, and Customs will have to refund it to us (unless we are able to deduct it from the output tax we have collected).

- The basic activity in computerized accounting is simple keyboard work, which anyone can learn in a single morning. The dealer who sells you the hardware and software will induct you into the simple procedures necessary and for the first few days will answer any calls you make if you come up against some difficulty. A well-written and proven piece of software will give you very little trouble and within a few weeks you will be perfectly happy with the system.

- The actual accounting records for a small business can be completed in about half an hour a day. Therefore the proprietor who establishes a simple system – for example putting all items due to be entered in a file cover or a tray as they arrive and then dealing with them at a convenient moment – keeps on top of the accounts and does not fall hopelessly behind with the records.

- The computer does the work, with plenty of user-friendly guidance as you make the entries, and the results are always correct (no mistakes in addition, subtraction, multiplication, etc.).

- Since computerized accounting programs are always devised by knowledgeable and qualified accountants you can rely absolutely on the correctness of the accounting work done with each piece of data you input into the system. Many systems will go right through to Final Accounts, and will ask you for any figures you need to input if they get stuck. For example, in preparing the Final Accounts they might ask: 'Please insert the figure for Closing Stock now.' If you have just carried out your stocktaking the figure will be available and the computer will accept it and carry on with the preparation of the Trading Account, Profit and Loss Account and Balance Sheet.

12

To discuss computerized procedures it is essential to choose a particular system. Since there was some discussion of Simplex book-keeping earlier in the book it is convenient to discuss Micro-Simplex, the computerized version. This has been followed by a discussion of one other system, that offered by Micro-Retailer Systems Ltd. Finally, in Chapter 13, there is a complete list of the systems available, provided from *Croner's Reference Book for the Self-Employed and Smaller Businesses*, which is referred to in that chapter as a useful authoritative source of information on all small business activity.

Micro-Simplex accounting

Micro-Simplex is a registered trade mark owned by George Vyner Ltd, who originally devised the Simplex system. The company licensed it for exclusive use to Micro-Retailer Systems Ltd, 84 Mill Street, Macclesfield, Cheshire SK11 6NR (telephone 0625 615375).

The system works off a series of programs stored on a single floppy disk fed into a device called a *disk drive unit*. The disk drive has a read-write head, which can read the information stored on the disk, and if necessary revise it, by writing back corrections to it. However, the program disk rarely needs to be changed in this way. The actual accounts are prepared on another disk, called the *data disk*, and this does need to be updated every time we make an entry. This is explained below.

The main menu

All computers work off lists of programs called *menus*. Each item on the menu is a different program, and by touching a single key you can load the program you require. For example, the Micro-Simplex main menu reads as follows:

1. Data entry
2. Data view
3. Data print
4. Summaries
5. Payment of unpaid bills
6. VAT
7. Audit trail
8. Profit and Loss Account
9. Close down

Select menu option

The screen display shown above invites us to select the menu option we wish to use. Suppose we wish to make an entry for the purchase of business stock. We select option 1, 'Data entry'. The computer says, 'Loading data entry', and a new menu appears:

1. Departmental headings
2. Expense headings
3. Receipts/paid to bank

4. Payments for business stock
5. Payments other than for stock
6. Weekly bank
7. Weekly cash
8. Unpaid bills
9. Goods taken for own consumption

Key shift X for main menu

Suppose we have just paid a delivery driver for some goods purchased for resale. The cheque was for £161, payable to T. Jones and Co. We now touch the 4 key, because 'Payments for Business Stock' is option 4.

Payments for business stock – option 4

This is the option where we record our purchases, the purchase of things that are to be resold, or worked up into finished goods or services.

It is used only for payments made on delivery of the goods, not for the payment of a bill we have already entered as an unpaid bill. The display is as follows:

> Payment No.
> Anal. code
> Date/cheque
> To whom paid
> Amount
> VAT content

- *Payment No.*   This is used for amending payments made during the week and is a little tricky. We will ignore it here.
- *Anal. code*   In the computerized Simplex system we can analyse purchases into ten departments, using codes 1–10 which are reserved for payments for business stock. If we suppose we are putting everything in General Purchases we just key in code 01. The description 'General Purchases' appears on the screen (see Fig. 12.1).
- *Date/cheque*   Here we can type in either the date or the cheque number. If you are paying by cheque, record the cheque number. If entering a date use a six-figure date, e.g. 3 April 1983 = 030483. In this case we will use this date.
- *To whom paid*   We now type in the name of the payee from whom the stock was purchased, T. Jones and Co.
- *Amount*   Here we type in the full amount paid, inclusive of VAT – say £161.

- *VAT content*   We now enter the VAT content if we have it on the document. If not the computer will calculate the value for us if we touch the V key, provided the goods are at standard rate.

The computer then says:

> Press 'C' for cash or 'Q' for cheque?

Since this is a payment by cheque we press 'Q'.

> Is this entry correct   (Y/N)?

If we press Y it then asks: 'Are you sure   (Y/N)?' If we again press Y it then tells us:

> This transaction number is 01.

We enter 01 on the document we are looking at. Enter it in the top right-hand corner clearly. This display is shown in Fig. 12.1.

The computer says: 'Press any key to continue.' When we do this the machine will make the entries and ask us if we have any more transactions for this option. If the answer to that is N for 'No', it returns us to the data entry menu.

A typical computer configuration for Micro-Simplex at the cheapest

```
        1234.56          SIMPLEX-64      123.45
  BANK                                          CASH
               PAYMENTS FOR BUSINESS STOCK

        PAYMENT NO

        ANAL. CODE        01 GENERAL PURCHASES.

        DATE/CHEQUE       030483

        TO WHOM PAID      T JONES & CO

        AMOUNT            161.00

        VAT CONTENT       21.00

            THIS TRANSACTION NUMBER IS 01
```

Fig. 12.1 Entering a payment for business stock
(*courtesy of Micro-Retailer Systems Ltd*)

Fig. 12.2 Working out the gross profit by microcomputer
(*courtesy of Micro-Retailer Systems Ltd*)

end of the market will cost about £550; a more sophisticated configuration about £2,500. These systems include a computer, disk drive, VDU, printer and transformer as well as the software. The system is available on Commodore, BBC, Einstein, Apricot, IBM, Amstrad and Sanyo computers and is being developed for other machines.

One of the cheaper configurations, the Amstrad, is shown in Fig. 12.2.

Outputs from the computer

There are two outputs from the computer: the screen output and a printout. If you wish to see what the figures are on a particular summary you can call it forward on the VDU using the data view program. You simply view it on the screen. If you require a permanent record for your accountant or the VAT inspector, or for your own satisfaction, you can print this out by attaching a printer. This will give you a complete audit trail of every entry made, which can be stored in suitable printout binders.

More sophisticated accounting for retailers

More sophisticated systems to exploit all the potential of the computer in the small and medium business fields are available. We can perhaps best consider the full range of systems by looking at all the different features available from a typical system, the Micro-Retailer system, available from Micro-Retailer Systems Ltd. A host of routine double entry records and management control information is available, as outlined below.

Sales and banking

- Full analysis by department of cash and credit sales by 50 headings for each branch.
- Banking analysis between cash, cheque, credit cards and paying-in branch.
- Multiple bank accounts with on-screen display.
- Handles all special retailers' schemes A–J and Pharmacy B.
- Summary reports available to screen or printer.
- Operates weekly or monthly.
- Optional links to customer credit accounts and point of sale systems.

Purchases

- Micro-Retailer has powerful facilities for recording and analysing details of payments made by cash or cheque (Cash Book) and bills to be paid at a later date (Purchase Ledger with up to 2,600 suppliers' accounts).
- Entry and full analysis by 50 departments for goods for resale and by 50 categories for overheads and expenses for each branch.
- Multiple VAT rate facility.
- Handles cash and credit purchases, credit notes and returns.
- Invoice approval facilities.
- Calculates and monitors selling prices, gross margin and mark-up for retail stock control and special retailers' VAT schemes.

- Provides for settlement discounts and payments on account.
- Allows for payment by cheque, clearing house, due date and/or supplier.
- Remittance advice note production.
- Reports to screen or printer of unpaid invoices with 'ledger card' and aged creditors' facilities for suppliers.
- Entry of bank charges, interest and standing orders.
- Journal facility for transfers between headings or recording goods transferred between branches.
- Summary of expenditures by department or category for the period and the financial year.
- Audit trail by invoice, supplier or cost heading to screen or printer for either range or year to date.
- An optional link to financial stock control is available.

Trading and Profit and Loss Accounts

- Micro-Retailer has information stored so that a Profit and Loss Account is available at the press of a key. It can be prepared *weekly* or *monthly* with period and year-to-date figures in a format you set up for yourself. Individual reports are produced for head office and each branch, with a company consolidation. You can view your profit progress every week if you so wish.

VAT reporting

Micro-Retailer is unique in the way it caters for the needs of all businesses having to prepare VAT returns. Special schemes A to J, Pharmacy B and normal method VAT systems are catered for, with the VAT return displayed on the screen or printed at the press of a key.

Reports to management

Micro-Retailer produces many reports, most of them on request so that you don't end up with lots of paper. Most reports are available on the screen or the printer and historical data is available for the whole of the financial year.

A number of specialist modules are also available, including a Financial Stock Control module, a Retail Sales Ledger system and a Market Purchases module for those who buy fresh stock daily (greengroceries, florists, etc.). Installation and training are provided and a telephone hotline is always available to support customers with any difficulty.

Services of the Accounting Centre

One disadvantage of computerized accounting for new businesses is that a dedicated system (one designed to fit a particular trader's exact requirements) is difficult to introduce, expensive to set up and is almost sure to have teething problems. This is precisely what the new small business does *not* want.

If we can use the existing expertise of an established computer centre, which has afforded the most expensive and versatile programs, has well-proven systems and a developed organization, with a consultancy facility to give advice, or warn of dangers looming ahead, we shall enjoy the best of all possible worlds. Such a service is provided by the Accounting Centre, Elscot House, Arcadia Avenue, Finchley Central, London, N3 2BR (telephone 081-349 3191).

What the Accounting Centre does is place the facilities of an advanced and sophisticated computer at the service of the small business. After a relatively brief analysis of your requirements, such of the various services available as are needed are linked together to give you a dedicated system which meets all your requirements. The basic services are:

(a) Sales ledger services, including credit control, monthly statements, sales analysis and customer history.

(b) Bought ledger services including analysis of purchases, remittance advice notes, cashflow control and supplier history.

(c) Payroll services, including PAYE and NI administration, payslips, and end of year returns.

(d) Monthly management accounts, including cash and cheque movements, profitability, cashflow management, future planning and end-of-year Final Accounts.

(e) Local consultancy services – a 'hand-holding' service, provided by local accountants where necessary, to give tailor-made advice and general supervision of book-keeping and VAT accounts, and assist in the interpretation of the monthly management accounts supplied by the computer.

Once you have provided basic details of sales, purchases and cash received and paid, the Accounting Centre turns it into not only financial records but management accounting records, to give you a total picture of your business's performance. Profits, cashflow, debtors and creditors, bank balances, overheads, etc., are all at your fingertips within a few days, and updated monthly. The added financial management and credit control eliminates a large part of the risks and uncertainties so common to businesses which have no computerised analysis of results on a regular basis.

There is an initial charge for the evaluation and adaptation of the computerized programs to give a tailor-made service, followed by a monthly payment which is a deductible expense for tax purposes. No specialist staff need be employed, no capital equipment needs to be purchased (and no need for expensive bank loans to purchase it). Lengthy consultations with accountants are not required because the system is organised month by month and records are always in apple-pie order. Any consultancy services which you do require will be discussions of a financial situation which the computer has made crystal clear, and prompt, inexpensive advice will therefore be forthcoming.

In particular there are no onerous long-term contracts, tied to expensive monthly payments. The well-established system depends for its success on mutual advantages – based upon client satisfaction and enduring relationships between the Accounting Centre, the small business client and the local consultant (if required).

Conclusions about computers for small businesses

Such a vast range of computer hardware and software is available today that that no one can be familiar with it all; it is too time-consuming. Most dealers have to be content with limiting themselves to a few titles within the range of commonly requested items and applications. In that way they can stay reasonably knowledgeable about these selected programs while remaining aware of most of what the industry has to offer.

The name in most common usage today is IBM (International Business Machines), which not only identifies IBM's own products but describes the industry standard personal computer, the IBM compatible. In recent years Amstrad has come to dominate the lower end of the market and its competitively priced products have made computing available to everyone. One specialist who kindly supplied material for these 'conclusions' said that he gets ten enquiries for Amstrad to every one for any other make.

Everybody who buys a PC needs word processing capability and Amstrad's PCW series offers that in a unique and total package: processor, screen, keyboard, printer and software at under £350 plus VAT represents remarkable value for money. The top machine in this series offers 512k of RAM (random access memory), a 720k floppy disk drive, wide-carriage daisy wheel printer and word processing software including spellchecker and mailmerge facilities at a total cost of £499 plus VAT.

With the advent of low-cost hardware, software houses have had to follow the trend. Compiling a comprehensive list of currently available, low-cost and powerful software would be a daunting task. Almost any application you can think of will be catered for. The most widely used categories of word processing, database, spreadsheet and accounting programs have prices ranging from £20 to several hundred pounds and specialist applications can run into many thousands of pounds.

It follows that the proprietor of a small business who wants computer facilities for accounting, word processing, etc., should rely on his or her local dealer and discuss the facilities required. Alternatively, the suppliers mentioned in this book will offer advice and supply both hardware and software. A full list is given in Chapter 13, and the director of one of them, Paul Tugby of Central Computer Services Ltd, Unit 22, Roxwell Trading Park, Argall Avenue, London E10 7QE (telephone 081-556 5331), kindly advised about these 'conclusions' on computers for small businesses.

The ideal place to select your system is at the annual 'Which Computer?' show, organized by the Reed Exhibition Company, Oriel House, 26 The Quadrant, Richmond, Surrey, TW9 1DL. Their Press and Publications Department will give details of the venue, etc. (telephone 081-948 9800). Readers may also wish to refer to *Computerisation in Business* in this Series.

Checklist

1. Computer programs are now available for a very wide range of business uses and accounting aspects are particularly well catered for by the software houses.
2. A microcomputer configuration consisting of a computer, visual display unit, keyboard, printer, etc., can be obtained for about £350, and in many cases add-on packages for particular specialist functions are available.
3. Some simple manual systems have been computerized, for example Micro-Simplex throws the ordinary manual Simplex system on to the screen, with its identical rulings, so that those familiar with the manual system can convert to the computerized system very easily.
4. The chief advantage of computerization is that once a piece of data has been fed into the computer, the programs will do with it everything that should be done – for example, a sale to a debtor will be debited into the debtor's account, credited in sales account, the VAT will be extracted and worked into the VAT records, and so on.
5. Computerized final accounts mean that a set of final accounts can be prepared by pressing a single key – every day if necessary.
6. A complete audit trail is made available so that every transaction can be traced, and its validity established to the satisfaction of the owners, the accountants and the Inland Revenue.

13 A complete set of manual and computerized accounting systems

Croner's Reference Book for the Self-Employed and Smaller Business □ Nature of the tabulations □ Invitation to other suppliers.

Croner's Reference Book for the Self-Employed and Smaller Business

Croner's Reference Book for the Self-Employed and Smaller Business is the standard reference book for all self-employed people. It gives up-to-date coverage of the legal and administrative situations of all small businesses, updated monthly and fully indexed. There is no point of difficulty in VAT, taxation, National Insurance, employment, health and safety, consumer law and company law that you cannot clarify from the book, which you will find in the reference section of most public libraries, or you can obtain a personal copy from Croner Publications Ltd, Croner House, London Road, Kingston upon Thames, Surrey KT2 6SR. The company has kindly given permission for the reproduction of the pages in Figs. 13.1 and 13.2, which give the names and addresses, subjects covered, etc., of all the manual and computerized systems for small businesses, available at the date shown. Users of the book will find this list updated from time to time.

13

Nature of the tabulations

The tabulations are given in alphabetical order in two parts: manual systems and computerized systems. Not all systems cover all aspects, so it is well to study the indications – a cross in any box indicates that the system concerned can handle the aspect named in the 'Coverage' class at the top of the page.

In choosing a system for use in your business it is advisable to scan the information given very closely and approach the publishers or suppliers of the systems that seem most appropriate for your class of business.

ACCOUNTS

DECEMBER, 1988

SIMPLE ACCOUNTING SYSTEMS
(See page Z10 for computerised systems)

Name of System	Bank	Cash	Sales	Purchases	Receipts	Payments	Payroll	VAT	Trading Account	Profit and loss account	Balance sheet	Handbook available	Free advice service	Advice service with nominal charge	Other features	Cost (Prices subject to revision)	Available from RS=Reputable stationers P=Publisher (see end col.)	Address of Publisher or Supplier
Ataglance VAT Account Book for Retailers	X	X	X	X	X	X		X					X			£4.70	P	Ataglance Publications, 16 Sawley Avenue, Lytham St. Annes, Lancs FY8 3QL. Tel: 0253 727107
Small Trader Book	X	X	X	X	X	X							X			£2.35 Plus VAT	P	
Collins Self Employed Account Book	X							X							Sub-contractors covered	£11.30	RS	
Collins Complete Traders Account Book	X				X	X		X								£11.30	RS	
Evrite Traders Account Book	X				X	X		X								£8.00	P	Evrite Publishing Co. Ltd., Haden Road, Cradley Heath, Warley, West Midlands.
FINCO	X	X	X	X	X	X	X	X				X	X		Financial control sheet included	£39 + VAT	P	Casdec Ltd., Broadwood View, Ropery Lane, Chester le Street, Co. Durham DH3 3NJ. Tel: 0385 880421
FINCO One-year System	X	X	X	X	X	X	X	X								£8.50 Plus VAT	P	
Guildring VAT Account								X								£19.49	RS	

Z8

	Cashflow forecast	Age analysis	Stock valuation	Budget	Petty cash and local installation service	Livestock Record	Refills and replacement stationery widely available from stationers	Price		Supplier
Kalamazoo Small Business Pack	X	X	X	X	X	X	X	£130 upwards	P	Kalamazoo Business Systems, Mill Lane, Northfield, Birmingham B31 2RW. Tel: 021-411 2345 (or see local telephone directory)
Kalamazoo Payroll Pack	X	X			X	X	X	£97	P	
Safeguard "One-write" Starter Pack	X	X		X	X	X	X	£126.80	P	Safeguard Systems GB Ltd., Centurion House, Gateway, Crewe, Cheshire CW1 1XJ. Tel: 0270 500921
Simplex Account Books "D" Cashbook	X	X	X	X	X	X	X	£5.23	RS or P	George Vyner Ltd., Simplex House, Mytholmbridge Mills, Holmfirth, Huddersfield HD7 2TA. Tel: 0484 685221 (Handbook is called *Simplified Book-keeping for Small Business*)
VAT Book	X	X	X	X	X	X	X	£7.77	RS or P	
Wages Book	X	X	X	X		X	X	£4.75	RS or P	
Licencees Book (for public houses and restaurants)	X	X			X	X	X	£9.31	RS or P	
Farm Account Book (Simplex Everall)	X	X	X	X	X	X	X	£8.35	RS or P	
Newspaper Round Book	X	X				X	X	£0.40	RS or P	
Twinlock Payemaster 87 Wages and Salaries System	X	X	X	X	X	X	X	£109.95	RS	Twinlock, Napier House, London Road, Wrotham Heath, Sevenoaks, Kent TN15 7RS. Tel: 0732 883555
Twinlock Triform 73 Book-keeping System	X	X	X	X	X	X	X	£189.95	RS	
Twinlock Variform Loose-leaf Account & Analysis Books	X	X		X	X	X	X	From £19.00	RS Money back Guarantee	

Fig. 13.1 Simple manual accounting systems

Note: Every attempt has been made to give a comprehensive coverage of the systems available. Publishers wishing to change the record shown, or to have their system included, are invited to submit details for evaluation and inclusion.

13

ACCOUNTS

DECEMBER, 1988

There are countless organisations offering specialised packages for all sorts of business purposes, and the state of the computer industry is such that it is very difficult to keep track of developments. The organisations shown below offer different services which may be of interest. We shall be glad to add other systems to this display if firms offering particular packages will kindly give us full details.

COMPUTERISED SMALL-BUSINESS SYSTEMS
(See page Z8 for manual systems)

Name of System	Is hardware supplied?	What software packages are available	Costs	Back-up provided	Other details
The Accounting Centre, Elscot House, Arcadia Avenue, Finchley Central, London N3 2JE. Tel: 081-349 3191	Yes, for some applications	Management accounts Sales and bought ledgers Payroll Cashflow statements Budget comparisons Balance sheets Profit and loss accounts Credit control	Contact company for details of service required.	Local consultant.	Manuals available.
Small and medium Business Accounting Systems by: Central Computer Services Ltd., 22 Roxwell Trading Park, Argall Avenue, London E10 7QE. Tel: 081-556 5331	Yes Amstrad Advanced Systems (and repair centre)	Payroll & SSP Invoicing Sales Ledger Bought Ledger Nominal Ledger Stock Control Also In-house Software department for complete programs and modifications.	£500-£5000 for complete systems.	Fully comprehensive maintenance by own service organisation plus full software support.	Total Support Provided.

Z10

Name & address		Description	Price	Support	Notes
KALAMAZOO Kalamazoo Business Systems, Mill Lane, Northfield Birmingham B31 2RW. Tel: 021-411 2345 (or see local telephone directory)	Yes	Pegasus and Tetra accounting packages A range of specialist packages for various trades and professions. "One-up." A complete package for first-time users.	From £350 per module. £1,799 package includes printer, software, etc.	Telephone advice service Software support Training Installation Hardware maintenance.	
LASS Ledgerless Account System, Work Flow Ltd., Edenbridge Kent TN8 7HA Tel: 0342 86357	Yes	LASS accounting system designed for the small business. Day book VAT listings with totals. Expenses analysis Trial balance. Gross/Nett profit. Bank reconciliation etc.	LASS comes complete with Tandon computer, 100cps matrix printer, all necessary cables, full instructions, etc. £1,995 plus VAT (software only—£750)	LASS includes 1 year on site, time and parts maintenance by Dictaphone Ltd.	LASS sample print-outs and detailed specs sent on receipt of large sae, or a demo-disk is available for £25.
MICRO-SIMPLEX 84 Mill Street, Macclesfield Cheshire SK11 6NR Tel: 0625 615000/615375	Yes	A full simple account service is offered. Sales, purchases, other payments, cash bank, debtors, creditors, VAT (all schemes), print-outs, final accounts. Available on most popular computers from £99 incl. VAT	£8-£12 per week according to system selected. Outright purchase is also possible. (£1,000-£3,000 according to system)	Full back up available.	Detailed manual available.
MICRO-SIMPLEX PLUS 84 Mill Street, Macclesfield, Cheshire SK11 6NR. Tel 0625 615000	Yes	An expanded version of Micro-Simplex with greater capacity for purchases and Sales analysis and final accounts. IBM compatible £295 plus VAT.	As above	As above	As above

Fig. 13.2 Computerized accounting systems for small businesses

13

Z11

ACCOUNTS

DECEMBER, 1988

Name of System	Is hardware supplied?	What software packages are available	Costs provided	Back-up	Other details
OB-SERVE RETAILER PLUS First floor, Portman House, Salisbury Street, Blandford Forum, Dorset, DT11 7AU (formally called The Cash Trader) Tel: 0258 51299	Yes	Accounting package incorporating cash book with sales and purchase ledgers, all VAT schemes, detailed analysis of sales and expenditure with full audit trails, year end summaries and profit and loss reports.	£185.00 + VAT	Full back-up available	Detailed manual and tutorial available.
Safeguard Plus System Safeguard System Centre. 4th Avenue, Gateway, Crewe. Cheshire CW1 1XJ. Tel: 0270 500921	No	Accounting software package 'Safeguard Plus' including manual data input system, software disks covering sales and purchase ledger, payroll, stock control, and continuous stationery	£575 approx.	Installation and training Hotline support	
TAXCOMP Integer Computer Systems, 430 Bury New Road, Prestwich, Manchester M25 5BD. Tel: 061-798 7307/7619	Yes	A range of accounting and business software covering sales, purchase and nominal ledgers, stock, sales, order processing, invoicing, payroll, word processing, spreadsheets, and databases.	These are negotiable according to system supplied	Full back-up available.	Detailed manual available.

Note: Pages Z13–Z16 have not been used.

Z12

Invitation to other suppliers

It is just possible that systems do exist that are not included in *Croner's* charts, although in recent years every attempt has been made to contact those offering such systems. If any publisher wishes to have a system that does not appear in the chart included in the next edition of this book or, even more important, included in *Croner's*, we shall be delighted to hear from them. Similarly, any amendment to existing entries should be indicated, preferably to Croner Publications at the address given above. The Croner Handbook would then be updated at the next monthly revision, and this Pitman/NatWest book would be updated on reprint.

13

14 The Final Accounts of a business

Introduction □ Adjustments and Final Accounts □ Manufacturing Accounts □ How to bring out a manufacturing profit □ A full set of Final Accounts for a sole trader

Introduction

In Chapter 6 we learned how to do a set of final accounts for a sole trader business, and found that a set of Final Accounts consists of a Trading Account, a Profit and Loss Account and a Balance Sheet. The starting point for a set of Final Accounts is the Trial Balance of the Ledger taken out after the close of business on the last day of the financial year. If you are not using a double entry system you do not have a Trial Balance, and have to draw up your Final Accounts from the various summaries provided by the system you are using. This is quite easy with a system like the Simplex system, because all the details you need are provided in the summaries and you are guided through the preparation of the Final Accounts very clearly. It is not quite so easy with some of the abbreviated systems described earlier (e.g. FINCO) and it may be necessary to turn your records over to an accountant and allow him/her to prepare your Final Accounts for you.

The aim of this chapter, and the next two chapters, is to encourage you to attempt to prepare your own set of Final Accounts, rather than passing them over to an accountant. The advantage is that you find out a lot more about your business if you prepare these accounts yourself, and you will do them more quickly than an accountant, who usually has a large backlog of work especially at the end of the calendar year (in December) and the tax year (in March). These are the times of year when most people finish their accounting years. If you finish your accounting year on the anniversary of starting your business you may finish at any time of the year, and this is of course quite acceptable to the tax man.

Later in this chapter we will be looking fairly closely at one further element in preparing Final Accounts, the Manufacturing Account, which is necessary for manufacturing businesses and which precedes the Trading Account, the Profit and Loss Account and the Balance Sheet. We shall then have a full sequence, as follows:

- The Manufacturing Account, which gives us a *manufacturing profit*, if we wish to work this out separately.
- The Trading Account, which gives us the *gross profit* of the business.
- The Profit and Loss Account, which gives us the *net profit* of the business, and
- The Balance Sheet, which is a snapshot of the current state of affairs of the business at a given moment in time – the last second of the last day of the financial year. The next day we start again, at 'Dawn on day one' of a new year.

Before beginning with the Manufacturing Account we must first mention one or two special points about adjustments.

Adjustments

What are adjustments?

At the end of the year there are several situations we need to know about, which come under the general heading of 'adjustments'. However, many small business proprietors do not understand adjustments and might get hopelessly muddled and worried if the Inland Revenue insisted too fussily that they do a lot of adjustments at the end of the year. Therefore the Inland Revenue allows such people to keep their books on a 'Receipts and Payments' basis. All this means is that you are allowed to ignore adjustments. If you receive any money, right up to the last second on the last day of the year, you have to treat that receipt as a receipt of the present year. If you pay any money, similarly, right up to the last second of your present year, and if it is a deductible business expense, you can treat it as a payment of the present financial year – even though, for example, you might only use the materials you purchased in the next financial year. If you are told that you must keep your books on a 'Receipts and Payments' basis that is what it means.

14

If you understand double entry book-keeping you will understand adjustments, and if you employ an accountant he or she will of course understand adjustments, and you will then have your books done on an 'accruals basis' which means that all necessary adjustments will have been done. The word 'accruals' means 'things that have become due'. Adjustments simply adjust the final accounts to include anything that had become due and must count as a profit (or a loss) for this year. They also exclude anything that has not become due, but ought properly to be deferred and treated as a profit of next year, or a loss of next year. That is all adjustments do, but as there are rather a lot of them, and they sometimes call for very clear thinking about principles of accounting, they can be worrying to the beginner.

Take one very simple example to illustrate the point. Suppose you have a sub-tenant who pays you £500 a quarter for rent. This is a little bit of profit for your business. Suppose it is due on 31 March, 30 June, 30 September and 31 December. In the year 19X9 the Rent Received Account looks like this:

Rent Received A/c   *L21*

19X9		£
31 March	A. Tenant	500.00
30 June	A. Tenant	500.00
30 September	A. Tenant	500.00

Fig. 14.1 An incomplete rent account

The tenant, who lives in Glasgow, has gone home for Hogmanay and you have not received the money on 31 December. If you were keeping your books on a Receipts and Payments basis the rent received for the year would be £1,500. However, everyone can see that this does not give a true and fair view of the profits of the business, because the Rent Received Account should read £2,000 for the year. Therefore the accountant would transfer £2,000 to the Profit and Loss Account as a profit for the year. The accounts would then look like these:

Rent Received A/c   *L21*

19X8		£	19X8		£
31 Dec. Transfer to			31 March	A. Tenant	500.00
P & L A/c		2,000.00	30 June	A. Tenant	500.00
			30 Sept.	A. Tenant	500.00
			31 Dec.	Balance c/d	500.00
		£2,000.00			£2,000.00
19X9		£			
1 Jan. Balance b/d		500.00			

Profit and Loss A/c for year ending 31 December 19X9   *L97*

	19X9	£
	Gross profit	27,295.60
	Rent received	2,000.00

Fig. 14.2 Closing off the rent account at the end of the financial year

Notes

- As A. Tenant has not paid the last £500 it appears as a debit balance on the Rent Received Account.
- Remember that any debit balance on an account is either a loss, or an asset (see Fig. 6.5). As the Rent Received Account is a profit account it cannot be a loss – it must be an asset. We have a debtor, A. Tenant, who owes us £500. As soon as he gets back from Hogmanay he will give us the money, and we shall pay it into the bank. It will then be an asset, cash at the bank, and the £500 balance on the Rent Received Account will disappear as we credit the account with the £500 received.

It is impossible at this stage to go into all the possible types of adjustments. Anyone who is really interested should obtain a copy of *Book-keeping Made Simple*, by the present author.

Adjustments and the Balance Sheet

Whenever we do an adjustment we finish up with a balance on an account which, had there been no adjustment, would have been clear. Thus in Fig. 14.1, if the tenant had been up-to-date with the rent and paid the full £2,000 for the year, the £2,000 would have been transferred to the Profit and Loss Account, and the Rent Received Account would have been clear. Instead it finished up with a balance on the Rent Received Account of £500, a debt from a debtor, A. Tenant. Now, every balance at the end of the year, on any account, must appear on the Balance Sheet, which is, as its name implies, a list of the outstanding balances which are being carried forward to the next year. Since the balance left on any account must either be an asset (something the business owns) or a liability (something the business owes) the balances that result from adjustments appear on the Balance Sheet either as assets or liabilities. In the case of the debtor, A. Tenant, the £500 rent due is an asset – we own this debt – and the figure

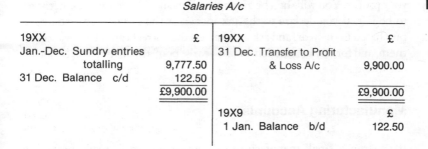

Salaries A/c

19XX		£	19XX		£
Jan.-Dec. Sundry entries			31 Dec. Transfer to Profit		
totalling		9,777.50	& Loss A/c		9,900.00
31 Dec. Balance c/d		122.50			
		£9,900.00			£9,900.00
			19X9		£
			1 Jan. Balance b/d		122.50

Fig. 14.3 Salaries accrued due at the end of the year

of £500 will appear on the assets side of the Balance Sheet as 'Rent due from sub-tenant, £500'.

Taking a different example, supposing the salaries for the year total £9,777.50 but we owe one employee £122.50 because he is in hospital and his salary has not yet been taken to him. The adjusted salaries figure is therefore £9,900.00. The Salaries Account looks as shown in Fig. 14.3.

This credit balance is a liability (we owe the man his salary) and this will therefore appear on the Balance Sheet as a liability, 'Salaries due £122.50'.

The general names for these outstanding balances are 'Accrued Charges' for the liabilities and 'Payments in Advance' for the assets.

Depreciation – a special type of adjustment

One adjustment which affects small businesses in a special way is depreciation. Depreciation is a reduction in the value of a capital asset as a result of fair wear and tear. The principle of it is that since all assets wear out as the years pass they should diminish in value on the Balance Sheet as the years pass, and each year the fair amount of loss in value should be written off the Profit and Loss Account as a loss for the year. Since the amount to be treated as depreciation is to some extent left to the discretion of the trader concerned there is a danger that, from the tax point of view, a trader could take advantage of the tax system. For example, suppose as a trader I am making good profits, I could decide to write off more than a fair amount of depreciation. This would reduce my profits and consequently reduce the tax payable.

To avoid such problems Parliament has decreed that a set rate of capital allowances shall be given. At present this is 25 per cent of new capital expenditure. The balance of the capital expenditure goes into a 'pool' and 25 per cent of the pool may be deducted in subsequent years. This is therefore 25 per cent of a diminishing balance, not 25 per cent of the original value. For this reason whatever sum you decide to write off as depreciation will be ignored by the tax inspector, who will add it back to your profits. You will then be given the allowance Parliament has declared to be fair. If you declare to the tax inspector the capital items you have purchased in the year, and ask to be given the correct capital allowance for them, and for any balance left in last year's 'pool' the matter will be sorted out for you.

Manufacturing Accounts

If you run a small manufacturing business you must really prepare a Manufacturing Account as part of your Final Accounts. The point here is that you cannot begin trading until some goods have been made, with which to trade. This means that the value of the goods manufactured has to be worked out and transferred into the Trading Account ('Cost of Goods Manufactured' instead of 'Purchases') and then these goods can be sold and a profit arrived at. The procedure is fairly simple, but a few pieces of vocabulary need to be explained first. These are:

- *Prime costs*. Prime costs are the first costs incurred in manufacturing, and are usually taken to include the costs actually embodied in the manufacturing of the products. They therefore include raw materials, any special components bought-in, the direct wages of workers employed in the production process and any other costs directly attributable to production, e.g. the power for machines. These costs are collected together in a section of the Manufacturing Account called the Prime Cost Section (see Fig. 14.4), and are then carried down into a further section called the Cost of Manufactured Goods Section.
- *Overheads*. Besides the prime costs of any manufactured goods there are a great many overhead expenses which have to be added to the prime costs to get the total costs of the manufactured goods. Since all these expenses have to be recovered from the customer we must build them into the 'cost of manufactured goods' before we work out a selling price. Typical overheads are supervision salaries, factory rent, lighting, repairs and depreciation.
- *Work-in progress*. At the end of the year we know that any trader will have stocks of goods unsold on the shelves, and these stocks must be taken into account when working out the Trading Account (see Chapter 4). In the same way any manufacturer will have partly finished goods going through the manufacturing process, and what is worse, they will be at all sorts of stages. Some will be still practically raw materials, having only just entered the production phase, and some will be almost complete. If we are going to take these stocks of work-in-progress into account we have to value them at some fair figure and this will usually mean we value them all as if they were half-finished (i.e. we take an average value). We can therefore say that work-in-progress is an adjustment made in the Cost of Manufactured Goods Section of the Manufacturing Account to take account of goods going through the manufacturing process, which are as yet incomplete.

To avoid having too many figures to look at when preparing a Manufacturing Account we will look at only part of a Trial Balance, which shows only the Manufacturing and Trading items. This will enable us to prepare a Manufacturing Account, and a Trading Account, but we will not go on to produce a Profit and Loss Account or a Balance Sheet. These will be explained later.

Notice that there will now be three lots of stock: stocks of raw materials, stocks of work-in-progress and stocks of finished goods. As with the Trading Account there will be opening stocks at the start of the period and closing stocks at the end of the period. Study the figures given in Example 1 below and the Manufacturing and Trading Accounts given in Figs. 14.4 and 14.5.

14

Example 1

R. Marshall is a manufacturer. Let's see how to prepare his Manufacturing Account and Trading Account for year ending 31 December, 19X9.

	£
Stocks at 1 January, 19X9	
Raw materials	27,824
Work-in-progress (valued at factory cost)	3,259
Finished goods	36,297
Purchases of raw materials	46,358
Sales	338,566
Returns in	1,566
Factory:	
Wages (prime cost)	24,268
Power (prime cost)	1,896
Factory:	
Salaries (overhead)	23,258
Rent (overhead)	5,960
Lighting (overhead)	1,265
Repairs (overhead)	1,792
Depreciation (overhead)	1,160
Warehouse: (Trading Account)	
Wages	29,254
Business rates	3,756
Stocks at 31 December, 19X9	
Raw materials	19,964
Work-in-progress (valued at factory cost)	4,416
Finished goods	27,348

Method

The Manufacturing Account is prepared first, as shown in Fig. 14.3 with its two sections: the Prime Cost Section and the Cost of Manufactured Goods Section. Then the Trading Account is prepared in the usual way as in Fig. 14.4. Notice that the Prime Cost Section simply collects together all the prime costs, and these are then carried down into the next section, the Cost of Manufactured Goods Section. In this section the overheads are added to the prime costs, the adjustment is done for the work-in-progress and the final cost of the manufactured goods is carried to the Trading Account. You are advised to work carefully through the example to see how the Gross Profit is finally arrived at.

Manufacturing Account
for year ending 31 December, 19X9
Prime cost section

		£		£
Raw materials:			Prime costs (carried to	
Stock at start		27,824	Cost of Manufactured	
Purchases	46,358		Goods Section)	80,382
Less returns	–			
		46,358		
Total available		74,182		
Less closing stock		19,964		
Cost of raw materials used		54,218		
Wages		24,268		
Power		1,896		
		£80,382		£80,382

Cost of Manufactured Goods Section

		£		£
Prime costs		80,382	Cost of manufactured goods	
			(transferred to Trading	
Overheads:			Account)	112,660
Salaries	23,258			
Rent	5,960			
Lighting	1,265			
Repairs	1,792			
Depreciation	1,160			
		33,435		
		113,817		
Work-in-progress:				
Stock at start	3,259			
Less Closing stock	–4,416			
		– 1,157		
		£112,660		£112,660

Fig. 14.4 A simple Manufacturing Account

Notes

• The work-in-progress needs a word of explanation. At the start of the year there was £3,259 of work-in-progress in the workshop and in Week One of the

new year this went through into production. At the end of the year the work-
in-progress closing stock was greater: £4,416. Therefore more was held back
(and carried over to next year) than was handed on to this year from last year.
The result is, in effect, that we must deduct the difference (£1,157) from the
cost of manufactured goods, since some of the raw materials, etc., used in the
year were not manufactured this year, but left behind for next year's output.
- The final result is a Cost of Manufactured Goods of £112,660. These finished
  goods were handed on to the Trading Account to be sold in the year. Now see
  the Trading Account in Fig. 14.5.

Trading Account
for year ending 31 December 19X9

	£		£
Opening stock of		Sales	338,566
finished goods	36,297	*Less* returns in	1,566
Cost of manufactured		Net turnover	337,000
goods	112,660		
	148,957		
Less closing			
stock	27,348		
Cost of stock sold	121,609		
Warehouse wages	29,254		
Business rates	3,756		
Cost of sales	154,619		
Gross profit	182,381		
	£337,000		£337,000

Profit and Loss Account
for year ending 31 December 19X9

		£
	Gross profit	182,381

Fig. 14.5 The trading account of a manufacturer

Notes
- This is exactly the same as any ordinary Trading Account, except that instead
  of purchasing goods for re-sale we manufacture them. Therefore the item
  'Purchases' does not appear and is replaced by 'Cost of Manufactured Goods'
  which comes in from the Manufacturing Account.
- One or two additional items have been included, for example warehouse
  wages and community charges (rates) have been added to the costs incurred
  (for operating the warehouse). The final result is that the Cost of Sales is
  deducted from the Sales figure (the Net Turnover) to give the Gross Profit.

Bringing out a manufacturing profit

Some traders like to bring out a manufacturing profit, because they want to know whether it is worthwhile having a factory at all. Would you do better if you bought-in everything you wished to sell, and did not have the worry of manufacturing?

To understand what is necessary to bring out a manufacturing profit look back to Fig. 14.4, where we have on the right-hand-side £112,660 Cost of Manufactured Goods. Suppose we can get a good idea of what these manufactured items would cost if we could purchase them. Suppose it was £140,000. This means that the manufacturing profit is £140,000 – £112,660 = £27,340. By simply putting the market value of the goods on the right-hand-side, instead of the 'Cost of Manufactured Goods' we can bring out the manufacturing profit, as shown in Fig. 14.6. This means that we will charge the Trading Account with the market value of the goods manufactured, not their cost. This will reduce the gross profit by £27,340, and we shall have in the Profit and Loss Account the same profit, but in two parts, a Manufacturing Profit and a Gross Profit on Trading. We can thus see that our factory is a valuable unit, contributing a useful sum to our total profitability. The final profit figure of £182,381 is the same as before, but we can now see that it is made up of two parts: (1) the results of the manufacturing effort and (2) the results of the trading activities.

You might like to work out what these profits would have been if the market value of the manufactured goods had been (i) £230,000 and (ii) £98,000. From the results you could then give an answer to the question, 'What should we do about our factory?'

Cost of Manufactured Goods Section

	£		£
Prime Costs	80,382	Market value of manufactured goods (transferred to	
Overheads:		Trading Account)	140,000
Salaries	23,258		
Rent	5,960		
Lighting	1,265		
Repairs	1,792		
Depreciation	1,160	33,435	
		113,817	
Work-in-progress:			
Stock at start	3,259		
Less Closing stock	–4,416		
		–1,157	
Cost of manufactured goods		112,660	
Manufacturing profit		27,340	
		£140,000	£140,000

14

Trading Account
for year ending 31 December, 19X9

	£		£
Opening stock of		Sales	338,566
finished goods	36,297	*Less* Returns in	1,566
Market value of		Net turnover	337,000
manufactured goods	140,000		
	176,297		
Less Closing stock	27,348		
Cost of stock sold	148,949		
Warehouse wages	29,254		
Business rates	3,756		
Cost of sales	181,959		
Gross profit	155,041		
	£337,000		£337,000

Profit and Loss Account
(for year ending 31 December, 19X9)

			£
		Manufacturing profit	27,340
		Gross profit	155,041
			£182,381

Fig. 14.6 A Manufacturing Account to bring out the profit on manufacturing

A Manufacturing Account for you to prepare

1. K. Hoyle is a manufacturer. From the information on p. 169 prepare his Manufacturing Account and Trading Account, and open his Profit and Loss Account for the year ended 31 December, 19X9:

Answer

Books of K. Hoyle: prime cost, £180,498; cost of manufactured goods, £222,056; gross profit £192,822.

Submitting accounts for a sole trader business

At the end of your financial year it is necessary to submit your accounts to the Inland Revenue. Some useful points about the Inland Revenue are

	£
Sales	375,281
Stocks at 1 January, 19X9	
Raw materials	29,464
Work-in-progress (valued at factory cost)	7,295
Finished goods	47,327

Purchases of raw materials	103,528
Stocks at 31 December, 19X9:	
Raw materials	17,247
Work-in-progress (valued at factory cost)	9,756
Finished goods	86,924

Factory:	
Wages paid	58,874
Wages due at 31 December, 19X9	625
Factory and machinery maintenance	6,725
Depreciation on plant and machinery	9,800

Factory power (prime cost)	5,254
Factory salaries	17,295
Factory expenses:	
Rent and Business rates	8,240
Lighting and heating	1,959

given in Chapter 19, the last chapter in this book. Here we are simply practising the preparation of Final Accounts for a sole trader, and in order not to neglect those who are involved in manufacturing, the first exercise shows a Trial Balance of a manufacturing business. Do not be dismayed by the look of this exercise. It is simple enough, because it shows the Trial Balance of the business at the end of the year. The rules for preparing a set of Final Accounts are as follows:

- The starting point is the Trial Balance of the books at close of business on the last day of the financial year. If you are using a specialist system like the Simplex system it will be the figures in the summaries collected together at the end of the year.
- You then prepare a Manufacturing Account if your business is engaged in manufacturing. If not you start with the Trading Account.
- You then prepare the Trading Account, but some businesses do not trade, they are fee-earning, and in that case you will not have a Trading Account. The Trading Account gives us the gross profit (see Chapter 4).
- You then prepare a Profit and Loss Account, starting with the gross profit. If you are a non-trading business all the fees earned will be

14

recorded in the Profit and Loss Account. Either way the result is the net profit of the business (see Chapter 5).

• Finally the net profit is carried into the Capital Account, and any drawings are also carried to the Capital Account where they reduce the profits available (because they have already been drawn). To clarify this procedure a simple example is given below.

Example 2

M. Thomas has capital at the start of the year of £6,785.00 and makes a profit in the year of £16,968.50. Of this he has already drawn out £650 a month for 12 months and has also taken home goods for personal use valued at £238.50. Show the Capital Account, the closing balance on the Profit and Loss Account and the Drawings Account after the preparation of the Final Accounts at the end of the year, 31 December 19X9.

Profit and Loss A/c (final profit only) 31 December 19X9   L194

19X9	£	19X9	£
31 Dec. Transfer to		31 Dec. Balance (net	
Capital A/c	16,968.50	profit) b/d	16,968.50

Drawings A/c (M. Thomas)   L15

19X9	£	19X9	£
Jan.-Dec. Sundry entries		31 Dec. Transfer to	
to a total of	7,800.00	capital A/c	8,038.50
Jan.-Dec. Goods	238.50		
	£8,038.50		£8,038.50

Capital A/c (M. Thomas)   L1

19X9		£	19X9		£
31 Dec. Drawings		8,038.50	1 Jan. Balance b/d		6,785.00
31 Dec. Balance	c/d	15,715.00	31 Dec. Net profit		
			transferred		16,968.50
		£23,753.50			£23,753.50
			19X9		£
			1 Jan. Balance b/d		15,715.00

Notes:

- First the profits are transferred to the Capital Account. The business now owes M. Thomas not only his original capital but also the profits earned.
- Then the drawings are transferred in, on the debit side because Thomas has already received them (debit the receiver). As a result we can see that the total funds now invested in the business by the proprietor are £15,715.00.

Exercises on the Final Accounts of a sole trader

1. Frank Dearden is in business as a manufacturer. On the last day of the financial year, 31 December 19X9, his Trial Balance is as follows:

	£	£
Stocks at 1 January		
Raw materials	9,560	
Work-in-progress	1,280	
Finished goods	13,925	
Purchases of raw materials	28,565	
Sales of finished goods		184,726
Factory Wages (prime cost)	34,768	
Power (prime cost)	1,295	
Factory overheads	48,954	
Office expenses	27,246	
Rent, insurance, etc.	5,980	
Commission received		18,256
Furniture and fittings	14,250	
Motor vehicles	16,750	
Debtors	3,248	
Creditors		4,921
Cash at bank	11,855	
Cash in hand	247	
Capital at start of year		16,250
Drawings	9,830	
Loan from bank		3,600
	£227,753	£227,753

14

Closing stocks at 31 December were found to be: raw materials £11,750; work-in-progress £3,960; finished goods £19,890. Prepare a full set of Final Accounts.

2. Mark Farmer is a professional person who does not manufacture or trade and who therefore starts his Final Accounts with what would be the Profit and Loss Account, but by choice he calls it a Revenue Account, since it contains details of his income and expenses for the year. The traditional name for incomes and expenditures is revenues. Here is his Trial Balance. Draw up his Revenue Account and Balance Sheet, taking account of the two adjustments shown below the Trial Balance. Remember that any adjustment not only adjusts the figures in the Revenue Account but also appears as a balance on the Balance Sheet, either as a liability (accrued expenses) or as an asset (payments in advance).

	Dr. £	Cr. £
Capital (at 1 January 19XX)		90,000
Drawings	24,000	
Premises	117,120	
Furniture, etc.	7,000	
Motor vehicles	48,000	
Fees received		134,625
Commission received		37,965
Rent from sub-tenant		2,350
Light and heat	1,865	
Cleaning	3,250	
Loans made to clients (current asset)	72,500	
Other debtors	4,850	
Creditors		1,264
Office expenses	3,266	
Office salaries	40,840	
Mortgage on premises		71,000
Advertising materials	3,750	
Computers, etc	2,318	
Cash in hand	240	
Cash at bank	8,205	
	£337,204	£337,204

Adjustments (at 31 December 19XX)

- An electricity bill for £240 is due and unpaid.
- Advertising materials (brochures) to the value of £650 are in stock and will be used up next year.

Answers

1. Books of Frank Dearden: prime costs, £62,438; cost of manufactured goods, £108,712; gross profit, £81,979; net profit, £67,009; capital at close of year, £73,429; Balance Sheet totals £81,950.
2. Books of Mark Farmer: net profit, £122,379; capital at close of year, £188,379; Balance Sheet totals £260,883.

Checklist

---

1. The last act of the book-keeper at the end of the financial year is to work out the Final Accounts of the business, and send them in to the Inland Revenue.
2. Some traders are allowed to prepare their accounts on a 'receipts and payments' basis. Others prepare their accounts on an 'accruals' basis, taking any adjustments at the end of the year into account.
3. If a business is a manufacturing business the first stage of the Final Accounts is a Manufacturing Account. This usually finds the Cost of Manufactured Goods, but if preferred it can also be used to find a manufacturing profit.
4. The 'Cost of Manufactured Goods' is made up of two parts, the prime costs and the overheads.
5. All manufacturers, and all traders, need a Trading Account in which the gross profit is discovered.
6. The gross profit is then carried into the Profit and Loss Account, where the net profit is found. Professional people, who do not trade, start their Final Accounts with the Profit and Loss Account which they often call the 'Revenue Account'.
7. The final part of a set of Final Accounts is the Balance Sheet, which is a snapshot of the affairs of the business at a given moment in time – the last second of the last hour of the last day of the financial year.
8. A copy of your Final Accounts should be submitted to the Inland Revenue, and in due course, perhaps after the odd enquiry about certain points, a letter agreeing your profit figures will be sent to you. Later, when you complete your annual Tax Return form, an assessment for tax will be levied on you, payable in two halves on 1 January and 1 July in the following year. Put your tax money away in a special Deposit Account at the bank, so you are able to meet your obligations.

14

15 Keeping the books of a partnership

What is a partnership? □ Partnership deed □ What are the differences between sole trader and partnership accounts? □ Appropriation Account □ Other partnership accounts

What is a partnership?

A partnership is legally defined as a relationship between persons carrying on a business together with a view to earning profits. It is a very ancient form of business arrangement and the legal rules surrounding it grew up over centuries until being finally set down in the Partnership Act of 1890. Partnerships come into existence at will, that is to say because the partners wish to work together, and may be dissolved at will. This means that one partner can give notice to the other partner, and to anybody else likely to be affected (such as suppliers and customers) that he/she no longer wishes to be associated with the other. An oral arrangement (one made by word of mouth) is sufficient to form a partnership, but to prove that it came into existence you need a witness.

Partnership deed

A written agreement is better, both because it is easier to establish that a partnership does exist, but also because in setting down in writing what is agreed between the partners a number of future difficulties may be aired and resolved. For example, it may be agreed that A, who is a good salesman, shall handle that side of the business, while B, who is good at accounts, and putting up most of the money, shall sign cheques. Best of all, if a solicitor is asked to draw up a formal partnership deed, the relationship will be more carefully investigated to cover many points that should be agreed between those who set up in business together. For example:

- The partners' shares of profits, and losses.
- The amounts of capital to be contributed.
- The areas of responsibility in the work to be done.

- Whether any partner is to have a salary, or interest on the capital subscribed.
- How much drawings should be allowed. Drawings are sums of money taken out in expectation of profits made. A partner has to live in the course of the year while the business is established, and is making its profits, and as the final profit figure is not arrived at until the end of the year some money must be released beforehand. If in fact the business is not making profits the sums withdrawn will be deducted from the capital subscribed, and the partners are said to be 'living on their capital'.

There are many more points. Solicitors will tell you that it is not unknown for partners who agreed to work together one week, to be at daggers drawn within a month or two, so the fullest airing beforehand of the likely problem areas forewarns the partners that a bit of give and take is essential if a partnership is to prosper.

What are the differences between sole trader and partnership accounts?

For the vast majority of simple transactions there is no difference between the accounts of a sole trader and partnership accounts. Manufacturing, buying and selling, the payment of overheads and the employment of staff are exactly the same. The differences lie in the arrangements for capital, drawings and the sharing of profits. Here the important points are as follows.

Capital accounts

Instead of a single Capital Account, each partner has a Capital Account on which is recorded the amount of capital contributed. It is usual to keep this figure on the Capital Account unchanged, except at very rare intervals when some fundamental rearrangement of the partnership's affairs takes place (as, for example, when a new partner is admitted). Partnership Capital Accounts are therefore said to be 'fixed'. With a sole trader it is usual to transfer the profits made to the Capital Account at the end of the year, and the Capital Account of a sole trader is therefore liable to fluctuate. This is not allowed to happen in the case of partnerships. As with all Capital Accounts, the balances on the accounts will be credit balances because they record what the business owes back to the owners of the business. The owners are 'creditors' of the business who have given the capital contributed to the business (credit the giver).

15

Current Accounts

If the Capital Accounts are fixed, it is necessary to have an account to which the profits earned by the partnership can be transferred, in the appropriate shares as laid down in the partnership agreement. Each partner, therefore, has a second account called a Current Account which does fluctuate from year to year and receives the partner's share of the profits earned. The balance on a Current Account will usually be a credit balance, because the business owes the profits to the partner, but it is possible to have an overdrawn Current Account, with a debit balance. For example, if a partner draws out more in the year than the business earns in profits, the debit entries on the Current Account will be greater than the profits earned on the credit side and a debit balance will result. This is not transferred to the Capital Account except if the partnership is being wound up, when the partner's balance will be cleared to the Capital Account and he or she will be unable to withdraw the full amount originally subscribed.

Drawings Accounts

Each partner also has a Drawings Account in which the sums of money drawn out can be collected together over the year, and a clear record of all sums drawn made available. Cash may be drawn on a regular basis. A partner is not allowed to have 'wages' in the normal sense of that word, since a partner is entitled to a share of the profits as the reward for his or her efforts. The cash drawn, as already explained, is 'in expectation of profits made'. Other forms of 'drawings' are sums paid by the partnership for the benefit of a partner; for example tax moneys due, pension contributions to private pension schemes, goods taken for own consumption and other items taken for personal use (for example, a partner might buy a redundant typewriter for his daughter to practise her typing).

These various accounts are set out later in this chapter but first we must mention one further account which is used to bring all these partnership accounts into order, and share out the profits in whatever way has been agreed. It is called the Appropriation Account.

Appropriation Account

The term Appropriation Account is used both in partnerships and companies to designate an account which is used to divide up the profits made and appropriate (or allocate) them to the particular uses which the partners, or the directors of a company decide is the best. In the case of a partnership, the most common usages are as follows:

- It is quite common to reduce the value on the books of any intangible asset, of which goodwill is the chief example. Goodwill is a sum of money paid to the previous owner of a business for the good opinion he or she has established in the minds of people in the locality – which it is believed will bring in profits to the business in years to come. One judge said, 'Goodwill is a payment for the probability that an old customer will return to the old place for further supplies at some time in the future'. If we pay out £1,000 for a piece of machinery we get an asset, a machine, in exchange for the money. When we pay out £1,000 for goodwill we get an asset 'goodwill' for our money, but it is a pretty intangible asset; it consists of a good opinion in the minds of the people in the locality. It is usual to write off this intangible asset out of profits in the first few years – say at 25 per cent a year.
- It is sometimes agreed that a junior partner shall have a salary, to ensure that a certain basic income is available to him or her. Since partners cannot really have wages or salaries, the sum agreed is regarded as a first charge against the profits, and is appropriated to the partner concerned as the first claim on the profits, after arrangements for goodwill have been completed.
- It is sometimes agreed that partners shall have interest on capital. Usually this is done where one party has contributed much more capital than the others. This interest on capital is treated as a prior charge on the profits before the residue of the profit is shared.
- Finally, the residue of the profit is shared between the partners in whatever manner is agreed.

The Appropriation Account is best illustrated by an example.

Example

Paul and Jean are in partnership, sharing profits ⅔ to Paul and ⅓ to Jean. The partnership agreement provides as follows:

- Paul to contribute capital of £20,000 and Jean £5,000.
- Interest on capital to be allowed at 8 per cent, to both partners.
- Jean, the younger partner, is to have a basic salary of £5,000 as a first claim on the profits. She is a fashion designer, whose designs the business is to market.

- They are to pay £2,500 for goodwill to the vendor of the business they are taking over. This intangible asset will be written off in equal instalments over the first five years of the business.

In the first year the profits are £39,285. Drawings in the year were: Paul £19,500 and Jean £12,600.

The Appropriation Account for this partnership is shown below, with some explanatory notes. The other accounts are shown in the next section.

Appropriation Account
for year ending 31 December 19X9

19X9		£	19X9	£
Goodwill		500.00	Profits (from P&L A/c)	39,285.00
Salary (Jean)		5,000.00		
Interest on capital				
Paul	£1,600.00			
Jean	£ 400.00			
		2,000.00		
Share of residue of profit				
Paul	£21,190.00			
Jean	£10,595.00			
		31,785.00		
		£39,285.00		£39,285.00

Notes

- The net profit comes in from the Profit and Loss Account as a credit entry (it is what the business owes to the partners for the year's profitable activities).
- The goodwill instalment is then written off – bringing the Goodwill Account down to a balance of £2,000 only. This is a capital transaction, not revenue expenditure, so it cannot be claimed as a reduction from the profits in the Profit and Loss Account. It is an appropriation of profit.
- Jean is then given her salary. It is taken to her Current Account, on the credit side.
- Each of the partners is then given the interest on capital. Again this is taken to their Current Accounts.
- Finally, the residue of the profit is shared in the agreed ratio, and taken to Paul and Jean's Current Accounts. This leaves the Appropriation Account clear; all the profits have been given away or used for the purpose the partners intended.
- For the rest of the accounts see the next section.

Other partnership accounts

In Partnership Accounts each partner has three accounts, a Capital Account, a Drawings Account and a Current Account. If we now look at these accounts, continuing the example given above, we find that the accounts of Paul and Jean are as shown below. Each set has some notes attached.

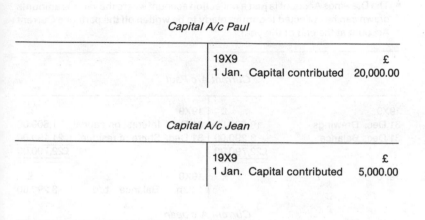

Capital A/c Paul

				19X9		£
				1 Jan.	Capital contributed	20,000.00

Capital A/c Jean

				19X9		£
				1 Jan.	Capital contributed	5,000.00

Notes

- The accounts are opened on the day the business starts, in order to record the original capital contributions.
- As these are fixed Capital Accounts, no further entries will be made except if some fundamental rearrangement of the partnership takes place (perhaps on the admission of a new partner). The accounts therefore remain as shown year after year, and appear on the Balance Sheet as shown later in this section.

Drawings A/c Jean

19X9		£	19X9		£
31 Jan.	Bank	1,000.00	31 Dec.	Transfer to current A/c	12,600.00
28 Feb.	Bank	1,000.00			
	etc., etc., each month				
14 Dec.	Computer A/c	600.00			
31 Dec.	Bank	1,000.00			
		£12,600.00			£12,600.00

15

Notes

- Only one Drawings Account has been shown – the other would be similar.
- The younger partner Jean draws £1,000 a month for living expenses and also took over a computer which was surplus to requirements, making the total drawn £12,600. These are all debit entries because the partner has received the cash, etc.
- This total drawings is carried to Jean's Current Account, leaving the Drawings Account clear to start a new year.
- The Drawings Account is just a collection account where the various amounts drawn can be collected together, ready to be written off the partner's Current Account at the end of the year.

Current A/c Paul

19X9		£	19X9		£
31 Dec.	Drawings	19,500.00	31 Dec.	Interest on capital	1,600.00
31 Dec.	Balance	3,290.00	31 Dec.	Share of residue	21,190.00
		£22,790.00			£22,790.00
19X0		£	19X0		£
			1 Jan.	Balance b/d	3,290.00

Current A/c Jean

19X9		£	19X9		£
31 Dec.	Drawings	12,600.00	31 Dec.	Salary	5,000.00
31 Dec.	Balance	3,395.00	31 Dec.	Interest on capital	400.00
			31 Dec.	Share of residue	10,595.00
		£15,995.00			£15,995.00
			19X0		£
			1 Jan.	Balance b/d	3,395.00

Notes

- It is the Current Account in partnerships that fluctuates with the earning of profits and their withdrawal by the partners.
- All the items due to the partners appear on the credit side, because the money is owed to the partner by the business.
- Against these profits earned, the drawings are debit entries because the partner has received the money (or goods for personal use). The balance is still owing to the partners and will be carried over to the next financial year.
- Imagine that Jean had drawn the same as Paul, £19,500.00. This would have meant she had overdrawn on her Current Account, and instead of a credit balance there would have been a debit balance: she would have been a debtor of the business for the excess amount drawn.

Goodwill A/c

19X9		£	19X9		£
1 Jan.	Goodwill acquired	2,500.00	31 Dec.	Appropriation A/c	500.00
			31 Dec.	Balance c/d	2,000.00
		£2,500.00			£2,500.00
19X9		£			
1 Jan.	Balance b/d	2,000.00			

Notes

- The asset 'Goodwill' is an intangible asset – there is not much to show for it really.
- If we decide to write it off, we must do so out of profits – it is not deductible as a revenue expense in the Profit and Loss Account.
- The result here is that the asset, goodwill, is reduced in value to £2,000.00.
- Accountants talk about the *paradox of goodwill*. When we take over a business with goodwill, we have on our books an asset at a high valuation. The truth is that at that time the public bears us no goodwill at all, for they do not even know that we exist! The goodwill they bear is to the previous owner. As the years pass we write off the intangible asset by a series of appropriations of profit. The goodwill gradually reduces until it is written off completely. At the same time, the public have now learned to know us; they realise our goods or services are reliable and they now bear us some goodwill. This is the 'paradox' of goodwill; it is valued at a high figure on the books when it is worthless, and at nothing on the books when it is quite valuable.

If you are in business as a partnership, or if you are thinking of setting up in business with a partner, try the following exercises. The first is an exercise to get you used to Appropriation Accounts. The second is a full set of Final Accounts.

Special note about the Balance Sheets of partnerships

The following special features of a partnership Balance Sheet should be noted:

- As there are two fixed (unvarying) Capital Accounts these appear on the liabilities side, simply added together.
- The partners' Current Accounts would normally have credit balances (meaning that the business owes the partners some undrawn profits at the end of the year). These would appear on the liabilities side, and once again they would be added together to show the total owed to the partners. However, it is possible for one, or both, of the partners to be

15

overdrawn on their Current Accounts, i.e. they have drawn out more money as drawings than they earned as their shares of the profits. In that case the balance will be a debit balance, and must be carried over to the assets side. It is probably best to treat this as an unusual asset, neither 'fixed' nor 'current' and it would therefore appear below the 'fixed assets' and above the 'current assets'.

Today, because the Enterprise Allowance is available to both husbands and wives if both are genuinely unemployed and seeking to become self-employed, there are a great many people setting up 'husband and wife' partnerships. There is a specimen set of partnership accounts available free of charge from George Vyner Ltd., Holmfirth, Huddersfield, HD7 2TA. The Balance Sheet of this specimen set is shown below as Fig. 15.1.

BALANCE SHEET of a PARTNERSHIP

LAST YEAR	Liabilities		THIS YEAR	LAST YEAR	Assets		THIS YEAR
	CAPITAL ACCOUNT				FIXED ASSETS		
3000 00	(i) MR. A.	3000 00		1250 00	Goodwill	1000 00	
18000 00	(ii) MR. B.	18000 00	21000 00	25000 00	Premises	25000 00	
	CURRENT ACCOUNT			2400 00	Fittings	2000 00	
186 00	(i) MR. A.	602 86		2500 00	Plant & Machinery	2000 00	
– –	(ii) MR. B.	1053 72	1656 58	1350 00	Motor Vehicles	1080 00	31080 00
21186 00	LONG TERM LIABILITIES			32500 00	CURRENT ASSETS		
				4200 00	Stock	4500 00	
15800 00	MORTGAGE		15000 00	2950 00	Debtors	2750 00	
	CURRENT LIABILITIES			3500 00	Cast at Bank	3850 00	
6763 00	Sundry creditors	4736 02		185 00	Cash in Hand	225 00	
66 00	Accrued charges	54 00	4790 02	480 00	Payments in Advance	41 60	11366 60
43815 00		TOTAL	42446 60	43815 00		TOTAL	42446 60

Fig. 15.1 The Balance Sheet of a partnership

Exercise on Partnership Accounts

1. Brighton and Hove go into partnership on 1 January 19X9 with capitals of £25,000 and £5,000, respectively. Their partnership agreement provides

   - that Hove will have a salary of £4,000 per annum as a first call upon the partnership profits
   - that both partners will get interest at 8% on capital
   - that any profit after these prior claims have been paid will be shared in the ratio 3/5 : 2/5 with Brighton taking the larger share.

   Net profit for the first year was £48,250. It was agreed on the last day of the year that the goodwill of £9,000 paid to the previous owner of their business, and standing at that figure on the

Goodwill Account, should be written off the profits to the extent of 50 per cent, before any other appropriations of profit were made. Draw up the Appropriation Account on that date.

2. Kadar and Sharif conduct a trading business in partnership on the following terms:

- interest is to be allowed on partners' Capital Accounts at 8 per cent per annum
- Sharif is to be credited with a partnership salary of £6,000 per annum
- the balance of profit in any year is to be shared by the partners in the ratio ¾ to Kadar, ¼ to Sharif.

After preparing their Trading and Profit and Loss Accounts for the year ended 31 March 19X9, but before making any provision for interest on capital or for partnership salary, the following balances remained on the books:

	Dr. £	Cr. £
Capital Accounts:		
Kadar (as on 1 April previous year)		22,000
Sharif (as on 1 April previous year)		3,000
Current Accounts:		
Kadar (as on 1 April previous year)		2,500
Sharif (as on 1 April previous year)	2,000	
Drawings Accounts:		
Kadar	13,700	
Sharif	11,000	
Profit and Loss Account – net profit for year		28,652
Stock at end of year	4,250	
Goodwill Account	2,000	
Plant and machinery	14,000	
Office equipment	3,600	
Fixtures and fittings	4,000	
Hire purchase loans		2,950
Trade debtors and creditors	2,942	1,823
Loan from Helpful Bank plc		3,000
Rent owing		200
Insurance unexpired at 31 March (current asset)	258	
Cash at bank, Current Account	6,375	
	£ 64,125	64,125

15

It is agreed by the partners to reduce the book value of goodwill by writing off £500 at 31 March, 19X9 (to be charged to the Appropriation Section of the Profit and Loss Account).

You are asked to prepare the Appropriation Section of the firm's Profit and Loss Account and the partners' Current Accounts for the year ended 31 March, 19X9, together with the Balance Sheet on that date.

Answers

1. Books of Brighton and Hove. Shares of residue: Brighton, £22,410; Hove, £14,940.
2. Books of Kadar and Sharif. Shares of residue: Kadar, £15,114; Sharif, £5,038. Current Account balances: Kadar, £5,674 credit; Sharif, £1,722 debit. Balance Sheet totals £38,647.

Checklist

1. Partnership is a relationship that exists between persons carrying on a business together with a view to earning profits.
2. It is desirable to enter into a written agreement about the terms of the partnership, and if this is drawn up by a solicitor as a formal agreement it is called a partnership deed.
3. As far as accounting goes the ordinary business transactions are the same as for a sole trader. The differences arise in preparing the Final Accounts of the partnership.
4. Each partner has a Capital Account to which the capital he or she subscribes is credited at the start of the business. This account is fixed at the original figure, except if some fundamental rearrangement of the partnership takes place (for example the admission of a new partner).
5. Each partner also has a Current Account, which can vary as profits are credited to it and drawings are debited to it. Each partner also has a Drawings Account where the drawings for the year are collected together before being written off the Current Account at the end of the year.
6. To allocate the profits at the end of the year in the manner agreed between the partners the net profit is transferred to an Appropriation Account (sometimes called the Appropriation Section of the Profit and Loss Account) where it is appropriated to the partners in the agreed way.
7. The Balance Sheet of a partnership is similar to the Balance Sheet of a sole trader, except that there will be two Capital Accounts added together, showing the original capitals contributed, and there will be two Current Accounts, usually shown as liabilities (the business owes the partners any profits not as yet drawn). If a partner should be overdrawn on his or her Current Account the debit balance will appear on the assets side of the Balance Sheet as an asset which is neither fixed nor current.

15

16 The Final Accounts of a company

Nature of a company □ Reasons for choosing the company format □ Setting up as a limited company □ The Final Accounts of limited companies □ The Balance Sheet of a Limited Company □ Checklist

Nature of a company

In this book we are covering accounting for small businesses and it is a fact that thousands of companies are very small and most start life as '£2 companies', which means they have a capital of only £2. A company is an organization with a separate legal status from the people who form it. Two or more people may form a company by subscribing their names to a Memorandum of Association (which records the fact that they wish to join together in a company for some lawful purpose). When this and other formalities associated with the registration procedure have been complied with, the company will be *incorporated* ('given a body') and will then become a legal 'person' able to do all the things an ordinary person can do, except the very personal ones. It can own property, employ workers, buy plant, machinery and motor vehicles, have a bank account, and become a debtor and a creditor. It cannot fall in love, marry, have children, or die, for these are personal acts.

Some companies are so large, have such prestigious premises and own such enormous amounts of property that there is a popular belief that all companies are rich, powerful, stable, reliable, etc. It is also believed that company directors are always honest, upright and respectable. Many of them are of course, but one cannot rely on it. For example, if Mr. A, a penniless, ill-educated, lazy individual sets up as Builders' Suppliers (Wilmot) Ltd, with a total capital of £2, he may call himself a company director, but will it turn him into a prosperous, skilful, energetic, go-getter overnight? Manifestly it will not! Always be wary of companies, and expect the worst from them. More of this later.

Reasons for choosing the company format

The sole reason for the development of the company format is that those who become members of the company, and own it by having shares in it, have limited liability. They can lose their money and be responsible for the debts of the business only to the extent of the money they have invested in the company. If it is a £2 company it means that there is only £2 which can be recovered by any creditor of the company. This means that those who supply companies must be very wary of providing them with large orders until they have a proven track record of payment. If you do supply them and payment is not forthcoming, you cannot sue the person who received the goods or the directors personally for the price of those goods. Your action lies against the company, and even if the company is insolvent but the directors display every appearance of prosperity, you cannot sue them for your money.

An interesting sidelight on limited companies is that by law the name of the company must end in 'limited' or the Welsh equivalent, unless it is a public limited company whose shares may be quoted on the Stock Exchange. Such a company's name must end in the wording 'Public Limited Company' usually abbreviated to PLC, or the Welsh equivalent. These words, Ltd, or PLC, are meant by Parliament to act as a warning that the companies concerned have limited liability and should not be supplied with goods on credit unless the supplier is prepared to take the risk or has confidence in the company's viability and ability to pay on the due date. Remember this every time you receive an order from a limited liability company and ask yourself whether you are absolutely confident that the company will honour its debts in due course.

If you decide to set up as a company yourself, you will probably do so in order to have limited liability so that your home, personal belongings, etc., cannot be taken to pay off the debts of the business. You will not expect then to receive large orders from suppliers on credit, for they will naturally be unwilling to supply. You should therefore be prepared to pay cash for supplies until such time as the company has established a track record for prompt payment. Of course you could give a personal guarantee, but that would lose you the privilege of limited liability which is the reason for taking up company status in the first place.

One great advantage of company status is that a company cannot die. The company has a separate status from the founder members, and from the directors and shareholders. If they die the company still continues, and there is no need for it to go out of existence. The only way a company can cease to exist is for it to go through a process called *liquidation*. We may go into *voluntary* liquidation, in which the members decide to discontinue the company, or *compulsory* liquidation, where the Court orders the company to be wound up. 'Liquidation' in acccountancy means that all the assets are converted to the liquid asset, cash. The cash is then paid in a correct order of priority to those entitled to claim it. The list starts with

16

those with a right to repayment prior to other creditors – usually the Inland Revenue, other official bodies and the secured creditors (who have a debenture or a mortgage on the property). Then the unsecured creditors may claim, and finally the shareholders may get their money back, together with any profits ploughed into the business over the years.

Setting up as a limited company

It is simple enough to promote a company, but the simplest way of all is to buy one 'off the shelf' from a local company registration agent. They cost about £130. You will find local firms listed under 'company registration agents' in the Yellow Pages. If in difficulty, a phone call to Natcom Services, 28 Kings Parade, Soham, Ely, Cambridgeshire CB7 5AR (telephone: 0353 722460) will bring you all the help you need. Alternatively, your accountant (and if you set up in business as a company it is advisable to have one) will make the arrangements for you, at a reasonable fee. Once a company is set up it is possible to change the name, ownership, names of the directors and the company secretary by a simple procedure. Most registration agents keep a variety of companies 'on the shelf' and if you want one to manufacture, or to engage in retail trade, they will have one or two for you to choose from.

The 'objects' clause

The Registrar of Companies only approves companies to operate in a particular field, as laid down in the objects clause. Thus, if you wish to operate road haulage vehicles and you started to trade on the sugar market, you would be outside your objects clause, and outside the law (*ultra vires*). If you buy a company off the shelf and its objects clause is not quite appropriate to your business, you must register a change in the company's objects before you start engaging in any activities.

Routine accounting for companies

Routine accounting for companies is exactly the same as that for sole traders and partnerships. However, as it is a requirement of the Companies Act 1985 that all companies must appoint auditors who are members of one of the bodies of accountants recognized as professionally qualified (either chartered or certified), it is important to keep your records in good order, and preserve all documents for inspection as proof of the various purchases, sales, expenses incurred, etc. Never be careless about documents in any business, but especially so in the case of companies, because your auditors have to sign that they believe the books to be a true record of your activities, and your final accounts to give a 'true and fair view' of the affairs of the business. Any reputable local firm of accountants will be happy to take you on their books and act as your auditors. See the *Yellow Pages* for a suitable firm in your locality.

The Final Accounts of limited companies

The chief difference between the accounts of sole traders and partnerships and those of limited companies is that, being a separate legal entity from the members of the company, the profits earned belong in the first place to the company. How much of the profits earned is actually distributed to the shareholders depends upon the recommendation of the directors at the Annual General Meeting. They will normally recommend a reasonable dividend, but any undistributed profit will remain as a balance on the accounts and is called a '*revenue reserve*'. Revenue reserves *do* belong to the ordinary shareholders, who can expect to receive them at some future time, but the reserves are often used to expand the business. In that case, the only way the shareholders may eventually receive them is in the form of bonus shares, when the company passes a resolution to recognize that the revenue reserves have been turned into fixed capital (by being spent on extra premises, machinery, etc). It then decides to issue shares to recognize that these profits have now been turned into capital assets.

It is possible for a business to have another kind of reserve called a '*capital reserve*', arising from profits which were not earned in the normal way as laid down in the objects clause, but in some other way. For example, if a company's premises were valued on the books at the purchase price of £25,000 (many years ago) it might be deemed desirable to raise the book value to the present value, say £100,000. Increasing the assets by £75,000 means we must increase the liabilities side of the Balance Sheet by £75,000 and this would be a capital profit (not a revenue profit). The figure would be entered on the credit side of an account, 'Appreciation of Premises A/c' to show the extent by which the premises had risen in value and contributed to the capital value of the business. Capital reserves may not be distributed to the shareholders as a dividend, but they may be capitalized and distributed as bonus shares to existing shareholders.

As with partnerships, the net profit of a company is transferred to an Appropriation Account (or an Appropriation Section of the Profit and Loss Account). The profits are then distributed or used in the ways recommended by the directors and approved by the shareholders at the Annual General Meeting. We can follow what happens most easily if we take a simple example.

16

Example 1

Triumvirate Ltd, made profits in the year 19X8 of £183,267. At 1 January 19X9 the balance on the Appropriation Account of undistributed profit from 1 January the previous year was £27,301. The directors recommended as follows:

- that a reserve of £60,000 be set aside for Corporation Tax
- that £25,000 be put in Plant Replacement Reserve and £25,000 in Computer Renewals Reserve
- that a dividend of 20% be paid on the Preference Shares of £50,000, and a dividend of 32% on the Ordinary Shares of £100,000
- £40,000 will be placed in General Reserve A/c and any balance left, in the Appropriation A/c.

The Appropriation A/c of Triumvirate Ltd would look as follows. One of the reserve accounts has been shown as well, so that the reader can see how these accounts would look after these transfers have been made. A few imaginary figures have been inserted to make the account realistic.

Appropriation Account: Triumvirate Ltd

19X8		£	19X8		£
31 Dec.	Corporation Tax Reserve	60,000	1 Jan.	Balance	27,301
	Plant Replacement Reserve	25,000	31 Dec.	Net Profit	183,267
	Computer Renewals Reserve	25,000			210,568
	General Reserve	40,000			
	Preference Share Dividend	10,000			
	Ordinary Share Dividend	32,000			
		192,000			
	Balance c/d	18,568			
		£210,568			£210,568
			19X9		£
			1 Jan.	Balance b/d	18,568

Fig. 16.1 The Appropriation Account of a limited company

Corporation Tax Reserve A/c

19X9	£	19X9	£
3 Jan. Inland Revenue	48,421	1 Jan. Balance b/d	67,500
31 Dec. Balance c/d	79,079	1 Jan. Appropriation A/c	60,000
	£127,500		£127,500
		19X9	£
		1 Jan. Balance b/d	79,079

Fig. 16.2 A typical nominal account to hold reserves of profits

Notes

- Accounts like this receive sums from the Appropriation Account on the liabilities side. The reason for this is that all the balances on these accounts really belong to the ordinary shareholders (because they are profits that have not been distributed). The shareholders cannot have them because the directors have decided that they shall be used for other purposes – in this case, to pay the Corporation Tax.
- Eventually, as these accounts are used for the purpose intended, they will be debited as the profits in reserve are paid away to the Inland Revenue or the preference shareholders, or to buy new plant, computers, etc.

The Balance Sheet of a Limited Company

The Balance Sheet of a limited company is similar in many ways to other Balance Sheets in that it has the assets set against the liabilities and the two sides should balance. However, limited companies are controlled by the Companies Act 1985, which sets out in Schedule 4 two alternative presentations of the Balance Sheet which companies are to use. One of these presentations is in continuous style, which means it is a Balance Sheet in vertical style. The other is in horizontal style, with the assets first (i.e. on the left-hand side) and the liabilities second (i.e. on the right). We therefore have the Balance Sheet in the correct European style in the way shown in Fig. 18.3(b) (*see* p. 223). This is the same style as the Trial Balance, with assets on the left and liabilities on the right.

This is not the place to go into too detailed an account of all the special features of limited company accounts because most small businesses are only private limited companies, and they rarely have more than £1,000 capital. However, the chief features of a company Balance Sheet are listed and explained below, and then illustrated in Fig. 16.3.

16

Balance Sheet of Triumvirate Ltd, as at 31 December 19X8

Assets	£	£	Liabilities				
Fixed Assets							
Intangibles			*Preference Shareholders'*			*Authorized*	*Issued*
– Patent Rights		12,000	*Interest in the Co.*			50,000	50,000
Tangibles			Preference shares of £1 fully paid				
– Land and Buildings	140,000						
Plant and Machinery	44,500		*Ordinary Shareholders' Interest*			*Authorized*	*& issued*
Fixtures and Fittings	19,742	204,242	*in the Co.*			100,000	
			Ordinary Shares of £1 fully paid				
Current Assets			Plant Replacement				
Stock	49,460		Reserve	17,000			
Debtors	5,984		+ additions	25,000	42,000		
Investments	132,186		Computer Renewal Reserve (new)		25,000		
Cash at bank	27,250		General Reserve	32,000			
Cash in hand	240	215,120	+ additions	40,000	72,000		
			Balance on Appropriation A/c		18,568		
			Ordinary Shareholders' interest			257,568	
			Corporation Tax Reserve			79,079	
			Current Liabilities				
			Creditors		2,715		
			Preference Dividend due		10,000		
			Ordinary Dividend due		32,000	44,715	
		£431,362				£431,362	

Fig. 16.3 The Balance Sheet of a company

The assets side of the Balance Sheet

The divisions of fixed assets

Fixed assets are divided into three classes: intangible assets, tangible assets and investments.

- *Intangible assets* are assets which cannot be touched – there is nothing real about them. We have already discussed 'Goodwill' as an intangible asset. Other intangible assets are trade marks, patents, licences, etc.
- *Tangible assets* are the real assets we are familiar with – buildings, cars, etc.
- *Investments* are divided into two classes, one of which is regarded as a fixed asset. These are investments in subsidiary companies (companies where we have 51 per cent of the voting shares) and related companies (where we have a substantial, but not a controlling, interest). All such shares could be sold off, but if we did sell them we should lose control of the subsidiary or our influence with the related company, and it is therefore better to regard them as fixed assets. They used to be called *trade investments*, since they were in companies in the same trade as ourselves.

Current assets

These are the usual current assets, stocks, debtors, etc., but we must add *investments*. This is the second class of investments, which are not kept for the purposes of control, but as a way of holding spare cash so that it earns interest. If we have profits put away in Plant Replacement Reserves or the General Reserve Account it is unwise to leave the money represented by these profits loose in the cash system. If we invest the surplus funds either on the money market or in stocks and shares they will earn some income for the future. Your banker will be happy to arrange this for you, e.g. you might put it on the money market for 28 days and then the bank will come back to you and say 'Well – shall we keep it on the money market, or do you want it back in your Current Account to buy new machinery?' It is a flexible arrangement which is useful both to you and to the bank.

16

The liabilities side of the Balance Sheet

The shareholders' interest in the company

The only unusual feature of the liabilities side of the Balance Sheet is to understand that the capital contributed by the ordinary shareholders originally, and all profits ploughed back into the business since it started, belong to the ordinary shareholders. If there are any preference shareholders they do not own any of the profits ploughed back, unless they own participating preference shares. You should now study Fig. 16.3.

Exercise on company Final Accounts

A limited company has an authorized capital of 200,000 Ordinary Shares of £1, of which 100,000 are issued and 50,000 9% Preference Shares of £1, of which 30,000 are issued. On March 31 19X9 it was found that the Net Profit was £93,420 for the year. There was also a balance on the Appropriation Account of £4,450 from 1 April the previous year. The directors resolved:

* to put £25,000 to a new General Reserve and £18,500 to a new Plant Replacement Reserve
* to reserve £25,000 for Corporation Tax
* to pay the 9% Preference Dividend
* to recommend a 20% dividend on the Ordinary shares.

Show the Appropriation Account and the Balance Sheet. In addition to the current liabilities resulting from the Appropriation Account there were £2,300 of debts to creditors outstanding. Fixed assets totalled £178,000 and current assets £52,170.

Answers

Balance on Appropriation Account £6,670; Balance Sheet totals £230,170; Ordinary Shareholders' Interest £150,170; Current Liabilities £25,000.

Checklist

1. A company is an incorporation, i.e. a legal entity which has been given its personality by force of law. The usual way to form a company is to register it under the Companies Acts 1985 and 1989.
2. In practice we buy companies 'off the shelf' from company registration agents, or ask them to register a specific company for us.
3. Limited companies must have names that end in the word 'Limited' or 'Public Limited Company' or the Welsh equivalent. This is a warning to suppliers that the directors of the company have limited liability.
4. Do not think that all companies are rich and powerful, many of them are only £100 companies – which means creditors can only expect to recover £100 between them in the event of liquidation (apart from what can be realized by selling the company's assets).
5. If you set up as a company do not expect to be given credit (unless you give a personal guarantee) until you have established a track record as a good payer.
6. The accounts of a company have to be audited by a professional firm of accountants, and they will usually supervise the preparation of accounts for you if you wish it.
7. The final accounts must conform to Schedule 4 of the Companies Act 1985. It is worthwhile buying a copy of the Act as one often needs to refer to it. Phone HMSO for a copy on 01 873 9090. You can pay for it on any credit card and it will be sent to you by post.

16

17 Aspects of controlling the small business

Importance of control □ The order position □ Controlling cash flow □ Controlling stock □ Credit control □ Credit control over purchases □ Staff performance □ Control over profitability □ Break-even analysis □ Budgetary control □ Checklist

The importance of control

Control is the process of supervising every aspect of a business so that it is able to continue, and grow. A business has to make enough profit to give a reasonable standard of living to the proprietor/s, but in the early years survival may be more important than enjoyment of current income, and the budding entrepreneur is more concerned with ploughing profits back into the business than in enjoying a high lifestyle.

When we think of control we do usually think of financial control, and businesses most often fail because they run out of cash. Cash is spent at every level, e.g. we can overspend by buying too many capital items or raw materials, too much stock, or paying too many people too much. Financial aspects enter into all areas of business activity and are of the greatest importance in a book which is concerned with accounting, but other aspects of control may be touched on, e.g. production, marketing, personnel and research are all areas which must be controlled and developed if any economic activity is to be successful.

Control may be exercised at any time, particularly in the small business, where the eagle eye of the proprietor can detect waste and bad practices as they occur, and economies as they become possible. At the same time, control operates best in a formal way, with a structure which gives each aspect of the business a known, established procedure, which is reviewed regularly. For example, pay increases should not be granted at the whim of the proprietor, or at the urgent request of an employee, but should be given as the result of a review procedure, either six-monthly or annually. The formal review designates a time when the pattern of wages will be considered. It delays impetuous demands for rises, is seen to be fair and to reward steady work rather than petulant behaviour, and measures the wages to be paid against the over-all prosperity of the firm or company.

Even the smallest firm or company should have regular meetings, with a proper agenda, and particular aspects of the work that are due for review featuring in the agenda in rotation. Thus the order book may be a feature of every agenda, but 'health and safety at work' may come up for annual review only. In this way proper plans can be drawn up to cover the item to be featured, reports of weaknesses revealed in recent months can be presented and considered and a blueprint laid down for the year ahead. Without the formality of regular meetings it is impossible to get all staff to know the true situation of the firm or company, problems are dealt with on an *ad hoc* basis, perhaps at the whim of the proprietor, and labour turnover may be higher than it otherwise would be as individuals become dissatisfied with sudden changes of procedure made in a haphazard way.

The order position

The order position is a vital component in the conduct of the business because it influences the rate of production, the stocks we feel we need to hold, the purchases we need to make, the cash flow position and staffing levels. We not only need to know what the current figures are but preferably comparable figures for a year ago – since orders fit into a pattern of activity which tends to repeat over the years. This is especially true in businesses like the fashion or toy trades, but some sort of pattern will be apparent in most.

Where a firm has only one product the important figures are the new orders (the current month's figures), the cumulative position since the start of the year, and the average per month since the start of the year. Where a firm has several products it will be necessary to analyse the figures within the product range, since the over-all figures might give a distorted view. For example, if 50 per cent of the orders were for one particular line it would be necessary to produce more of that line than the others. This is carried out more easily with a computerised system if there are numerous products. This analysis might be made in terms of units rather than cash. Figure 17.1 shows a typical order summary, in value terms, for a particular month.

The fulfilment of orders

The ability to fulfil orders should be reviewed whenever order book figures are looked at. Ideally, orders should be fulfilled at once, since this pleases customers, allows invoices to be despatched and cash flows inwards to

	Current Year			Previous Year		
	This month £	Total to date £	Average per month £	This month £	Total to date £	Average per month £
1. Balance C/Fwd at 1/5/19X9	23,500			14,800		
2. Orders Received	15,000	72,000	14,400	11,500	62,000	12,400
3. Orders Fulfilled	19,500			13,000		
4. Orders Cancelled	500			1,000		
5. Orders C/Fwd at 31/5/19X9 (1 + 2 – 3 – 4)	18,500			12,300		

Fig. 17.1 Order summary (in value terms) 31 May 19X9

Notes

- In the current month new orders were just above average for the year so far, which is satisfactory.
- Compared with the same figures last year, orders are up by 30% on the month ($\frac{3,500}{11,500} \times 100$) and 16% on the first five months of the year ($\frac{10,000}{62,000} \times 100$).
- Fewer orders have been cancelled than in the same month last year – which is encouraging.
- Our ability to fulfil orders has improved by 50%.

increase. Where a manufacturing or fabricating procedure is to take place, immediate fulfilment is impossible, but we should give estimated delivery dates and these should be checked up on by some sort of progress-chasing procedure. If the order book is growing and a backlog is developing, we may need a review of procedures. Is the factory too small? Are there bottlenecks in production or in the supplies of components from sub-contractors? Do we need new machinery, more staff, more skilled labour in some area? More seriously, do we need to increase the scale of our business, with all that means in terms of extension of premises, purchase of plant and machinery, capital finance, and so on?

Controlling cash flow

The most common cause of business failure is the problem of cash flow. It is no good having a full order book if the people placing the orders do not pay. Clear terms of payment when allowing customers to place orders are essential. Strict credit control procedures must be applied and prompt action taken where payment is not forthcoming. Where customers are paying in a proper manner but cash flow problems still arise, there can be a number of reasons for the difficulty. All these must be looked at so that we understand the problems.

Why is cash flow such a problem? The answer is because we must ourselves pay our way, and if we don't we can expect someone to whom we owe money to take steps to recover it, and put us out of business. If we are to avoid this and we face cash flow problems, we must borrow working capital from the bank. Since interest rates are high, this creams off a lot of our profit which goes into the bank's or finance company's pocket instead of our own.

To study our cash flow position we start with a cash flow forecast which estimates what receipts and payments will be in the months ahead. It is usual to have a rolling forecast over a period of three or six months. As the months pass we roll the forecast forward, filling in the figures for the months ahead as they become easier to forecast. For each month we have a 'Budget' column and an actual column. We fill in the actual column at the end of every month, and then compare the two figures. Any difference between the two is called a *variance*, which can be positive or negative. First, consider the cash flow budget given in Fig. 17.2 and the notes below it.

Analysing cash flow variances

Suppose the budgeted and actual cash flows in January are as shown in Fig. 17.3. By placing a sheet of paper alongside them we can make a note of the variances and suggest reasons for them in each case. (See p. 202.)

Cash flow smoothing is a procedure whereby we move cash payments which can be moved to a position in the payments year where we are flush with cash and can pay most easily. Payments such as insurance premiums, car/tax, loan repayments, etc. can be re-arranged to be made at a time when we know we will have funds. The purchase of capital items can be postponed to the most appropriate time for us (rather than when the supplier would like us to purchase the item).

17

	January Budget (£)	January Actual (£)	February Budget (£)	February Actual (£)	March Budget (£)	March Actual (£)
1. Cash at start (cash & bank)	2,340		12,100		-5,793	
Receipts						
2. Sales in cash	10,000		12,000		15,000	
3. Debts collected (1 mth old)	4,500		5,600		4,250	
4. " " (2 mths old)	2,750		2,250		2,800	
5. " " (3 " ")	1,650		2,750		2,250	
6. Other receipts	250		550		850	
7. Extra capital contributed	–				2,000	
8. Loans arranged	–				5,000	
9. Total receipts (2 to 8 inclusive)	19,150		23,150		32,150	
10. Total cash available (1 + 9)	21,490		35,250		26,357	
Payments						
11. Business stock	5,390		18,560		6,620	
12. Overheads & consumables	850		2,428		1,250	
13. Wages & salaries	2,425		2,955		3,500	
14. Capital items	125		16,500		–	
15. Payments out (11 to 14 inclusive)	8,790		40,443		11,370	
16. Drawings	600		600		600	
17. Total payments (15 + 16)	9,390		41,043		11,970	
18. Final cash balance (c/fwd) (10–17) or (17–10)	+12,100		-5,793 Must arrange loan (£5,000) and inject new capital (£2,000)		+14,387	

Fig. 17.2 Cash flow forecast

Notes

- The budgeted receipts for the month include the estimated sales, and the estimated receipts from debtors. It is believed, in this example, that 50% of the debtors will pay within one month and 25% each will pay in two and three months respectively. Thus in January we have £4,500 coming in from last month's debtors, and £2,250 coming in during February and March respectively.

- The total receipts are added to the estimated cash balance at the start of the month to give the total cash available.

- The external payments are made up of those to suppliers for stock, consumables and capital items, and those to employees for wages and salaries. The drawings of the proprietor have to be added to this figure to give the total payments for the month.

- When total payments are deducted from the total cash available we have the final cash balance envisaged at the end of the month.

- The actual figures can only be inserted at the end of the month, and when we do insert them we shall be able to see what the variance is between the estimate and the actual figures. This is discussed in Fig. 17.3 (see p. 202).

- As the February budget shows, the cash flow forecast can reveal that a shortage of cash will develop in the months ahead. There are all sorts of reasons why this should be so, e.g. a dealer in fireworks lays in huge stocks in August and September for sale in October and November. He/she may be short of cash in August and September, but in funds again by November. In this case re-stocking in February and the purchase of capital equipment is the cause of the shortage. Forewarned, arrangements are made to cover the deficit by a loan from the bank and the contribution of further capital from the proprietor's savings.

- Where possible, *cash flow smoothing* should be tried. This is explained in the main text.

17

	Budget (£)	Actual (£)	Variance (£)	Reason
1. Cash at start	2,340	4,250	+1,910	Good Xmas cash sales
Receipts				
2. Sales in cash	10,000	7,400	−2,600	Competition from Y Ltd
3. Debts collected	4,500	3,800	− 700	Economy depressed
4. " "	2,750	2,400	− 350	− no bad debts
5. " "	1,650	990	− 660	envisaged.
6. Other receipts	250	850	+ 600	Sale of spare van
7. Extra capital	–	–	–	
8. Loans arranged	–	–	–	
9. Total receipts	19,150	15,440	−3,710	
10. Total cash available	21,490	19,690	−1,800	
Payments				
11. Business stock	5,390	4,250	−1,140	Reduced orders in view of (2) above
12. Overheads etc.	850	1,150	300	Water rate increase
13. Wages & salaries	2,425	2,025	− 400	Part-time staff dismissed
14. Capital items	125	–	− 125	Postponed this expenditure
15. Payments out	8,790	7,425	−1,365	
16. Drawings	600	750	+ 150	Promised wife to increase this
17. Total payments	9,390	8,175	−1,215	
18. Final cash balance	+12,100	+11,515	− 585	

Fig. 17.3 Cash flow variances – January

Notes

- A negative variance on receipts is an unfavourable variance, since receipts are less than they should be.
- We can't do much about any of these negative variances, but it is hoped all the debtors will eventually pay.
- To offset what seemed to be happening, prompt action was taken to reduce outgoings by reducing orders to suppliers and dismissing part-time staff.
- The result was that some of the cash lost by reduced receipts was offset by reduced payments. A negative variance on payments is a favourable variance, since payments were less than they were expected to be.
- The result overall is an unfavourable variance of £585, with a final cash balance of only £11,515.

Controlling stock

There are three aspects of stock which need controlling:

(a) The general stock position
(b) Stock losses of various sorts
(c) Stocktaking for accounting purposes.

(a) *The general stock position.* Close control of stock positions is required, since we never want to be out of stock if we can avoid it, yet at the same time to be over-stocked means that capital is tied up in unsold stock, which is not selling and therefore not yielding any profit. It is only when stock turns over that a profit is made, so that slow-moving stock ('shelf-warmers') are a great disadvantage. Such slow-moving stock is a sign of bad buying, and may call for reprimands to buyers. Considerations about stock may be listed as follows:

- What is the achievable monthly sales or utilisation figure for each type of stock, and how does it vary from month to month? Many items are seasonal, and sell at particular times of the year. Orders must be placed to allow stocks to be high at peak-selling periods and low (or non-existent) at other times.
- Can suppliers be relied on to deliver on time, or should we keep higher stocks to allow for possible short deliveries?
- If we are manufacturing components ourselves we may need to manufacture batches of components to meet anticipated production targets. Sometimes idle-time on machines can be filled by producing small batches of parts we know will be required at a later date.
- We can rarely achieve 100 per cent consumer satisfaction, because to do so requires us to keep stocks of even very slow-moving items, with such items it is better to order them as requested and to add some margin to the price to cover the expense of any 'small-order' procedure that is required.
- Except in the very smallest businesses where personal supervision of stocks is possible, a stock control procedure should be implemented to keep control of each type of stock, with a bin card or similar document being completed as stocks arrive or are issued. Such procedures do cost money and take a lot of time, so the cost of the procedures have to be weighed against the losses that will occur if less strict controls are instituted. A typical bin-card is illustrated in Fig. 17.4.

(b) *Stock-losses of various sorts.* Stock losses arise from a variety of causes and measures must be instituted to correct them. Some of them are

17

BIN CARD

Description .. Socket (white)   Maximum stock .. 100 ...

Bin number .. 28 ....   Minimum stock .. 30 ...

Code number .. P 517 ....   Re-order level .. 40 ...

Unit of issue .. 5 ......   Re-order quantity .. 60 ...

Received			Issued			Balance
Date	Ref.	Quantity	Date	Ref.	Quantity	Quantity
1 Jan 19..						65
			8 Jan	Req 217	30	35
19 Jan 9..	Order 126	60				95
			24 Jan	Req 297	40	55

Fig. 17.4 A bin-card

known as 'merchandise' qualities, which are 'inherent vices of the goods.' Strawberries rot, bananas go bad, crockery breaks, materials fade, powders blow away, insects attack many products, etc. We must train staff to understand the merchandise they are handling and help them reduce losses which are the result of 'inherent vices' in the goods themselves. Don't order perishables in large quantities; don't put clumsy people in charge of fragile goods; firmly discourage horse-play, etc.

Other stock losses occur because of staff malpractice. Theft is not uncommon; 'passing out' (the giving of goods to friends without payment) is common; turning a blind eye to shop-lifting by friends and relatives is rather similar. The same sort of practices occur with money (giving excess change is not uncommon). To reduce such losses it is essential to train staff so that they know the detection of any such practices is highly likely, and the consequences will be unpleasant. Emphasize the serious nature of having a police record, even for tiny offences; the impossibility of getting a character reference; the chances of dismissal. Even in these days when unfair dismissal is a serious matter for employers, summary dismissal for theft is generally regarded as not being unfair, and a succession of offences, with formal warnings, is certainly cause for dismissal.

Certain events throw up situations where such malpractices may be discovered, for example stocktaking. If stocktaking is carried out randomly without warning, with a particular type of merchandise being carefully checked and costed, any discrepancies will be discovered. If staff are unwilling to take holidays, or days off, or work late regularly, or arrive early on a regular basis, the circumstances should be investigated. Of course everything may be all right, but the investigation will warn others that any departure from standard procedures is, to some extent, suspicious. Customer complaints are another source of information which may lead to investigation. It is best to open all mail yourself if that is possible. If you read every letter you will know what is going on. Complaints about non-delivery, short delivery, damaged goods, etc., should always be investigated.

(c) *Stocktaking for accounting purposes.* Technically speaking we only need to do stocktaking for final accounts purposes once a year, but it is preferable to do a full stocktake more frequently. Every three months we have to complete a VAT Return, a situation which calls for a quick review of sales, purchases and daily takings. This is a suitable time to do stocktaking, and we can then take out a set of interim final accounts, just to see how the profits of the business are coming along.

When stocktaking we have to count all the items in stock at a given time, as already explained (see p. 51). By going through the stocktaking procedure, serious stock losses may become apparent, and may be shown up as a drop in gross profit percentage (see p. 217) when the interim Final Accounts are worked out. Making a fuss about the stock losses tightens up procedures and warns anyone engaging in malpractices that the proceeds are not worth the risk.

Credit control

Credit is the supply of goods or services without immediate payment. When we supply goods or services the time of payment is a matter between the parties, who must make it clear to one another what terms they are trading on. Thus, a person who is only prepared to supply for cash should make this clear in any pre-contract negotiations. In a shop we often see notices reading 'Please do not ask for credit as a refusal may offend'. For shop trading these days the problem of granting credit hardly arises since the use of credit cards has separated the credit problem from the selling problem, and the credit card companies have assumed the credit risks. Become a credit card trader, an easy and almost cost-free arrangement, and enjoy the benefits.

17

If we trade on cash terms it means that payment must be made at the same time as the goods or services are supplied. If the customer is to be allowed to pay by cheque, a cheque card should be insisted upon. Recording the card number on the back of the cheque is sufficient to guarantee payment, provided the value does not exceed the card limit (usually £50, but some cards have a £100 value). The card must be current (i.e. not expired). If the payment is to be made by credit card no cheque is required; the credit card voucher is made out by the supplier and signed by the customer. There is a 'floor' value above which the supplier must phone for authorization, but sums of any amount may be paid in this way provided the payment is authorised. One South-coast marina phoned to say a customer was trying to buy an £80,000 yacht with his credit card. The purchase was authorized without any hesitation.

Supplies which are not made against cash payments are said to be 'on credit'. If we are to allow customers credit we should only do so if we know them to be creditworthy: this usually means that only after they have become regular customer placing steady orders, and after we have taken up references upon them, should we agree to deal with them on 'open account'. 'Open account' means that we deal with them in the way that is usual in the trade. This often means that they pay monthly in arrears. Thus they are sent a statement once a month showing what they owe to the date of the statement, and they must then pay the statement within 30 days. These terms can be varied, e.g. payment within 7 or 15 days is quite common.

Shorter credit terms may be agreed. For example, payment within 7 days of invoice date means that they have to pay each invoice as they receive it. This is less convenient for the customer, since it may mean several payments in a month, but it is advantageous for the supplier because cash flow improves.

The general principles of credit control are:

- Do not supply goods on credit to new customers except in very special circumstances – for instance, if they have been known to you personally for a very long time, or if you have a clear statement from a bank that they are of excellent reputation. The sort of cautious banking reference 'Believed to be good for normal business transactions' is not enough to justify credit.
- Be more careful about giving credit to companies than to sole traders or partnerships. Company directors have limited liability which means that the business is a separate entity in law from the directors, and they cannot be held personally liable for debts. If you contract with a company you cannot enforce the contract against a director unless you have asked him/her for a personal guarantee. Where a company asks

to be supplied on credit do not agree until you have had time to sort out their creditworthiness to your satisfaction. You can ask for a banker's reference, and for trade references – firms who have supplied them in the past. Check with such people personally both by telephone and by correspondence to find out their opinions about the potential customer. You may be advised to do a company search. The idea here is that since directors of a company have limited liability (limited to the amount of capital they have invested in the business) all the creditors can look to is the capital of the company. This may be as little as a few pounds, and is often less than £1,000. By asking a specialist firm to do a company search for you, you will at least find out what that capital is. It is a good idea to draw up a set of 'Terms of Payment' which states the terms on which you expect to be paid. Send a copy of such conditions to your customer when you start to allow a credit period, and insist upon acknowledgment of the conditions before supplying the first batch. If you are a member of a trade association of some sort they will usually let you use their set of 'Trading Conditions', for a nominal charge.

Many large firms insist on negotiating more favourable credit terms than are usual in the trade, and often insist on larger discounts. You have to weigh up the advisability of dealing with such firms against the cash-flow difficulties they create. You need to be sure that you can survive the first period before payment becomes due. Problems can often be avoided by planning ahead.

- If you do decide to allow a customer time to pay, set a credit limit on them by marking it on their account. Do not let this credit limit be exceeded. It is a common practice by unreliable traders to place one or two small orders and pay promptly, but then put in a very large order for which there is no real intention to pay. A single big bad debt can cripple a small firm. Never let any order go out if the previous statement has not been paid. If the payment date has not yet arrived and the new order brings the total due above the agreed credit limit, don't fulfil the order. Phone and ask for payment first.

- It is always advisable to send statements out promptly. Firms never pay until they get a statement, and the earlier they get it the sooner you should have your money. Check that there are no petty errors in the statement since these are often used as an excuse to delay payment.

- Do not be bashful about asking for payment the moment an account is overdue. The person who demands payment and makes a fuss is more likely to be paid than a person who does not ask. A telephone call, or a personal visit if the customer is local, is more likely to produce a result than a mere letter, but if this does not produce an immediate result send a letter stating a deadline for payment. If you arrange with your solicitor to refer all debts to him/her as soon as the deadline you set in your

17

request for payment is exceeded, a formal letter requesting payment will be sent at once. Failure to respond to such a letter can be followed by legal action to recover and is therefore a threat to the slow payer. Payment will usually be forthcoming. A poor payer who has a number of debts to pay will usually pay the person who is bothering him/her rather than the person who is not yet complaining. A useful booklet, '*Prompt Payment Please*', is available from the Small Firms Service.

Credit control over purchases

Although credit control is usually thought of as an activity which exercises control over customers and ensures that bad debts are avoided, it is just as bad to fail to exercise control over payments for purchases. A business cannot be laid low by its debtors; it is the unpaid creditors who can force the business into bankruptcy. We should pay our bills promptly for the following reasons:

- Because, on the principle of 'Do as you would be done by', we should be as careful of our supplier's welfare as of our own. If we wish to be paid promptly for our own goods or services, in accordance with the agreed contractual terms, we should be equally prepared to honour our own debts according to contract.
- Because prompt payment is the best way of building a sound supplier – customer relationship. The supplier who knows we pay promptly is unlikely, even at times of shortage, to divert our goods to another customer, and will honour urgent requests for supplies promptly.
- A good name is an invaluable asset and can only be established slowly over a period of years. It can quickly be lost by a single late payment, and totally destroyed by a succession of them.

It is the common practice of new suppliers to ask other suppliers for an opinion of our reliability should we be seeking supplies for them, and an unhesitating confirmation that we pay promptly is the best recommendation.

A satisfactory procedure on payments for supplies is as follows:

- Always open the mail yourself, since you will then know exactly what has been purchased in your name and will be able to detect any fraudulent behaviour at the earliest possible moment.
- If you have to pay on the invoice, work out the due date and file the invoice, or a reminder to pay it, on a date just prior to the due date so

that you are sure it is paid in time, yet you have taken advantage of whatever credit period is available.

- Always sign all cheques yourself. If you are paying on a statement rather than a single invoice, check that all goods charged for have in fact arrived and that any returns have been credited.

- If your organization is growing, establish a proper control procedure to check that all goods ordered are received, are in good order, are not paid for before the credit period is approaching its end, and that cheques are signed only by authorized officials. It is wise to put a limit on the cheque values that may be signed by people other than yourself, and to notify the bank that your personal signature is required on cheques above this limit.

- If cash flows are good it may be desirable to take cash discounts by paying more promptly and not using the full credit period.

- If cash is short and some payments have to be delayed, it is well to review all payments and pay those where the moral obligation to pay is strong, or where the natural objection of the supplier can be least easily borne.

- All payments to suppliers are reduced if proper control of stocks prevents the placing of unnecessary orders. This means having maximum stock and re-order levels, and designating someone as the sole 'purchasing officer' to prevent haphazard small orders being placed by individuals unaware of the cash flow position.

- One final point about scrutinizing invoices as they arrive is that the prices shown are the latest prices, and may have important implications for pricing goods for re-sale, costing jobs, and estimating or quoting prices to customers. The small business is often much too slow in raising prices. It is most unwise to get left behind in an inflationary spiral – we need to price ahead of inflation or our profit margins will be eaten into. Alert staff to the need to re-price and keep yourself familiar with the price elements built into your costing activities so that you are quick to spot a raw material that is becoming more expensive.

Staff performance

No single element of control is as important as the control of staff. We need staff to perform various aspects of our work, and for this reason we must check that they have the skills we require, or at least the potential to acquire these skills. Once employed, staff are difficult to get rid of, and poor staff are even harder to get rid of because they have little incentive to go elsewhere.

Besides the skills we require them to have, we also hope to have a

17

reasonably agreeable working environment. People who cannot get on with others or work willingly without endless supervision soon become a bore. Impress upon new arrivals before they are appointed that you are looking for co-operative, helpful people; self starters who don't need to be driven all day but believe in a fair day's work for a fair day's pay. Build such sentiments into letters of appointment so that if, at some future time, the employee behaves unreasonably, that in itself (after several warnings) will justify dismissal.

This does not imply that we can be anything less than scrupulous in our own behaviour. Good control of staff requires leadership, example, fair treatment and consultation, rather than a niggling rectitude.

Just as production, marketing and distribution require a clear organisational structure to secure control, the area of employee relations needs a definite structure if it is to ensure proper control of the workforce. The embryo firm is under the personal supervision of the proprietor and as such the structure is clear and control is exercised directly. As the business grows it becomes necessary to establish a framework of clear responsibilities of key staff over certain areas of the work. Job descriptions which define the tasks to be done by any person appointed (but also call for adaptability and willing co-operation across boundaries where the situation requires it) are part of this framework. Clear statements of employee conduct on punctuality, self-certification of sickness, racial discrimination, sexual discrimination, etc., are desirable. Arbitrary management should be ruled out as unfair, authority should be clearly specified, discretion within a policy conceded, and appeal to a higher level laid down as a natural right. The principles of natural justice, which are that everyone has a right to be heard and that no-one shall be judge in a dispute in which he/she is one of the parties, must be applied.

It may be asked 'What has all this to do with accounting?' The answer is, 'A very great deal'. Employer-employee confrontations have enormous impact upon the financial stability of firms. The inability of management to manage is a frequent cause of failure, but equally, arbitrary management brings costs in higher labour turnover, stoppages, awards for unfair dismissal, fines for breach of regulations, loss of licences, etc. Anything that raises costs, interrupts delivery dates, or causes disaffection in the surrounding locality is of interest to accountants.

Control over profitability

This subject is best dealt with by looking at the various accounting ratios which can be calculated once the Final Accounts, or the interim final accounts, are worked out. These are dealt with fully in Chapter 18.

Break-even analysis

A business only breaks even when its sales to customers bring in enough income to cover all the costs that have been incurred. Suppose the prime costs of an article are £15 (these, remember, are the costs of the raw materials and labour actually embodied in the finished product). Suppose also that we can sell it for £35. We thus have a contribution from each article sold to profits of £20. However, that contribution is not enough to lead us into profit until it has covered all the 'overhead' costs of the business, both the manufacturing overhead (see Chapter 14 for the Manufacturing Account) and the selling, distribution and general over-heads for the rest of the business. The prime costs are the variable costs (because they vary without output) but the overheads are called fixed costs, because they do not vary with output. For example, if we make 200 articles we shall need 200 lots of raw materials, and if we make 2,000 articles, 2,000 lots. By contrast, whatever output we produce we only need one factory (although eventually we could need another one). Overhead costs are to a very considerable extent fixed costs.

To break even we must cover both variable costs and fixed costs. Where will this point occur? We can see it if we draw a break-even chart like the one shown in Fig. 17.5. In this diagram we have fixed costs of £40,000 and

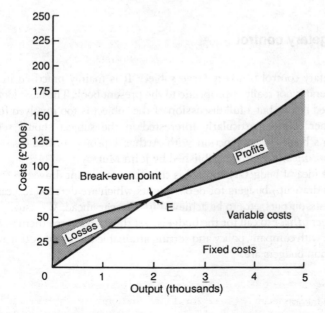

Fig. 17.5 A break-even chart (*notes overleaf*)

17

Notes

- The fixed costs are £40,000 as indicated by the horizontal line on the graph.
- On top of these fixed costs we have variable costs of £15 per unit, which at an output of 5,000 units makes a total of £75,000; on top of £40,000 fixed costs, £115,000 in all.
- By selling the articles at £35, one thousand units brings in £35,000 and 5,000 units brings in £175,000.
- We can see that the break-even point is at an output of 2,000 units, (E on the diagram) where the sales proceeds cover both the fixed and the variable costs and we start to make profits.
- From that time on each unit sold brings in a contribution to profits of £20.
- You might like to answer the following questions:
  - What loss will be made if only 1,500 can be sold?
  - What profit will be made if output and sales reach 4,500 units?
- You could now draw a similar diagram if the selling price that could be achieved was £40, not £35.

variable costs of £15 per unit. The selling price is £35 per unit giving a contribution towards fixed costs (and eventually to profits) of £20 per unit. We can see that at £20 profit per unit we shall need to make and sell 2,000 units if we are to cover £40,000 of fixed costs (2,000 × £20 = £40,000). Therefore the break-even point is going to be at an output of 2,000 units. Study the chart in Fig. 17.5.

Budgetary control

Budgetary control is a very large subject. It is mainly practised in large firms and is not really appropriate to the present book. The basic ideas are outlined below, but a full discussion of the subject is too involved for the beginner. Those particularly interested in the subject should see the author's book (in conjunction with Arthur Upson) entitled *Success in Accounting and Costing*, published by John Murray.

The idea of budgetary control is that the accountant draws up (or has others draw up) budgets for departments which are detailed forecasts of the costs, outputs, etc., to be achieved in the year ahead. We usually need a *budget officer* to call for the budgets, vet them and agree them as being in line with company policy and setting attainable targets of performance. Common budgets are:

- sales
- production
- manufacturing (direct materials, direct wages, factory overheads)

- administration, selling and distribution costs
- purchases
- cash
- plant utilization
- capital expenditure
- research and development

The budget in each of these cases sets a standard against which all sorts of controls can be established. For example, a movement of raw material prices could be easily detected. Can we find a cheaper supplier? Can we use an alternative material? Can we rebut the price rise in any way? Can we push it on to the customer by raising our own prices? The reader will see at once that budgetary control sparks off a train of ideas from each *variance* that becomes apparent between budgeted and actual costs.

Budgetary control may be defined as a technique for relating the responsibilities of an executive to the requirements of policy through a system of budgets. It enables comparisons to be drawn between budgeted and actual costs and performances to correct any adverse variances, or, if they are insusceptible to correction, to revise the budget and feed the revision through to final prices so that budgeted profits are still achieved.

A full system of budgetary control is an advanced technique, inappropriate to this book, but an awareness of the basic principles can still have implications for the proprietors of small businesses.

Checklist

---

1. Every aspect of a business requires control. With sole traders the control is direct and easily exercised. As businesses grow we must establish an organisation which gives control over all aspects both in routine matters and emergency situations.
2. Control over the order book is often a first requirement. We must attract a steady flow of customers and ensure that we can fulfil all the orders we accept.
3. Cash flow control is an essential element of management. A cash budget should be drawn up and shortages anticipated and financed. Cash flow smoothing should be practised wherever possible.
4. A *variance* is a difference between a budgeted and an actual figure. If you analyse the variances that arise you may be able to control costs, or at least act quickly to pass them on as increased prices to customers (and thus prevent your profit margins being eroded).
5. Stock should be controlled by a system that specifies maximum stocks, re-order points, re-order quantities, etc. Be aware of the dangers of stocklosses by pilfering, inherent vices of the goods and bad buying, which cause stocks to be sold off at cut prices to prevent deterioration.
6. Control over purchases is important. Open mail yourself so that you see the invoices and know what has been ordered in your name. Pay bills just before the due date to take full advantage of any credit period, unless you decide to take the settlement discount offered by paying earlier. Be solicitous of your suppliers' needs to be paid, and thus establish a good name in the trade for prompt payment.
7. Exercise good control over staff, so as to obtain a fair day's work for a fair day's pay, and avoid disruption due to petty disputes, claims for unfair dismissal, etc.
8. A break-even chart is a useful diagram for predicting when a new product will prove profitable.
9. As the business grows, implement a system of budgetary control to keep costs and performance under constant review.

---

18   Accounting ratios

Nature of accounting ratios □ Analysis of the Trading Account
□ Analysis of the Profit and Loss Account □ Analysis of Balance
Sheets

Nature of accounting ratios

A ratio is a quantitative relationship between two figures which clearly
brings out how many times one goes into another. For example, if our
average stock of a particular item is £1,000 at cost and we sell £26,000 of
it per annum (at cost of sales price) then it is clear that our average stock
turns over 26 times in a year. A rate of turnover of 26 is a very good for
many items (but it would not do for newspapers because it would mean
that on average each paper sold was 2 weeks old). This type of figure is
helpful to know, but we can only interpret it in the light of our knowledge
of a particular business. For the self-employed person the business we are
interested in is our own business, and these simple ratios can tell us a lot
about it. They are even more important when we have collected them over
several years and can compare this year's performance with last year's. A
further point is that if we take out a set of Final Accounts more frequently
than once a year (say quarterly) we can compare results of not only this
quarter with last quarter, but more importantly, this quarter with the same
quarter last year, and that gives us a very good idea of how we are getting
along.

The use of accounting ratios, then, is to tell management what is
happening to the business and bring out the *relative* not the *actual*
changes. Suppose an advertising campaign increases sales by 500 items –
this might seem a satisfactory increase. If the previous sales were 40,000
and the increase brings them to 40,500 we see that the relative increase,
expressed as a percentage, is:

$$\frac{500}{40,000} \times 100\% = 1.25\%$$

The increase in sales does not seem much when you can see it *relative*
to the original sales. Relative figures are usually more informative than
actual figures.

Accounting ratios are found by an analysis of the Final Accounts. They
include the following:

- Analysis of the Trading Account reveals:
  - (*a*) the gross profit percentage
  - (*b*) the rate of stock turn.
- Analysis of the Profit and Loss Account reveals:
  - (*a*) the net profit percentage
  - (*b*) the expense ratios (for all expenses).
- Analysis of the Balance Sheet reveals:
  - (*a*) the 'working capital ratio' or 'current ratio'
  - (*b*) the 'liquid capital ratio' or 'acid test ratio'
  - (*c*) the return on capital employed (ROCE)
  - (*d*) the return on capital invested (ROCI).
- Analysis of the Balance Sheet of a company reveals:
  - (*a*) the ordinary shareholders' interest in the company
  - (*b*) the value per share.

Analysis of the Trading Account

Here is the Trading Account of 'Tasty Sweets', an imaginary sole trader business.

Trading Account for year ending 31 December 19X9

19X9		£	19X9	£
Opening Stock		5,250	Sales	139,500
Purchases	42,160		*Less* Returns	1,500
Less Returns	410		Net turnover	138,000
Net Purchases		41,750		
Total stock available		47,000		
Less Closing Stock		4,500		
Cost of stock sold		42,500		
Gross Profit		95,500		
		£138,000		£138,000

Fig. 18.1 A Trading Account for appraisal

From this Trading Account we can work out the ratios listed in Fig. 18.1 above.

Gross profit percentage

The formula is:

$$\text{Gross profit percentage} = \frac{\text{Gross profit}}{\text{Turnover}} \times 100$$

Substituting the figures from the Trading Account we have:

$$\text{Gross profit percentage} = \frac{\text{£}95{,}500}{\text{£}138{,}000} \times 100$$

$$= \frac{9{,}550}{138}\ \%$$

$$= \underline{69.2\%}$$

Comments on this percentage

- Gross profit percentage should always be quite a high figure because we have to cover a great many overhead expenses with this gross profit. One of the commonest causes of failure in business is not taking a big enough gross profit percentage. You simply cannot keep going on a gross profit of 20 per cent – you need at least 50 per cent, and 200 per cent or 300 per cent is not uncommon. If your circumstances are so competitive that you cannot charge a high enough margin, leave the industry and seek a more lucrative outlet for your talents.

- The important point about gross profit percentage is that it should be the same from year to year (i.e. it should be a constant) unless you yourself are doing something to make it change (like introducing more efficient methods of working). Always compare this year's ratio with last year's. Suppose last year you were making 75 per cent gross profit percentage. What can have happened to cause the decrease? It can only be something within the Trading Account. What could it be?

  (*a*) It could be the manager/manageress stealing the sales money.

  (*b*) It could be some member of staff stealing the sales money. Who, on the staff, is looking like a million dollars these days? It could be your million dollars they're looking like!

  (*c*) It could be that stocks are down because of (*i*) theft by the staff or (*ii*) theft by customers or (*iii*) 'passing-out' (giving of stock to friends and relations).

  (*d*) It could be increased purchase prices which have not been passed on as increased selling prices to customers.

  (*e*) It could be stock losses due to poor buying (perishables thrown away or slow-moving stock sold at marked-down prices). It could be skylarking in the crockery department. Anything that means a lower stock means a lower gross profit, and hence a lower gross profit percentage.

18

The rate of stock turnover

The rate of stock turnover can be found using either of two formulae:

- Rate of stockturn $= \dfrac{\text{Cost of stock sold}}{\text{Average stock at cost price}}$

- Rate of stockturn $= \dfrac{\text{Net turnover}}{\text{Average stock at selling price}}$

The point is that the two figures used must be in the same form – either both at cost price or both at selling price.

Using the cost price figures from Fig. 18.1 we have:

$$\text{Rate of stockturn} = \frac{£42,500}{\text{Average stock}}$$

$$\text{Average stock} = \frac{(\text{Opening stock} + \text{closing stock})}{2}$$

$$= \frac{£5,250 + £4,500}{2}$$

$$= \frac{£9,750}{2}$$

$$= £4,875$$

$$\therefore \text{Rate of stockturn} = \frac{£42,500}{£4,875}$$

$$= \underline{8.7 \text{ times a year}}$$

Whether 8.7 times in a year is a reasonable rate of turnover or not depends upon the type of goods being sold. It gives us a better picture if we turn the figure into another related figure, namely the amount of time the average stock is on hand before it is sold. We can do this by dividing the rate into the number of days, weeks or months in the year. Thus:

$$\frac{12}{8.7} = 1.4 \text{ months an average item is in stock}$$

$$\frac{52}{8.7} = 6.0 \text{ weeks an average item is in stock}$$

$$\frac{365}{8.7} = 42.0 \text{ days an average item is in stock.}$$

Whether the sweets dealt in by this trader would be in a satisfactory condition after about 6 weeks in stock is a matter for management to ponder.

Analysis of the Profit and Loss Account

Here is the Profit and Loss Account of 'Tasty Sweets' at the end of the same year.

Profit and Loss Account for year ending 31 December 19X9

19X9	£	19X9	£
Mortgage interest	5,250	Gross Profit	95,500
Light & Heat	2,350	Rent Received	2,500
Telephone expenses	1,460	Discount received	350
Salaries	27,640		98,350
Insurance paid	420		
Interest paid	350		
Community charges (rates)	4,875		
Motor Vehicle expenses	2,536		
Packaging and selling			
expenses	4,419		
	49,300		
Net Profit	49,050		
	£98,350		£98,350

Fig. 18.2 A Profit and Loss Account for appraisal

From this Profit and Loss Account and the turnover figure in the Trading Account we can work out the ratios in Fig. 18.1 above.

Net profit percentage

The formula is:

$$\text{Net profit percentage} = \frac{\text{Net profit}}{\text{Turnover}} \times 100$$

$$= \frac{£49,050}{£138,000} \times 100$$

$$= \frac{4,905}{138}$$

$$= \underline{35.5\%}$$

18

Comments on this percentage

- Net profit percentage can vary enormously between firms according to the type of industry concerned and the competitive state of the industry. One wants the return one earns from risking one's capital in business to be higher than the 8–10 per cent one could earn from a safe investment in a building society or a gilt-edged security. 35 per cent is well above this level.
- What was the net profit percentage last year? If we know that it was 38.5 per cent, we could ask ourselves why it has fallen this year. Provided the gross profit percentage had remained more or less the same, the fall in net profit percentage must be due to something within the Profit and Loss Account. Has a particular expense item risen considerably in the current year? We can find out by taking out expense ratios (see below). Has some source of profit we enjoyed last year (other than gross profit) fallen considerably, or even ceased to be earned for some reason? We can look at these situations. For example, if Rent Received has fallen because we had to use rooms formerly let off for our own expansion, there is nothing we can do to recover the sums lost. If we have failed to pursue possible profits we should take steps to recover them in the coming year.

Expense ratios

Expense ratios are those where we relate particular expenses to turnover, to arrive at a percentage. Thus the Salaries Ratio is found by the formula:

$$\text{Salaries ratio} = \frac{\text{Salaries paid}}{\text{Turnover}} \times 100$$

$$= \frac{\pounds 27,640}{\pounds 138,000} \times 100$$

$$= \frac{2,764}{138}$$

$$= \underline{\underline{20.0\%}}$$

20 per cent of our turnover was used up in salaries: suppose last year the figure was 16.5 per cent. Clearly there is a problem here. Some people collect employees, because it makes them feel powerful if they have a little empire of 'hangers on'. If extra staff have been appointed with little real effect on the expansion of the business (an increased turnover) we should want to know 'Why?'. If every expense ratio is calculated and compared with the same ratio in previous years we shall be able to pinpoint areas

where action is necessary. If we cannot avoid the increases in overheads we must pass the increases on to our customers by raising prices.

To familiarise yourself with these ratios you should now try the exercises below. The answers are given at the end of the exercises.

Exercises on evaluating the Trading Account and Profit and Loss Account

1. A. Trader had in stock on 1 July 600 articles costing £2.00 each. During the month he bought 1,800 more of these articles at £2.40 each and sold 2,020 at £4.00 each, of which 20 of the most recent items were returned. He sells stock on a first in, first out basis. Draw up a statement showing the Gross Profit earned and express the Gross Profit as a percentage of the turnover.

2. On preparing the Trading Account of R. Lyons, a retailer, for the financial year ended 31 March 19X9, it was found that the ratio of Gross Profit to sales was 15 per cent, whereas for the previous financial year the corresponding ratio had been 25 per cent. State, with your reasons, whether or not the following may have contributed to cause the decline:
   (a) The stock at 31 March 19X9 was undervalued.
   (b) The cost of a new delivery van had been included in the purchases for the year ended 31 March 19X9 and charged to Trading Account.
   (c) The sales for the year ended 31 March 19X9 showed a decline compared with the previous year.
   (d) In both years R. Lyons and his family had been supplied with goods from the shop but the value of these goods had not been recorded in the books of the business.
   (e) On the last day of the financial year an employee was successfully convicted of dishonesty with regard to the theft of takings from the tills.

3. A trader carries an average stock of £8,000 (valued at cost price) and turns this over five times a year. If he marks up his stock by 25 per cent on cost price, what is his Gross Profit for the year?

4. A trader carries an average stock valued at cost price of £6,250 and turns this over 14 times a year. If his mark up is 20 per cent on cost and his overheads came to £6,200, what is the Net Profit for the year?

Answers

1. Gross profit = £3,440; gross profit percentage = 43 per cent.
2. (a) Yes – undervalued closing stock increases the cost of sales and reduces the profit, and hence the gross profit percentage.

(b) Yes – including a motor vehicle in purchases increases the cost of sales as in (a) above.
(c) No – decline in sales should not affect the ratio, which is a constant.
(d) Possibly. These goods reduce the stock and consequently affect the gross profit percentage as in (a) above. However, since it happened last year too, it would only affect the gross profit percentage if the quantity of goods taken was greater this year than last year.
(e) Yes – theft of sales money reduces the sales figure and consequently the gross profit.
3. £10,000 gross profit.
4. £11,300 net profit.

Some comments on Balance Sheets

Before looking into the analysis of Balance Sheets there are one or two points that may confuse the reader whenever the Balance Sheet is studied. The idea of a balance in everyday life is that two sides of a situation should be weighed against one another and considered to see whether they are of equal weight. We can see this idea if we think of the statue of Justice on the Old Bailey in London, where Justice holds up the scales to see whether the 'good' or the 'evil' in a case is greater. A balance, both in the scientific laboratory and in justice, must be horizontal.

The Balance Sheet was invented in 1536 by Simon Stevin of Bruges, and he called it a Statement of Affairs. This a very good name, for it describes exactly what a Balance Sheet is, a statement of the affairs of a business at a given moment, the last second of the last day of the accounting period. Unfortunately, since a Balance Sheet is derived from a Trial Balance, where the assets are on the left hand side and the liabilities are on the right hand side, it is a great pity that Stevin got in a muddle when he drew up his Statement of Affairs, and crossed the Balance Sheet over to put the liabilities on the left and the assets on the right. This became the traditional British Balance Sheet, as shown in Chapter 6. Other nations quickly changed the Balance Sheet round the correct way, so that most European nations and the United States do their Balance Sheets the correct way round.

However, the most confusing thing for traders today is that the United Kingdom's accountancy bodies started to do Balance Sheets in vertical style, with the assets above the liabilities or, perhaps, the liabilities above the assets. This makes a mockery of the name Balance Sheet, let alone Justice. It is as sensible to have a Balance Sheet in vertical style as it would be for Justice to have the good side of a case on top of the evil side, or *vice versa*. If, therefore, your Balance Sheet from your accountant is in vertical style, remember that really it should be horizontal, and we are trying to weigh the assets against the liabilities to ensure that they are equal.

To explain the points made in this section the Balance Sheet we are about to analyse has been presented in all three forms.

Balance Sheet of 'Tasty Sweets' as at 31 December 19X9

19X9		£	19X9		£
Capital			*Fixed assets*		
At start		43,332	Premises		68,000
Add Net Profit	49,050		Plant and machinery		28,500
Less drawings	18,750		Motor vehicles		13,820
		30,300	Furniture, etc		9,250
		73,632			119,570
Long-term liabilities			*Current assets*		
Mortgage	50,000		Stock	6,500	
Bank loan	5,000		Debtors	1,850	
		55,000	Cash at bank	5,214	
			Cash in hand	738	
Current liabilities					
Creditors		5,240			14,302
		£133,872			£133,872

Fig. 18.3(a) A Balance Sheet for appraisal in traditional UK style

Balance Sheet of 'Tasty Sweets' as at 31 December 19X9

19X9		£	19X9		£
Fixed Assets			*Capital*		
Premises		68,000	At start		43,332
Plant and machinery		28,500	Add net profit	49,050	
Motor vehicles		13,820	Less drawings	18,750	
Furniture, etc		9,250			30,300
		119,570			73,632
Current assets			*Long-term liabilities*		
Stock	6,500		Mortgage	50,000	
Debtors	1,850		Bank loan	5,000	
Cash at bank	5,214				55,000
Cashh in hand	738				
			Current liabilities		
		14,302	Creditors		5,240
		£133,872			£133,872

Fig. 18.3(b) A Balance Sheet for appraisal in correct 'European' style

18

Balance Sheet of 'Tasty Sweets' as at 31 December 19X9

	At Cost £	Less Depreciation £	Value £
Fixed assets			
Premises	68,000	–	68,000
Plant and machinery	35,000	6,500	28,500
Motor vehicles	18,000	4,180	13,820
Furniture and fittings	12,000	2,750	9,250
	£133,000	£13,430	119,570
Current assets			
Stock		6,500	
Debtors		1,850	
Cash at bank		5,214	
Cash in hand		738	
			14,302
			£133,872
Financed by:			
Capital at start			43,332
add net profit		49,050	
less drawings		18,750	
			30,300
			73,632
Long-term liabilities			
Mortgage		50,000	
Bank loan		5,000	
			55,000
Current liabilities			
Creditors			5,240
			£133,872

Fig. 18.3(c) A Balance Sheet for appraisal in vertical style

Note

One can see the advantage of the vertical style Balance Sheet – it is much easier to set out across a typewritten page. For example, the details of the depreciation to date have been set out in full. However, this can be done just as easily with the European style if the Balance Sheet is set out across a double page. The term 'Balance Sheet' is then much more appropriate, for the two sides do 'balance'. A balance is essentially a horizontal affair, and the vertical style is therefore not really appropriate.

Interpreting the Balance Sheet

Remember that since a Balance Sheet is taken out at the very end of the financial year it is essentially a historical statement – this is how things were at the end of the accounting period. When we come to analyse it, it is too late to correct anything – all we can do is learn lessons for the future.

The working capital ratio or current ratio

Before considering the working capital ratio we must learn the vocabulary of Balance Sheets. We know that *fixed assets* are those which last a long time (more than a year) and *current assets* are those which are not held for long-term use but are only temporary (they last less than one year). For example, we hope we shall sell all our stock in the first few weeks of the new year, and we hope our debtors will pay us within one month (or any other agreed credit period). We often call the fixed assets *'fixed capital'* because the capital we have spent on them is tied up in long-term assets and is no longer liquid-money-capital. The current assets are often called *'working capital'* because they are used to keep the business working, pay wages, buy more raw materials or goods for re-sale, etc. Shortage of working capital is one of the chief problems of businesses, for these reasons. It is the working capital (particularly the cash in hand and the cash at the bank) which we use to pay off our current liabilities, i.e. our creditors. If we have insufficient working capital to pay our creditors, one who cannot be paid may start legal proceedings against us and we may finish up in the bankruptcy courts. Buying too many fixed assets and leaving ourselves too few current assets is called over-trading.

The best definition of working capital is:

$$\text{Working capital} = \text{Current assets} - \text{Current liabilities}$$

In the case of Fig. 18.3 it is:

$$\text{Working Capital} = £14,302 - £5,240$$
$$= \underline{£9,062}$$

The more useful management figure is:

$$\text{Working Capital Ratio} = \frac{\text{Current assets}}{\text{Current liabilities}}$$

$$= \frac{£14,302}{£5,240}$$

$$= \underline{2.7 \text{ times}}$$

18

In other words we could, if we realised all our current assets, pay our creditors 2.7 times over. Thus we are perfectly safe, and no creditor could possibly put us out of business because we have plenty of funds to pay everyone.

The usual guiding rule is that the working capital ratio should be at least 2.0, i.e. we can pay all our debts twice over.

The 'acid test' ratio, or liquid capital ratio

Although the working capital ratio referred to above is a good guide to the state of our business as far as capital goes, there is an even more vital ratio – such a strict ratio that it is called the 'acid test' ratio. This states that when we test for our current viability we should not include the stock in our current assets, because stock can be notoriously hard to sell, and if we do want to realise it (i.e. turn it into cash) we often have to reduce it in price. Liquid capital is therefore defined as (current assets – stock) – current liabilities. The acid-test ratio formula is:

$$\text{Acid test ratio} = \frac{\text{Current assets} - \text{stock}}{\text{Current liabilities}}$$

In the case of Fig. 18.3 it is:

$$\text{Acid test ratio} = \frac{£14,302 - £6,500}{£5,240}$$

$$= \frac{£7,802}{£5,240}$$

$$= \underline{\underline{1.5 \text{ times}}}$$

This is a satisfactory liquid capital ratio. Accountants hold that with our liquid assets we should be able to pay all our creditors, i.e. the liquid capital ratio should be at least 1.0. However, just suppose the figures had had rather more stock in them. Say:

	£
Stock	9,500
Debtors	2,850
Cash at Bank	1,214
Cash in Hand	738
	14,302

We should then have had:

$$\text{Working Capital Ratio} = \frac{14,302}{5,240} = 2.7 \text{ times}$$

$$\text{Liquid Capital Ratio} = \frac{4,802}{5,240} = 0.92 \text{ times}$$

Clearly we have not enough liquid capital to pay all our debts, and there is some chance that we could be in financial difficulties.

The return on capital employed

When we discover the return on capital employed we are to some extent comparing our business as an investment with other investment opportunities open to us. There are a variety of measures used (not everyone has the same ideas about what we should include under the term 'capital employed'). For example, if we look at any Balance Sheet it is a simple fact that whatever assets we have on the assets side have been obtained with the capital listed on the other side. For example, in Fig. 18.3 the total assets are worth £133,872. How have these been obtained? The answer is that the proprietor originally provided £43,332 and has also ploughed in profits earned worth £30,300, making the total of the proprietor's contribution £73,632. Then we also used capital from a building society or bank mortgage, and a bank loan of £55,000, and we managed to persuade creditors to lend us £5,240. All these various bits of capital financed the purchase of the assets.

It is usual to leave out the creditors (because to some extent anyway they are balanced up by the debtors on the other side who are using *our* capital to finance their business activities). It is also usual to average out the profits ploughed back and say, 'Well, really, we've only had the use of that capital for half the year on average'. A similar averaging process would be necessary if we borrowed the long-term liabilities at some time during the year. However, we will pretend both the Bank Loan and the mortgage have been used for the whole year.

The capital employed is therefore worked out as follows:

$$\text{Capital employed} = £43,332 + £15,150 + £55,000$$
$$= £113,482$$

The return on capital employed is the profit we made in the year expressed as a percentage of that capital: this profit is £49,050. However, as we are counting the loan and the mortgage as part of the capital employed we must include the interest paid on these amounts as part of the profit – those figures were £575 and £5,250 respectively. This makes the full profit £49,050 + £575 + £5,250 = £54,875. Therefore we have:

18

$$\text{Return on capital employed} = \frac{£\ 54{,}875}{£113{,}482} \times 100$$

$$= \underline{\underline{48.4\%}}$$

This appears to be a very satisfactory return – comparing it, for example with the same capital invested in gilt-edged securities where we might get about 9 per cent. It seems it is well worthwhile being in business!

Return on Capital Invested

A more subtle ratio, which applies more particularly to the proprietor, is to work out the return on capital invested. This term refers to the capital invested by the proprietor at the start of the year. As with all sophisticated ratios we have to think carefully about the figures we are using and perhaps adapt them if necessary. The profit earned was £49,050 on original capital of £43,332 invested at the start of the year. However, to find out whether it has really been worthwhile being in business we have to see what extra benefit the proprietor is gaining. When we take up the opportunity of being self-employed we give up any chance of doing other things and these lost opportunities mean we have lost money. Thus, if we cannot now take a job, we have lost the opportunity to earn wages. We have also lost the opportunity of putting £43,332 in a safe bank account earning a high rate of interest. These losses are called the *opportunity cost* of being self-employed – the lost opportunities.

What were the opportunity costs in Fig. 18.3? We don't know, but let us imagine that the proprietor of 'Tasty Sweets' could have earned £8,500 a year as the manager of a sweet shop, and could have invested his/her savings in a high interest account earning 9.5 per cent. The opportunity cost is therefore £8,500 + £4,117 (the interest calculated at 9.5 per cent on £43,332 if it had been invested instead of being used in the business). This means the extra profit actually earned by being in business is:

$$£49{,}050 - £12{,}617 = £36{,}433$$

Therefore the Return on Capital Invested (ROCI) is:

$$\text{ROCI} = \frac{\text{Net Profit} - \text{Opportunity Cost}}{\text{Capital at start}} \times 100$$

$$= \frac{£49{,}050 - £12{,}617}{£43{,}332} \times 100$$

$$= \frac{£36{,}433}{£43{,}332} \times 100$$

$$= \underline{\underline{84\%}}$$

Clearly, it is well worthwhile being in business.

You should now try these exercises to familiarise yourself with these control ratios.

Exercises on the interpretation of a Balance Sheet

1. M. Brown's current assets total £27,300 and his current liabilities total £8,500. Work out the working capital ratio, and comment on its adequacy.

2. R. Bird's current assets are as follows:

	£
Stock	15,500
Debtors	3,400
Cash at bank	5,800
Cash in hand	200

Her only liability is to a single creditor, £8,600. Work out (correct to two decimal places) (a) her working capital ratio and (b) her acid test ratio. Say whether each of these is adequate.

3. Here is M. Ross's Balance Sheet. You are to answer the questions below (with calculations if needed).

Balance Sheet as at 31 December 19X9

19X9		£	19X9		£
Capital			*Fixed assets*		
At start		56,000	Goodwill		2,000
add Additions during year		2,000	Premises		36,000
		58,000	Plant and Machinery		24,000
			Motor Vehicles		4,000
					66,000
Add Net Profit	16,600				
less Drawings	7,200				
		9,400			
		67,400			
Long-term Liabilities			*Current Assets*		
Mortgage		10,000	Stock	9,192	
			Debtors	2,548	
Current Liabilities			Cash at Bank	2,762	
Creditors	3,228		Cash in Hand	144	
Accrued			Payments in		
Charges	194		Advance	176	
		3,422			14,822
		£80,822			80,822

18

(a) What is the capital owned by the proprietor at the end of the year?
(b) What is the capital employed in the business? You should assume that profits were earned at an average rate throughout the year and that current liabilities are not part of the capital employed. The additions to capital were invested on 1 January.
(c) What is the working capital?
(d) Calculate the working capital ratio (correct to two decimal places).
(e) What is the liquid capital?
(f) Calculate the acid test ratio (correct to two decimal places).
(g) Work out the return on capital invested (correct to one decimal place) assuming that Ross could earn £9,000 a year in an alternative position with none of the responsibilities of a small businessman and could invest his capital at a rate of 10 per cent if he had no business to use it in. Comment on the results.

Answers

1. Working capital = £18,800; working capital ratio = 3.2. This is more than adequate.
2. Working capital = £16,300; working capital ratio = 2.90; acid test ratio = 1.09. Both are adequate.
3. (a) £67,400; (b) £72,700; (c) £11,400; (d) 4.33; (e) £2,208; (f) 1.65; (g) 3.1%. The extra profit hardly seems worth the effort and risk. Perhaps there are non-monetary satisfactions.

Checklist

1. The Trading Account enables us to work out a gross profit percentage, using the formula:

$$\text{Gross profit percentage} = \frac{\text{Gross profit}}{\text{turnover}} \times 100$$

2. We can also work out a rate of stock turnover using the formula:

$$\text{Rate of stockturn} = \frac{\text{Cost of stock sold}}{\text{Average stock at cost price}}$$

3. The Profit and Loss Account enables us to work out a net profit percentage using the formula:

$$\text{Net profit percentage} = \frac{\text{Net profit}}{\text{Turnover}} \times 100$$

4. We can also work out expense ratios for each expense item, using the formula:

$$\text{Expense ratio} = \frac{\text{Expense item}}{\text{Turnover}} \times 100$$

5. Working capital is found by the formula: current assets *less* current liabilities.
6. The working capital ratio is found by dividing the current liabilities into the current assets. It tells us how many times we can pay our current liabilities with our available current assets.
7. The liquid capital ratio is the same sort of calculation, but the stock is left out of the current assets. It is the acid-test ratio of whether we can meet our obligations.
8. The return on capital invested tells us whether it is worthwhile being in business.

18

19   The Inland Revenue and your business

Nature of the Inland Revenue □ Notifying the Inland Revenue of a new business □ The accounting date □ Shared expenses – part business, part domestic □ The distinction between capital and revenue expenditure □ Submitting your accounts to the Inland Revenue □ The Tax Return and the assessment □ Checklist

Nature of the Inland Revenue

At one time the money needed to run the government of the United Kingdom was relatively small and could be obtained from taxes imposed on luxury goods entering the country such as furs, jewellery, wine and tobacco. Later, as government activities increased, it became necessary to impose taxes on wealth-creating activities at home – an *inland revenue* as well as customs duties on imports. Today, government activities are so enormous that about 38 per cent of the entire national income has to be taken in taxes to finance defence,health, education, law and order, and so on. In one recent year it was £168,000 million. It is the Board of Inland Revenue which is charged with the duty of collecting these enormous sums, according to well-defined rules laid down in a number of Acts of Parliament. These Acts are varied from time to time, but especially by decisions announced on Budget Day and enacted into law later in the year in the Finance Act.

The Inland Revenue has a tax office in every district, staffed by a number of 'inspectors' of taxes, and there are a rather smaller number of officials called 'collectors' who act like the cashiers to take the payments as they come in, issue receipts and pay the money into bank accounts. The funds eventually reach the Bank of England, where they are put in the Exchequer Account and are used to pay for all government activities. The local inspector of taxes is the person we all deal with in our tax affairs. We submit our accounts to the tax office at the end of the financial year and in due course answer any queries raised by the inspector. Eventually we have an 'assessment'. We may appeal against this assessment within 30 days, or if we accept it we pay the amount due on the date specified. For self-employed people payment is in two halves, on 1 January and 1 July in the year after the assessment is made. Companies pay in a single payment on 1 January each year.

There is a popular misconception that the Inland Revenue is an oversize crocodile lying in wait to devour unsuspecting entrepreneurs who are trying to earn an honest five pound note or two. Nothing could be further from the truth. They have no interest in destroying enterprise; they are overworked and underpaid (as evidenced by the large number of them who leave each year to take less stressful and better-paid jobs). All they want to do is to extract from the taxpayer the share of profits which Parliament has agreed is fair and correct in the nation's present circumstances. If you get into difficulties with the Inland Revenue it will almost certainly be your own fault. You can avoid any trouble by adopting the procedures outlined in Fig. 19.2 below.

Notifying the Inland Revenue of a new business

The Inland Revenue issues a booklet entitled *Starting in Business* which is full of useful information for those setting-up in business. In the middle of the brochure is Form 41G which can be torn out and completed to supply the local tax office with all the information it needs to open a file on you. You can obtain a copy from your local tax office (see your local telephone directory under 'Inland Revenue'). The form is reproduced as Fig. 19.1 below.

You should complete the form and submit it to the local inspector of taxes as soon as you are clear that you intend to set up in business on your own account, whether as a sole trader, a partnership business or a limited company.

If you are already in business and have not yet notified the Inland Revenue, do so at once. Phone up for a copy of the booklet and complete the form as soon as it arrives. It is inadvisable to wait until the end of your financial year, when it is almost time to submit your first set of accounts, because certain decisions have to be made right from the start.

You should also notify the Department of Social Security because your National Insurance contributions change if you become self-employed and failure to notify them may mean you build up a backlog of contributions, instead of paying the new amounts from the start. Even if you are still working as an employee part time you will still need to make arrangements about self-employed contributions.

If you are thinking of employing someone, even if it is only part time, you may need to deduct tax and National Insurance contributions from

19

Enquiries about the business	Replies
1. In what name is the business carried on, if not in your own name?	1.
2. What is the business address, including postcode, if different from your private address?	2. Postcode
3. What is the nature of the business?	3.
4. When did you start in this business?	4. 19
5. If you took over an existing business, from whom did you acquire it?	5. Name Address Postcode
6. To what date do you propose to make up your business accounts? If they are to be prepared by an accountant, please give his name and address including postcode.	6. 19 Name Address Postcode
7. If you are not already operating PAYE as an employer, have you any employees earning • more than £45.00 a week or £195 a month? • more than £1 a week who have other employment?	7. Yes No Please '√' appropriate box

Personal enquiries	Replies
8. Were you employed or were you self employed before you started this business? What was the name and address of the business or employer. Please provide this information even if you had a period of unemployment between leaving employment and starting your own business. If you still have the leaving certificate form P45 handed to you by your last employer, please attach it and give the leaving date.	8. Employed ☐ Self employed ☐ √ one box Name Address Postcode Date of leaving shown on P45 19
9. If this is your first occupation since leaving full time education on what date did the education cease?	9. Date education ceased 19
10. If in addition to running your business you are in paid employment, or are continuing an existing business, please give the name and address of the employer/existing business.	10. Name Address Postcode
Is this an existing business or employment?	Existing business ☐ Employment ☐ √ one box

If you are a woman state whether single, married, widowed, separated or divorced.

If you are married, please give your husband's first names

Signature   Date   19

Printed in the UK by HMSO, April 1988 Dd 8091856. C850 19565

Fig. 19.1 Notification of a new business
(*courtesy of the Controller-General, HMSO*)

their pay. Ask the Inland Revenue for their booklet *Thinking of taking someone on.*

You should also consider your VAT situation. This has already been referred to in Chapter 11. If you are intending to register voluntarily for VAT, so that you can claim back any input tax you pay on machines, furniture, vans, etc., or if you feel fairly sure that your takings will exceed the levels per quarter at which it becomes compulsory to register for VAT, do so at once through your local VAT office.

The accounting date

The basic principle behind the taxation of profits is that the net profit of the business is the income of the proprietor, or is shared between the proprietors if there are two (or more) partners. It is therefore important to ensure that profits are worked out in a easy way which is uniform for all businesses, so that the assessments eventually arrived at are fair as between one business and another. To ensure that this is so there are a number of rules. The first is that the accounts are prepared for a set 12 monthly period. It is up to you to decide what accounting date to pick, but if you are registered for VAT it is very awkward if you pick a date that is not the end of a month, because VAT records work on month-end dates and your financial accounts and VAT accounts will be out of synchronisation. The alternative dates are:

- The anniversary of the day you start business. This seems a logical date to pick but if you start business on a date which is not the first day of the month you will have the difficulty referred to above.
- The anniversary of the end of the month you started business in. This means that your first year may be a week or so longer than a real year.
- The end of the calendar year – 31 December. This means that unless you start business on 1 January your first 'year' will be short. For example, if you start on 1 February your first year will be eleven months long.
- The end of the month nearest to the end of the tax year. This is 5 April, so many people work out their accounts to 31 March each year.
- The end of the tax year, 5 April. This is an awkward date to pick because it puts your VAT records out of synchronisation with your financial records, as explained above.

One further point is that if you have a VAT date which varies from your financial records, even though it is a month-end date, it can be slightly awkward. Thus a trader who is VAT registered on a quarterly basis might have to submit VAT records on the last day of February, May, August and November. This is awkward if the accounting date chosen for the financial records is, for example 31 December. It is quite possible to manage with such a difference in dates, but it is a bit irritating to close off your financial records and have your VAT records still open. A letter to the VAT authorities to ask them to allow you to change your dates to fit in with your

19

financial records will sort this out, and they will let you have a long '4 month' quarter to get your records synchronised. Once that long quarter is over you will be sending in VAT records at the end of March, June, September and December.

To be truthful, it doesn't affect the Inland Revenue very much which accounting date you pick, but in the first few years they have special ways of deciding what figure to take as your 'profits' for the year. Generally, you are taxed in any year on the basis of the profits you made in the previous year. It follows that if Year 1 was a short year (say an 8 month year) you might benefit considerably if in Year 2 (which is a full year) you were only taxed on the figure for the short Year 1. They will therefore apply a special system to arrive at a fair figure.

If you want detailed advice about this you could ask an accountant to advise you about the best accounting date to choose but, once you have chosen it, it is usual to keep to the same date every year.

Shared expenses – part business, part domestic

In many small businesses there are certain expenses which are shared. For example, if we run our business from home, the rent, telephone charges, electric light, etc., are partly used for business and partly for domestic purposes. The rule here is that you must decide some fair share of the expense for business purposes and only put that part down as a business expense. The usual proportion is a simple fraction for each expense headings. Thus a car might be shared half and half, but the telephone might be two-thirds business and one third domestic. If you occupy one room in a five-roomed house you will be allowed one fifth of the expenses on lighting, heating, etc., but if you are able to argue that the garage is your archive for out-of-date documents the inspector may concede one quarter. Note, however, that if you claim these allowances as business expenses you would be liable to capital gains tax on any capital gain made on the part of the premises that are designated for business, if you move. This can be a considerable sum, and for that reason some people do not always charge such expenses to the business.

In deciding these simple fractions for shared expenses you have two courses of action open to you:

- You can make the decisions yourself, and not bother with the tax inspector's opinion until you send in your accounts at the end of the year. The fraction has to be a fair one for both parties, and if you carefully consider all aspects of each case you will probably arrive at a correct figure. An important point to note is that you cannot claim any part of your mortgage payments as a business expense. This is because the interest paid is already taken into account in another way when you fill out your tax return, and to give it to you as a business expense would be to give you an allowance twice. The other part, the repayment of capital, is not allowed as a business expense because it is capital expenditure, not revenue expenditure.

If you do decide to make your own decisions it is important to set them out in a letter to the Inland Revenue inspector when you send your accounts in, so that he/she knows what you decided. Any disagreement with the fractions used will then be discussed.

- Alternatively, you can ask for a meeting with the inspector to get a firm decision right from the start. This is perhaps the better way, but sometimes there is so much to do at the start of a new business that it is difficult to find time. The Inland Revenue are busy too, and while they will always find time to interview you if you wish it, they are also content to let it go. If everyone is reasonable about what is a fair proportion of such expenses there will be no difficulty at all. The only other thing to be said about meeting the inspector is that his/her manner will soon convince you that your tax affairs are an important point of being self-employed. While one hopes dealings with the Inland Revenue will always be amicable, it is your duty to keep honest records and to put away your tax money throughout the year so that you have the money ready to pay, when you need to pay it.

The Inland Revenue knows the exact position of every firm in the country. It can soon see if your records are suspect in any way because your results are manifestly different from what they expect to find, and they will call you in for a discussion if they are at all unhappy. The majority of bankruptcy cases start with non-payment of tax. Sometimes the kindest thing the inspector can do is to declare you insolvent. That is the one occasion when all the people who owe you money will *have* to pay up.

The distinction between capital and revenue expenditure

This has been referred to earlier, but it is important to remember all the time when making book-keeping entries. If an expense only brings in a short-term benefit, lasting less than one year, it is a revenue expense, and as long as it was incurred wholly and exclusively for the purposes of the business it is a deductible expense of the business. This means it may appear either on the Manufacturing Account, the Trading Account, or the Profit and Loss Account as a deduction from income. If it is a shared expense you should write the fraction on the document (for example two-

19

thirds and one third) and then adjust the amount of expense down to the correct figure. This reduced figure is the one to be used in both your VAT records and your financial records.

Capital items are not deductible expenses, and even depreciation, however you calculate it, will be added back if you deduct it from your profits. The inspector will then give you the capital allowance to which you are entitled instead. This has already been explained in Chapter 14.

Submitting your accounts to the Inland Revenue

At the end of the financial year you should draw up a full set of Final Accounts for the type of business you are operating. For most businesses this means a Trading Account, Profit and Loss Account and Balance Sheet. Anyone running a small factory will have a Manufacturing Account as well, and those who do not trade will have only a Revenue Account (a Profit and Loss Account with another name). Of course, you may ask an accountant to draw up your Final Accounts for you, but this will cost you a reasonable fee, according to how much work is involved and the state of the records you present to him/her. There is much to be said for doing your own accounts, but another method is to do your own set of Final Accounts but ask your accountant to put them into apple-pie order and actually submit them to the Inland Reveue.

If you are submitting your own accounts write the inspector a fairly full letter covering most of the points you think might present a difficulty. These would usually include:

- Telling the inspector how you have proceeded with shared expenses, the fractions you have used, and why you deem them to be fair.
- If the fractions had been agreed previously, confirm that you are still using them, and if for some reason you have changed one of the fractions, justify the change by a brief explanation.
- Detail any capital expenditure incurred during the year and ask to be given a proper allocation of capital allowance on these new items, as well as the allowance due on your 'pool' left over from previous years.
- Comment on your current year's figures in comparison with the previous year. If profits are up explain why are doing so well; if profits are down explain any special problems that you have faced (e.g. competition may be fiercer this year). If a particular expense item is greater or smaller this year, you might explain why (e.g. a heavy advertising budget may reflect a new product which you have been bringing to the attention of the trade outlets concerned).

Finally, you should offer to bring your books in for inspection if required. To present such a set of books in good order is reassuring to an inspector that you are reasonably well organized and can prove the figures you have used in your final accounts by pointing to the original documents, neatly filed in a lever-arch file or some other storage device.

It is a wise precaution to take a photocopy of the records you submit, since it is easy to forget what the figures are and what comments you made about them. If you are asked to clarify a point over the telephone it is helpful to have a copy in front of you.

Usually it takes a few weeks before you have any reaction from the inspector, and when a letter does arrive it may consist of a list of points which he/she wishes to clarify. Deal with these promptly, and if they give you any concern go to the tax office and ask for guidance on the point concerned. If necessary, ask for an interview with the inspector, but most routine matters can be sorted out by lesser mortals. Do not get upset. Ninety per cent of their queries are matters you will be able to clear up without any difficulty, and the other ten per cent are matters where you will learn something you did not know before. Generally, unless you know you have been giving in false records, the problems can be resolved without difficulty. If you *do* get into serious trouble it will almost certainly be your own fault. Keep honest records – that is the only safe policy.

The final communication from the tax inspector is a brief letter in which he/she states that your computations are accepted and your profit figure is agreed at £X,000. These figures will therefore be the profits on which you will be assessed for tax.

The tax return and the assessment

Everyone, whether employed or self-employed, has to fill in a tax return which arrives about the middle of April and has a 30 day time limit. It establishes not only what income you have received from all sources but also what allowances you are able to claim. Your profit figures as agreed with the inspector will be the main income you have received and a photocopy of the final letter proving what the agreed figure is should be sent in with the return on completion. Eventually an assessment will be made telling you how much tax you have to pay. You may appeal against this assessment within 30 days if you so wish. The full details of this procedure and many other minor points are given in the booklet *Starting in Business*.

Checklist

1. The Inland Revenue is a government department charged with the duty of collecting income tax, corporation tax, etc. It has no interest in killing enterprise, but it does have to collect the government's share of the proceeds of enterprise.
2. All those setting up in business should obtain a copy of publication *IR28 Starting in Business*, and should complete and submit Form 41G in the centre of the brochure.
3. An accounting date should be selected and should then be used year after year as the date to which accounts will be completed. These accounts should be submitted with a letter of explanation on any difficult points.
4. In drawing up these accounts it is essential to remember that the only deductions from income allowed are revenue expenses incurred wholly and exclusively for the purpose of the business.
5. Any shared expenses – part-business, part-domestic – should be divided on the basis of simple fractions like half and half, or two-thirds and one third. These fractions may be agreed with the inspector first if preferred. If this is not done a full explanation of the fractions chosen should be given in a letter sent with the first set of accounts when they are submitted.
6. The inspector may respond with a few queries which should be answered promptly. If necessary, a visit to the Tax Office may be the best way of sorting out any difficulty.
7. Eventually, an agreed figure for your profits will be arrived at which will be the figure used when your tax return is considered and an assessment of the tax payable is made.
8. For sole traders and partners, tax is paid in two portions, on 1 January and 1 July each year. For companies, the corporation tax is payable on 1 January in a single amount. Companies must have their books audited by professional accountants, and it would normally be best to allow the accountants to draw up the Final Accounts for submission to the Inland Revenue.

20 Accounts for clubs and charities

Clubs and charities as non-profit-making bodies

Business people often act as treasurers for local clubs and societies of every sort, so it is not inappropriate to introduce as the final chapter of this book a special chapter about club accounts. The general feature of club accounts and accounts for charities is that such bodies are 'non-profit-making', though many of them do in fact make profits. The point is that the organisation comes into existence for other reasons, notably to provide some centre of activity and organise functions which are of interest to the members. Thus the local Bowls Club will have its greens, club house, refreshment-making equipment, etc., and will run competitions and organise meetings of interest to the members. In the course of these activities it will receive a good deal of income, and make a great many payments on its members' behalf. At the end of the year it may have made a profit on some activities, but these were not deliberately aimed at. We therefore do not regard them as profits but as 'surpluses', excess amounts contributed by the members, surplus to the expenditure of the club. Similarly, if at the end of the year 'payments' exceed 'receipts' this will not be called a 'loss', but a 'deficiency'.

The person in charge of the accounts is called the **treasurer** and he or she will naturally be anxious to avoid a deficit on the year's accounts. Treasurers may not be keen to amass a large surplus, preferring that members enjoy their simple pleasures as economically as possible, but it may be club policy to build up adequate reserves to provide for the replacement or improvement of assets from time to time.

Accounts of a club

The accounts of a club therefore consist of a record of 'receipts' and 'payments'. One of the receipts for example is 'Subscriptions from Members' and another would be 'Refreshment Income'. Payments would be made for 'Equipment' (a capital expense) and 'Refreshment Materials' (a revenue expense). Clearly there would be many such receipts and

20

payments. When keeping this type of record we need an analysis cash book. There is such a book on the market, at a very inexpensive price: the Simplex Club Accounts Book. The illustrations in this chapter are taken from it, by kind permission of the publishers George Vyner Ltd., from whom it may be obtained. The address is George Vyner Ltd. P.O. Box 1, Holmfirth, Huddersfield, HD7 2RP. Bank managers, accountants and others who read this chapter might like to advise the treasurers of clubs whose accounts they appraise of the existence of the Simplex Accounts Book for Clubs. It includes one year's accounts and the summaries at the end lead straight into the 'Final Accounts', i.e. Receipts and Payments Account of the club, to be presented to the members at the Annual General Meeting.

The Simplex Club Account Book has space for all the receipts and payments of the club, on a monthly basis. The amounts received and paid are analysed off under various headings so that similar items can be collected together and monthly totals are built up under these various headings. These records occupy 36 of the 48 pages, and are explained below, and illustrated in Figs. 20.1 and 20.2.

Each month the various totals for receipts and payments are taken to summaries on the 'Summary of Receipts and Payments' page at the back of the book, while a Monthly Bank Report and Monthly Cash Report are also prepared (see Figs. 20.2 and 20.3 for these summaries). The Cash Report each month should of course agree with the Cash in Hand, while a Bank Reconciliation Statement (see Chapter 8) should be drawn up from time to time, and agreed with the Monthly Bank Report.

Finally the totals of the 'Summaries' for the whole year are used to prepare the Receipts and Payments Account of the Club, which is presented to the members of the Society at the Annual General Meeting (AGM).

Let us now look at these sections of the book in detail.

The receipts of the club

Figure 20.1 shows the 'receipts' side of the Club Account Book.

Amounts received are entered in the 'Cash' or 'Cheque' Column (Cols. 10 and 11) and analysed off into appropriate channels (Cols. 1–9). Some columns have printed headings, others are left blank to enable the treasurer to write in suitable classes of receipts. The receipts are totalled monthly and may be cross-totalled to check for accuracy. Columns 1–9 should total when cross-totalled to the same total as Cols. 10 and 11. The totals are then carried to the Summary at the back of the book (see Fig. 20.3).

Receipts for the month *(in cash and by cheque)*

Month of JANUARY Year 1976

Date	Details	P.C.V.	1 Subs. £ p	2 Donations £ p	3 Refr. Sales £ p	4 Raffles £ p	5 Theatre Visits £ p	6 £ p	7 £ p	8 Misc. £ p	9 Cash drawn from bank £ p	10 In Cash £ p	11 By Cheque £ p
			Analysis Columns — You may head the spare columns to suit your own club or school									Amount Received	
JAN 4	Subscriptions 5 members		10 00									10 00	
5	Gift – Mrs Clark			5 25									5 25
11	Refreshments				3 25							3 25	
12	Subs Jones + Family		6 00										6 00
18	Refreshments				3 55							3 55	
19	Theatre Visit						8 50						8 50
25	Refreshments				2 80							2 80	
26	Subs Brown + Smith		4 00									4 00	
30	Refreshments				2 95							2 95	
30	Raffle + Refreshments				4 20	2 45						6 65	
31	Cash from Bank										10 00	10 00	
	Totals *(cross-tot to check)*		20 00	5 25	16 75	2 45	8 50				10 00	43 20	19 75

©

If entries have been analysed correctly total of columns 1-9 will equal total of columns 10 and 11.
At the end of the month carry the 1-8 column totals to the 'Summary' pages at the end of the book. Use the totals of columns 10 and 11 in the cash and bank reports opposite.

Fig. 20.1 The receipts of the club

The payments of the club

Figure 20.2 shows the 'payments' page of the Club Accounts Book.

Again, the payments are entered either in the Cash or Bank columns and analysed off into appropriate headings of expenditure. Once again these are totalled at the end of the month and cross-totalled to check for accuracy before being carried to the Summary of Payments at the back of the book (see Fig. 20.3).

The monthly Cash and Bank Reports

As shown in Fig. 20.2, these monthly summaries present no difficulty to the treasurer and give him or her a monthly check on the accuracy of the book-keeping. As mentioned earlier, the Cash Report should agree with the total of cash in hand, while the Bank Report must be periodically checked by comparison with a Bank Statement and the preparation of a Bank Reconciliation Statement.

The Annual General Meeting

At the Annual General Meeting the treasurer must account to the members for the conduct of the club's financial affairs. He or she does this by presenting them with a Receipts and Payments Account which shows the members what the balance was at the start of the year, the receipts and payments made during the year and concludes with the final balance at the end of the year. The balance of cash in hand should be available at the meeting for checking, if required, and a Bank Reconciliation Statement should have been prepared as at the last day of the financial year.

If the club has appointed auditors from among the members, they should be asked to check the records for the year, and sign the statements submitted to the members. If duplicating equipment is available sufficient copies should be produced to meet the needs of the members in attendance. Figure 20.4 shows a typical Receipts and Payment Account prepared in the Simplex Club Accounts Book.

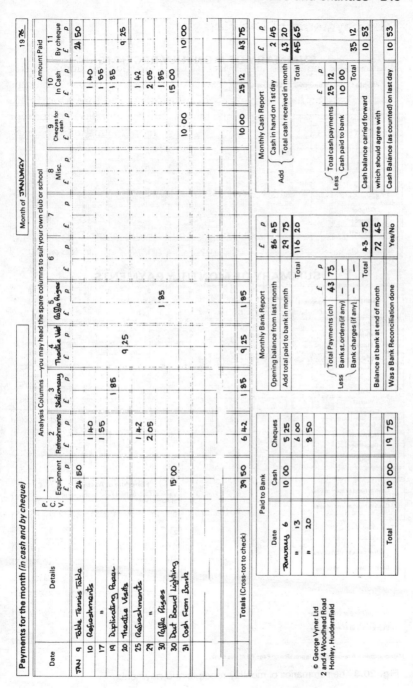

Fig. 20.2 The payments of the club, and the Cash and Bank Reports

SUMMARY OF MONTHLY RECEIPTS

Month	1 Subscriptions £ p	2 Donations £ p	3 Refreshment Sales £ p	4 £ p	5 £ p	6 £ p	7 £ p	8 £ p
January								
February								
March								
April								
May								
June								
July								
August								
September								
October								
November								
December								
Total								

SUMMARY OF MONTHLY PAYMENTS

Month	1 Equipment £ p	2 Refreshment Purchases £ p	3 £ p	4 £ p	5 £ p	6 £ p	7 £ p	8 £ p
January								
February								
March								
April								
May								
June								
July								
August								
September								
October								
November								
December								
Total								

Cash in hand at start of year	£ .		
Cash in hand at end of year	£ .		

Cash at bank at start of year	£ .
Cash at bank at end of year	£ .

Stock in hand at start of year	£ .
Stock in hand at end of year	£ .

Schedule of Assets	£	p
Value of Club/School Fund Assets at start of year		
Items Purchased during year.		
1.		
2.		
3.		
4.		
5.		
6.		
7.		
8.		
9.		
10.		
11.		
12.		

©
Memorandum – A re-order form is provided on Page 43 of this book.

Fig. 20.3 The summaries of monthly receipts and payments

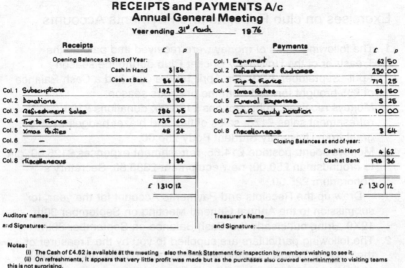

RECEIPTS and PAYMENTS A/c
Annual General Meeting
Year ending 31ˢᵗ March 1976

Receipts		£	p
Opening Balances at Start of Year:			
	Cash in Hand	3	54
	Cash at Bank	86	48
Col. 1 Subscriptions		142	50
Col. 2 Donations		8	50
Col. 3 Refreshment Sales		286	45
Col. 4 Trip to France		735	60
Col. 5 Xmas Parties		48	24
Col. 6 —			
Col. 7 —			
Col. 8 Miscellaneous		1	84
		£ 1310	12

Payments	£	p
Col. 1 Equipment	62	50
Col. 2 Refreshment Purchases	250	00
Col. 3 Trip to France	719	25
Col. 4 Xmas Parties	56	50
Col. 5 Funeral Expenses	5	25
Col. 6 O.A.P. Charity Donation	10	00
Col. 7 —		
Col. 8 Miscellaneous	3	64
Closing Balances at end of year:		
Cash in Hand	4	62
Cash at Bank	198	36
	£ 1310	12

Auditors' names
and Signatures:_____

Treasurer's Name_____
and Signature:_____

Notes:
(i) The Cash of £4.62 is available at the meeting – also the Bank Statement for inspection by members wishing to see it.
(ii) On refreshments, it appears that very little profit was made but as the purchases also covered entertainment to visiting teams this is not surprising.
(iii) A stock of refreshments valued at £26 is available (at the start of the year stocks were only £4). Other assets include camping equipment valued at £350, stored on the premises.
(iv) Creditors. A debt for repairing windows broken in the recent burglary is outstanding £7·25.
(v) There are no debtors.

Fig. 20.4 The Final Accounts of the club, ready for the Annual General Meeting

The club's membership record

A membership record is essential for club purposes, and the last three pages of the Simplex Club Accounts Book are devoted to a membership record, shown in Fig. 20.5.

Membership Register

Where the organisation using this book is a club, a register of the paid up membership may be kept here.

No.	Date paid	Name	No.	Date paid	Name	No.	Date paid	Name

Fig. 20.5 The club's membership register

Exercises on club Receipts and Payments Accounts

1. The following sums of money were received and paid by the Treasurer of the University Cricket Club during the season April–September 19X9. On April 1st the club had a Cash Balance of £55 brought forward from the previous season.
   Moneys received: subscriptions £125.00; donations £100; refreshment sales £178; sales of ties and blazer badges £165.50; grant from University Student Body £50.00.
   Moneys spent: postage £14.65; refreshment expenses £125.00; gift to groundsman £50.00; new equipment £386.50; Secretary's honorarium £25.00.

   Draw up the Receipts and Payments Account for the year, for submission to the Annual General Meeting on September 30th, 19X9. Bring out clearly the Cash Balance on September 30th.

2. The following particulars are supplied to you by the Treasurer of the Leyside Tennis Society, who asks you to draw up a Receipts and Payments Account. Take into account the point he makes in the note below the figures:

Cash balance	March 1st	£13.50
	October 31st	£ 7.84
Bank balances	March 1st	£48.24
	October 31st	£138.24

   Receipts during season: subscriptions £150.00; sales of spectators' tickets £129.50; entrance charges to functions £112.85; competition fees £48.50; refreshment sales £95.80; donations during season £135.99.
   Payments during season: refreshment materials £125.50; nets and waterproof sheeting £186.50; groundsman's charges £136.65; postage £18.50; stationery £14.85; light and heat £21.50; secretary's expenses £84.80.
   Note: A debt is owing for equipment, £42.00, which is to be included in the above costs as it will be paid at once by cheque, the bank balance being reduced accordingly.

Answers

1. Balance £72.35 Totals £673.50
2. Balances cash £7.84 Bank £96.24 Totals £734.38

Income and Expenditure Accounts and Balance Sheets for clubs and charities

While the Receipts and Payments Account described earlier is satisfactory for small organisations like the local tennis club it has certain defects. For example, it does not show:

- Whether a surplus or a deficiency has resulted from the year's activities (it only shows the 'cash in hand' and 'cash at bank' positions).
- Any debts owed by the club to creditors nor any sums payable to the club (for example, members who are enjoying the facilities without paying their club membership fee).
- Any assets owned (and usually clubs have quite a lot of assets of one sort or another). Nor does it show any liabilities (for example, there may be a mortgage on premises or loans repayable to members).

In particular, the rules for charities require that all trustees of charities must keep proper books of account and submit to the Charity Commissioners 'Statements of Account' which require rather more detail than can be found from a simple Receipts and Payment Account. The more advanced accounting statement that a club can prepare is called an Income and Expenditure Account, and it is followed by a Balance Sheet which reveals the full state of the club's affairs on the last day of the financial year. From this type of statement the sort of records required by the Charity Commissioners can easily be provided, while for other clubs the members can see the full position. Remember, some clubs are enormous organisations (for example the Automobile Association; with millions of pounds in subscriptions and hundreds of employees covering the entire country).

The records needed to prepare an Income and Expenditure Account and a Balance Sheet are as follows:

- We must have an Opening Balance Sheet, either drawn up on the first day the club started its activities or the one drawn up at the end of the previous year which becomes the starting point for the present accounting period.
- We need a Receipts and Payment Account prepared from the detailed figures of receipts and payments, however these were kept. They might for example be in a Simplex Club Accounts Book like the one described earlier in this chapter or they might be in a full set of double-entry book-keeping accounts.

20

From these records we can then go on to draw up an Income and Expenditure Account, which may be described as the Profit and Loss Account of a club. Like every Profit and Loss Account it has all the income for the financial year on the right-hand side, and all the expenditure (equivalent to the losses of a business) on the left-hand side. The difference between the two sides is of course the 'net profit' for the year, but as it is a club we do not call it a profit, we call it a 'surplus of income over expenditure'. Of course it could be a loss for the year, which we do not call a loss, but a 'deficiency'.

Sometimes a club which supplies refreshment, or has a bar or restaurant, will prepare a Bar Trading Account or Refreshment Trading Account. In that case the profit on the bar or the refreshments *is* called a profit, and appears as one of the items of income on the right-hand side of the Income and Expenditure Account.

Having arrived at the surplus or deficiency for the year we then ask the question 'What happens to the surplus?' or 'What do we do with the deficiency?' The answers are as follows:

- As there is no proprietor, the profits cannot go to the proprietor and the losses cannot be suffered by the proprietor.
- The surplus belongs to the members generally, and the losses must be borne by the members generally.
- This is done by adding any surplus to a fund called the Accumulated Fund (sometimes called the Capital Fund), or taking any deficiency away from the Accumulated Fund (or Capital Fund).
- If this means we have more in 'the funds' than we really need, we can use it up either by reducing the membership fee in the years ahead or increasing the services available (cheaper refreshments, etc.).
- Sometimes clubs put money away in special funds – for example a Rebuilding Fund.

The best way to see all this in practice is to do an exercise for a club of this sort. As we have already seen we must start with an Opening Balance Sheet and a Receipts and Payments Account.

Example

The Happy Valley Young Farmers' Club has the following assets and liabilities at 1 January 19X9:

Assets: Club house £18,500
          Games equipment £8,250
          Bar stocks £7,825
          Club house equipment £886
          Subscriptions due £60 (12 members at £5 each)
          Cash in hand £124
          Deposit Account at Bank £4,650

Liabilities: Loan from A. Member £8,000 (interest free)
               Creditors £426 (for bar supplies)

The Receipts and Payment Account at the end of the year is shown below.

Receipts and Payments A/C for year ending 31 December 19X9

Receipts	£	Payments	£
1 Jan Cash in Hand	124	Bar purchases	7,500
Subscriptions	3,560	Rates	1,378
Donations	284	Light & heat	298
Dance takings	1,266	Purchase of new club	
Refreshments takings	1,842	equipment	344
Bar takings	14,858	Postage & printing	89
		Dance expenses	553
		Refreshment expenses	469
		Club house repairs	272
		Transfer to Deposit Account	7,000
		Bar wages	3,100
		Cash in hand c/d	931
	£21,934		£21,934
Balance b/d	931		

From these figures and the following information prepare a Trading Account for the Bar, an Income and Expenditure Account and a Balance Sheet as at 31 December 19X9.

- The bar stocks at the end of the year were worth £6,125.
- At the end of the year subscriptions were due from 11 members at £5 each and three members had paid in advance for next year.
- At the end of the year £196 was owing for bar supplies, and a printing bill for £45 was due and unpaid.
- All the subscriptions for last year were eventually paid, and we expect this year's outstanding subscriptions to be paid in due course.

20

- The member who made the loan last year did not ask for any repayment in the year.

To solve this problem there are several points we must first sort out.
1. *The Accumulated Fund at the start of the year.* At the start of any year, just as with an ordinary business, we can draw up a Balance Sheet for the club, and the Accumulated Fund will be in the same position as the capital of a business. If we list the assets and liabilities of the club at the start of the year we find:

Liabilities	£	Assets	£
Loan	8,000	Club house	18,500
Creditors	426	Games equipment	8,250
	£8,426	Bar stocks	7,825
		Club house equipment	886
		Subs due (debtors)	60
		Deposit Account at bank	4,650
		Cash in hand	124
			£40,295

It is clear that the missing item is the Accumulated Fund – the capital of the club. It is £40,295 – £8,426 = £31,869. Putting in the Accumulated Fund on the liabilities side will make the two sides balance.
2. *Adjustments.* We can have adjustments in Club Accounts just as we do in an ordinary business. Once again the rule is to make every penny of this year's income be included in the accounts for this year, and every penny of this year's expenses be borne by this year's accounts. So, for example, on subscriptions we have the following points to consider:

- Subscriptions received in the year £3,560.
- This would include £60 from last year's subscriptions.
- £55 is due from this year's late payers.
- £15 has been received in advance for next year.

To find the subscriptions actually received for this year we must deduct the £60 for last year and the £15 for next year, and count in the £55 due from the late payers who have not yet paid:

Subscriptions = £3,560 − £75 + £55 = £3,540

Note that at the end of the year the subscriptions due will be an asset (the members are debtors for £55) but the subscriptions in advance will be a liability. (We owe the members a year's entertainment. They are creditors for £15.)

3. *The creditors for bar stocks at the beginning of the year.* These present a problem. If payments for bar purchases in the year were £7,500 this must include the money owed for last year, £426. The amount owing at the end of the year is for this year's stocks and must be counted in. So the purchases in the year are £7,500 − £426 + £196 = £7,270.

The Final Accounts will now be prepared as follows:

- Everything in the opening Balance Sheet must appear somewhere in the Final Accounts. This includes the Accumulated Fund at the start.
- Everything in the Receipts and Payments Account must appear somewhere in the Final Accounts.
- All the adjustments given in the extra information must appear twice in the Final Accounts, once in the Final Accounts and once in the Balance Sheet as they are carried over to next year.

The final accounts of the club are as shown below.

Bar Trading Account for year ending 31 December 19X9

	£		£
Opening stocks	7,825	Bar takings	14,858
Purchases	7,500		
Less last year's	426		
	7,074		
Add this year's due	196		
	7,270		
	15,095		
Less Closing stock	6,125		
	8,970		
Bar wages	3,100		
	12,070		
Profit on bar	2,788		
	£14,858		£14,858

Income and Expenditure Account for year ending 31 December 19X9

	£		£
Rates	1,378	Subscriptions	3,560
Light and heat	298	*Less* subs due at start	60
Postage and printing	89		3,500
Add sum due	45	*Add* subs due	55
	134		3,555
Dance expenses	553	*Less* subs in advance	15
Refreshment expenses	469		3,540
Repairs to club house	272	Donations	284
	3,104	Dance takings	1,266
Surplus for year	6,616	Refreshment takings	1,842
(to Accumulated Fund)		Profit on bar	2,788
	£9,720		£9,720

Balance Sheet as at 31 December 19X9

Accumulated Fund		£	*Fixed Assets*			£
At start		31,869	Club house			18,500
Add surplus for Year		6,616	Games			
		38,485	equipment			8,250
			Club house			
			equipment		886	
			Add new items		344	
Long Term Liability						1,230
Loan from A. Member		8,000				27,980
			Current Assets			
			Bar stocks		6,125	
Current Liabilities			Deposit			
Bar supplies	196		account	4,650		
Printing bill due	45		*Add* new			
Subs in advance	15		deposit	7,000		
		256			11,650	
			Cash in hand		931	
			Subscriptions			
			due		55	
						18,761
		£46,741				£46,741

More advanced final accounts for clubs and charities

Exercises

1. From the information below produce an Income and Expenditure Account and a Balance Sheet for the Amateur Photographer's Club for the year ending 31 December 19X8.

   On 1 January 19X8 equipment was valued at £1,630, there was a Bank balance of £120 and the Cash balance was £288. Subscriptions due amounted to £25 for the previous year and Subscriptions paid in advance for the current year were £50. During the year there were the following receipts and payments.

   Receipts and Payment Account for year ending 31 December 19X8

	£		£
Bank balance	120	Rent and rates	385
Cash in hand	288	Insurance	64
Subscriptions	1,825	Wages of part-time staff	360
Refreshments sales	288	Postage & printing	68
Competition fees	160	Refreshment materials	194
Collections	48	Prizes	85
Donations	425	Repairs	162
		New equipment	625
		Bank balance	630
		Cash in hand	581
	£3,154		£3,154
Bank balance	630		
Cash in hand	581		

   Additional information is as follows: On 31 December rates were due £42; wages due £46; subscriptions due £40. The insurance payment includes £23 for next year and subscriptions in advance for the year ahead were £75. Old equipment is to be depreciated by 20%.

2. The Leyside Cycling Club has assets and liabilities as follows at the start of its financial year, 1 April 19X9.

   Assets: Club premises £06,000; practice machines £3,485; furniture and fittings £1,765; subscriptions due £65; stock of spare parts £864; Bank balance £426; cash in hand £63.

   Liabilities: Subscriptions in advance £126; telephone expenses due £48; mortgage on premises £18,000.

   The Treasurer prepares two Receipts and Payments Accounts:

20

Receipts and Payments in Cash for year ending 31 March 19X0

	£		£
Cash in hand at start	63	Payments for spare parts	156
Subscriptions	2,950	Prizes	200
Competition fees	760	Refreshment expenses	125
Refreshment sales	827	Premises expenses	384
Sales of spare parts	825	Repairs	185
		Payment to bank	4,000

Receipts and Payments by cheque for year ending 31 March 19X0

	£		£
Balance at start	426	Rates	486
Rent from sub-tenant	2,080	Purchases of spare parts	2,255
Subscriptions	240	Telephone expenses	199
Cash banked	4,000	Mortgage interest	1,592
Sales of spare parts	1,624	Mortgage repayments	1,564

At the end of the year subscriptions of £126 were due and £185 had been received in advance for the next year. Stocks of spare parts were valued at £956. Show the calculation of the Accumulated Fund at the start of the year, a Receipts and Payment Account (Cash) and a Receipts and payment Account (Bank), a Trading Account for spare parts, an Income and Expenditure account for the year and a Balance Sheet as at 31 March 19X0. Note that mortgage repayments decrease the mortgage. They are not a revenue expense, but a capital movement.

Answers

1. Accumulated Fund at start £2,013; Surplus for year £1,027; Totals £3,203.
2. Accumulated Fund at start £23,494; Cash balance £375; Bank balance £2,274; Profit on spares £130; Surplus £3,866; Balance Sheet totals £43,981.

Accounts for charities

Although the accounts of charities are essentially club accounts, in that they are the accounts of non-profit-making organisations, there are some special points to be made about the general conduct of charities' financial affairs. Since the methods of collection are generally speaking fairly free and easy the funds subscribed are at considerable risk and it is a common complaint that only a small portion of the funds collected actually reaches the persons in need. This may be a quite unfair criticism – obviously a great deal of money subscribed in providing food for Ethiopia is going to have to be spent on transport, packaging, etc. This is essential and unavoidable. That being said it is a fact that the trustees of charities have the following duties:

- They must keep proper books of account, and prepare statements of account in the form of an Income and Expenditure Account and a Balance Sheet as described above.
- They must present these accounts to some official body. For permanently endowed charities this body is the Charity Commissioners, St. Alban's House, 57–60 Haymarket, London, SW1Y 4QX and such accounts must be submitted annually, without request. Other charities may at any time be asked by the Charity Commissioners to submit their accounts and must comply with such a request. Trustees of local charities for the poor must send copies of their accounts to the appropriate local authority, and must give public notice of the place where their accounts may be inspected by the general public. They must give copies on request to any person until the accounts are submitted to the local authority. Other local charities must send copies to the Parish Council or to the chairman of the Parish Meeting.
- Accounts must be preserved for at least seven years.

In this book we are dealing with the grass-roots work of keeping accounts; so what does the phrase 'must keep proper books of account' mean in the case of any local charity? The answer includes the following points:

- Whenever money is collected it should be done in as fool-proof a manner as possible, and in as public a way as possible. For example:
  (1) If money is collected in a meeting place, or at a social function of some sort it should be counted by the Treasurer in the presence of other members and the amount collected should be announced to the meeting. It is highly desirable that a receipt should be made out for the amount collected. The top copy – which would normally be given to the individual making a contribution to club funds – should be pinned on any notice board available and left up for at least one month.
  (2) If money is collected in collecting boxes, these should be efficiently sealed before use and should only be opened by the treasurer or an assistant treasurer in the presence of other people

including, if possible, the collector responsible for the box. A receipt for the amount collected should be made out and the top copy given to the collector. If several people took over the box during the day a note should be kept of the name of the person to whom the receipt is given. Preferably this note should be made on the receipt itself so it is carbon copied onto the counterfoil.

(3) If collecting boxes are displayed in shops, public houses, etc., the box should be opened and counted in the shopkeeper's presence and a receipt given in the shopkeeper's name.

(4) All donations by private individuals should be acknowledged by receipts. All receipt books should be numbered consecutively with the year, i.e. 1/91; 2/91; 3/91, etc. and kept for seven years.

- All money paid out should, so far as is possible, be paid against invoices or other documents, even if only a till receipt is available. These documents should be preserved in a lever arch file or some other storage device. Small receipts should be stapled onto larger sheets of paper for safety, and a petty cash voucher number should be written on them so that they can be easily traced. The aim should be to have a piece of paper sanctioning every payment and a receipt to cover every piece of income.

- All moneys received and paid should be recorded in an analysed cash book (like the Simplex Club Accounts book referred to earlier) and the columns should be totalled and carried to summaries for use in preparing the Receipts and Payments Account for the year. This account is the essential record for drawing up the Income and Expenditure Account and Balance Sheet in the manner already described above.

Note on the Charity Commissioners' official forms

The Charity Commissioners provide some very useful notes for charity trustees and a booklet which contains a digest of the Charities Acts 1960 and 1985 as they affect charity accounts. Those responsible for the accounts of charities should certainly read this material. The Commissioners also provide special forms on which the figures they require can be submitted. There is a simple Form AC(A) for smaller charities and a more detailed Form AC(B) for larger charities. The simpler form is reproduced in Fig. 20.6 (*see* pp. 260–3). The reader will see that all the figures required are available in the Income and Expenditure Account and Balance Sheet, while other details would be known to the Trustees from the minutes of meetings or the Trust Deed (if one was drawn up when the charity started).

To conclude we may say that keeping proper accounts for both clubs and charities is very important. Even though we give our own time voluntarily to serve on club and charity committees we need to be as professional as an amateur can be when handling money. Our good names are being held out in public as those of responsible and caring members of society. It is important to have all our records in impeccable good order, so that our good names are preserved and our reputations enhanced.

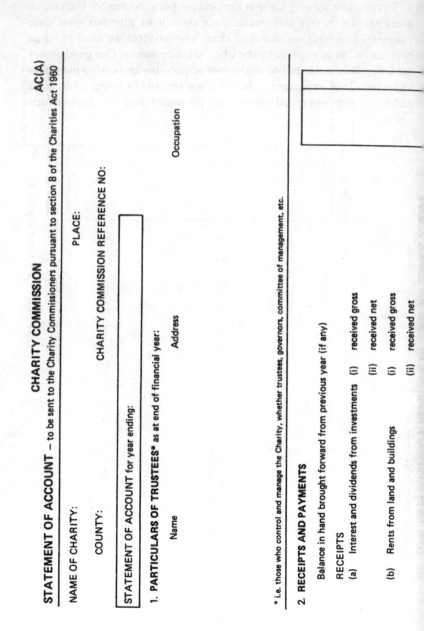

Fig. 20.6   The official Form AC(A) of the Charity Commissioners
(*reproduced by courtesy of the Charity Commission*)
Note: Form continues overleaf

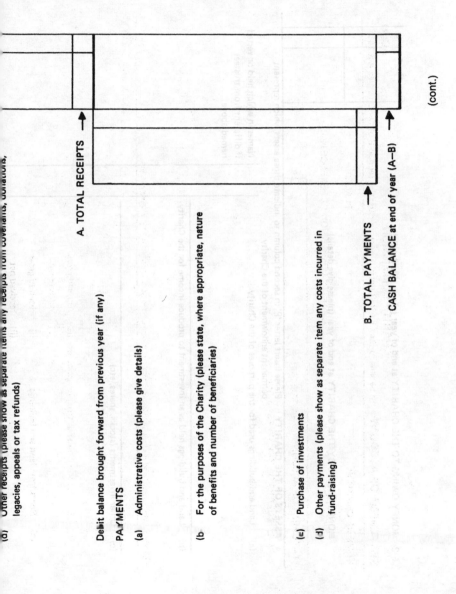

(a) Other receipts (please show as separate items any receipts from covenants, donations, legacies, appeals or tax refunds)

A. TOTAL RECEIPTS →

Debit balance brought forward from previous year (if any)

PAYMENTS

(a) Administrative costs (please give details)

(b) For the purposes of the Charity (please state, where appropriate, nature of benefits and number of beneficiaries)

(c) Purchase of investments

(d) Other payments (please show as separate item any costs incurred in fund-raising)

B. TOTAL PAYMENTS →

CASH BALANCE at end of year (A—B) →

(cont.)

20

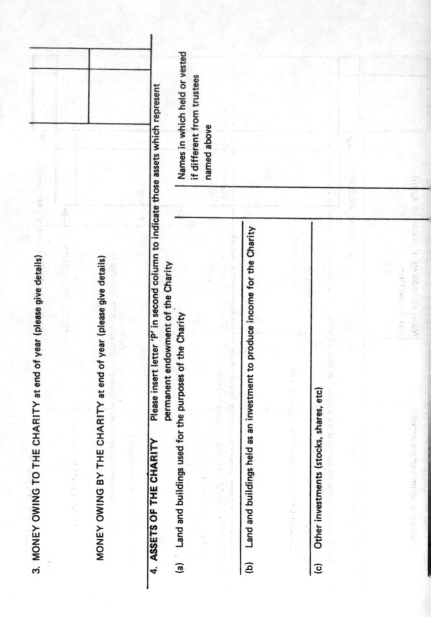

3. MONEY OWING TO THE CHARITY at end of year (please give details)

MONEY OWING BY THE CHARITY at end of year (please give details)

4. ASSETS OF THE CHARITY   Please insert letter 'P' in second column to indicate those assets which represent permanent endowment of the Charity

Names in which held or vested if different from trustees named above

(a) Land and buildings used for the purposes of the Charity

(b) Land and buildings held as an investment to produce income for the Charity

(c) Other investments (stocks, shares, etc)

(cont.)

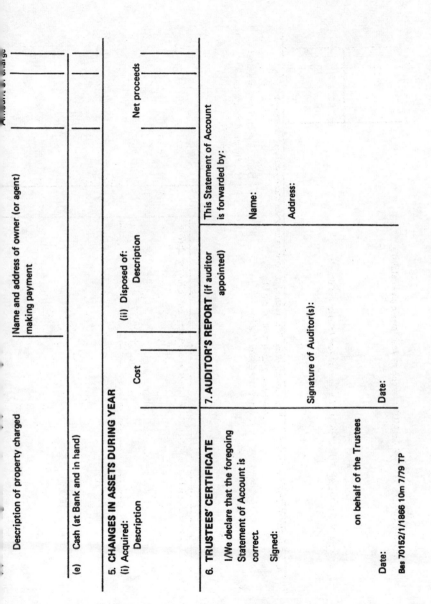

Description of property charged	Name and address of owner (or agent) making payment	Amount of charge

(e) Cash (at Bank and in hand)

5. CHANGES IN ASSETS DURING YEAR

(i) Acquired:

Description	Cost

(ii) Disposed of:

Description	Net proceeds

6. TRUSTEES' CERTIFICATE

I/We declare that the foregoing Statement of Account is correct.

Signed:

on behalf of the Trustees

Date:

7. AUDITOR'S REPORT (if auditor appointed)

Signature of Auditor(s):

Date:

This Statement of Account is forwarded by:

Name:

Address:

Bas 70152/1/1866 10m 7/79 TP

20

Index

Fill the gaps in your NatWest Small Business Bookshelf!

The books in the NatWest Small Business Bookshelf contain all you need to know about managing your small business. Written in a concise, readable style, each book is a handy and authoritative reference on important aspects of small business management.

Titles in the NatWest Small Business Bookshelf are:

A Business Plan
Alan West
A guide for strategic planning for profit. Evaluates key areas and includes case studies and spreadsheets

Starting Up
Gary Jones
How to find ideas for new enterprises and build up to a successful start-up

Selling
Peter Allen
How to understand customers and cashflow, choose your market position and sell correctly

Hiring and Firing
Karen Lanz
How to recruit, manage, pay and part with staff effectively and within the law

Small Business Survival
Roger Bennett
How to manage operational matters more effectively and turn your business into a profitable venture

Retailing
Gary Jones
How to open and run a shop of any sort effectively and profitably

Managing Growth
Maureen Bennett
A guide for the business on the brink of major expansion, focusing on resources management, finance and leadership

Book-keeping and Accounting
Geoffrey Whitehead
A guide for the small trader which looks at simple book-keeping systems, and explains business accounts, ratios and other performance indicators

Exporting
James Dudley
How to plan for export marketing, new markets and sell profitably overseas

Franchising
Peter Hall and Rob Dixon
A guide for both the business owner seeking to franchise a business and the would-be franchisor

Titles in the NatWest Small Business Bookshelf are available from all good bookshops. In case of difficulty, contact the publisher.

Sales Department, Pitman Publishing, 128 Long Acre, London WC2E 9AN
Tel: 071 379 7383